Gil
With best regards and
wishes arishes

Charles Hill

TRANSPORT LOGISTICS

The Wheel of Commerce

Issa Baluch
Charles H. W. Edwards

Ivy House Publishing Group

PUBLISHED BY IVY HOUSE PUBLISHING GROUP
5122 Bur Oak Circle, Raleigh, NC 27612
United States of America
919.782.0281
www.ivyhousebooks.com

ISBN: 978-1-57197-508-9
Library of Congress Control Number: 2010932968

Printed in the United States of America

DEDICATIONS

Issa Baluch

There are many great people to thank who made this book a
realization…and there a few special ones
who have served as my central influence in writing this book.
I would like to dedicate this to them.

My parents, who had both taught me to aim high and continuously
inspired me to go for greater heights—if they had been living today, I
am sure that I would have seen their pride register in some ways. To the
late Shero and Hamida Baluch—this book is for both of you.
You are deeply missed.

My in-laws, Mr. Harry Lewis Keheley and Mrs. Margaret Keheley, who
have never regarded me as a son-in-law, but like their own flesh and
blood. As a grateful son, I dedicate this book to both of you as well.
I cannot thank you enough for all the love you have showered upon
me, and I will forever cherish your precious words of encouragement,
endless support, untiring listening ear and wise counsel.

Finally, to my son who lives far away, but has always been diligently
in constant contact—may this book provide you with the inspiration
to never stop being positive about life and to continue basking in the
intricacies of the modern world. My son, Faisal, it is a privilege
for me to dedicate this book to you.

Charles Edwards

for Belle
my lovely and ever gracious wife of 30 years,
whose encouragement and support have made
my far-flung adventures in international logistics possible.

for Charles
my magnificent son, whose patience in the face of my international
travel has garnered my appreciation and my respect.

for Harris and Margaret
my devoted and inspiring parents, who taught me
the excitement of distant places and
encouraged me to set high goals.

ABOUT THE AUTHORS

Issa Baluch is credited with pioneering the thriving sea-air combined  transport freight business in the UAE. He holds a Master of Business degree from the University of Hull (U.K.) and has completed numerous aviation, transport, and freight logistics programs. He started as tally clerk at Gulf Agency Company in Dubai in 1973, rising to general manager. In 1989, he founded Swift Freight International, which quickly gained a reputation as one of the top freight logistics providers in the region. Baluch was recently re-elected as President of the Dubai-based National Association of Freight and Logistics, and serves on the Board of Directors of the International Federation of Freight Forwarders Associations (president, 2003-2005) and The International Air Cargo Association. He has served on the Advisory Board of Dubai Logistics City, and the Marketing Committee of Dubai Flower Centre. Baluch is the author of *Transport Logistics: Past, Present and Predictions,* which is available in four languages. He currently works as an industry consultant, providing counsel and advice to supply chain organizations around the world.

Charles H.W. Edwards has been engaged in the commercial aviation  and logistics industry since 1970. He held senior management positions with the North Carolina-based airline that started United Parcel Service Airlines and a U.K.-based charter passenger airline. He has managed a commercial airport and has been a senior advisor to public and private aviation projects in the United States, Germany, Thailand and Malaysia. Edwards was president of the U.S. subsidiary of the German company CargoLifter and executive vice president of Advanced Composite Structures. He holds a B.A. from the University of Toronto, M.Sc. from the University of Reading, and MBA from the Darden Graduate Business School of the University of Virginia. He has been a guest lecturer at North Carolina State

University and the University of New Mexico, and is a frequent speaker at aviation and logistics meetings globally. He is an Industry Fellow at the Kenan Institute for Private Enterprise, and serves on the Education and Research Committee of The International Air Cargo Association.

FOREWORD

L ogistics is a complex process that involves a chain of people and systems working together to move goods from one point to another in the most efficient, cost-conscious, prompt, and seamless manner.

When this process takes place across borders, across different time zones, and in different seasons among a diverse culture of people, global trade is the outcome. This is how logistics puts an economy into motion.

What could easily be a disastrous flow of interchange within the supply chain is converted into a straightforward process by creative and dedicated experts in the transport logistics industry.

We have one such expert in our midst—Issa Baluch.

Issa's contributions to the world of logistics have contributed significantly to the progress of Dubai as a global trading hub. As founder of a successful freight forwarding company in the UAE, Issa's clear-cut approach to providing logical logistics solutions to traders and businessmen has earned him a reputation as a respected industry leader.

For most of his peers, he is a leader in his roles as the past President of the International Federation of Freight Forwarders Associations (FIATA), a member of the Board of Directors of The International Air Cargo Association (TIACA), and adviser to many other various local and international organizations. For his supporters and friends, he is an expert who generously shares his knowledge and experiences through his colorful anecdotes, conveyed in his trademark wit.

And we can expect nothing less from him through his new book, *Transport Logistics: The Wheel of Commerce*.

This book takes the reader on a journey to Burundi, Ethiopia, Ghana, Kenya, Rwanda, Tanzania, Canada, Chile, India, Singapore, and the United Arab Emirates—where transport logistics plays a huge role in their rich histories and present economic standing. The case studies illustrate the complexities of transport logistics projects simply and clearly, while personalizing the unique stories that are featured in this book.

Issa teamed up with Charles Edwards for this particular book project and, together, the two authors succeed in demonstrating their in-depth understanding of the different facets that encompass transport logistics—sea, air, road, rail and multimodal transports.

This book is definitely a good read for practitioners, as well as a great tool, or a textbook for the academic world.

Ahmed bin Saeed Al-Maktoum
President, Dubai Department of Civil Aviation
Chairman, The Emirates Group

FOREWORD

M ost of us know Issa Baluch as the revered veteran logistician who was successful in leading the FIATA as president from 2003 to 2005, and is still making waves in the industry as an active member of the board.

Just when we thought we had the man pegged, he surprised us all with a remarkable contribution to the industry via the launch of his first book, *Transport Logistics: Past, Present, and Predictions.* I say remarkable because the book included topics that were never discussed before in the very few logistics manuscripts that exist. The book cleverly interconnected the stories of major earth-moving projects of the past, avant garde projects of that time, and a succinct forecast of what the future holds for the global logistics industry.

Naturally, the book was a success and was well received by his peers and academics alike. FIATA has always been a strong advocate of authors who magnanimously share their knowledge about the industry, especially since there has been a long-standing issue of not having enough comprehensive printed material on the study of logistics.

This is one of the reasons Issa's second book, *Transport Logistics: The Wheel of Commerce,* comes at a very opportune time, as it clearly provides the information that the industry needs at present amid the global economic downturn.

The book provides case studies of eleven countries that prove how transport logistics drives the economy while inducing energy to all other sectors of the industry, such as supply and demand, and import and export. It also details a comprehensive report on the financial performance of these countries and their significant contributions to the progress of moving freight via air, land, sea, rail, and multimodal transport. The emphasis in this respect is how transport logistics as an industry acts as the "wheel of commerce" that triggers the cycle of globalization. The book therefore becomes a vital reference for day-to-day operations of logistics personnel, as well as all those involved in movement of freight, particularly upcoming logisticians and students.

This time around, Issa has recruited co-author Charles Edwards from North America, who is also one of the most respected industry movers of our time, and a prominent figure in the academic world. To have these two gentlemen pair up in the creation of this book—despite their busy schedules and personal engagements—is a great example of true commitment and devotion for the transport logistics industry and its practitioners.

Jean-Claude Delen
President, International Federation of Freight Forwarders Associations (FIATA)

FOREWORD

So many times we get involved in our day-to-day business and tasks that we lose sight of the broader picture. Everyone at an airline such as Cargolux Airlines International is so focused on providing safe, efficient and effective service that we sometimes forget about all of the factors that control our operation as well as the impact that our services have on other people. There is an old saying that it is best to "know your customer's customer." By following that approach, you are better able to understand the needs of one's direct customer and to anticipate changes. This book provides a series of examples that the downstream impacts of transport and logistics services and operations have on the economic and social fabric.

As Chairman of the Board of Directors of The International Air Cargo Association I have the responsibility to lead the organization's goal of "advancing the interests of the air cargo industry." One aspect of that goal is the creation of an educational program for the many members of the air cargo industry. Thus it is with great pleasure to help introduce this book, *Transport Logistics: The Wheel of Commerce,* written by two members of TIACA and, coincidentally, members of the Education and Research Committee.

Issa Baluch is known far and wide for his insightful knowledge and long service to the international freight forwarding and logistics industry. As an innovator and leader he has given tirelessly of his time and knowledge. That includes his time as President of FIATA and as a valued member of the Board of Directors of TIACA. Now he has followed his first successful book—*Transport Logistics: Past, Present, Predictions*—with this new effort that illustrates the impact of transport and logistics on economic and social development. He and his colleague, Charles Edwards, another long-time member of the air cargo industry and TIACA, have highlighted unique and intriguing transport and logistics operations and services. The breadth of their knowledge of the industry is demonstrated in the different modes that they have studied. I look forward to Issa and Charles continuing their work with TIACA to develop the educational program and believe the book provides valuable material for the program.

The primary focus on Africa is particularly intriguing. While there are many challenges, which the authors unabashedly face head on, there are also many opportunities. As they point out, there are models of success in Asia and the Americas that can be applied around the world with the consequent benefits to everyone. While I never foresee an airline moving the vast quantities of fresh water from southern Chile, this an example of the unique logistics challenges that the industry faces every day.

In spite of the negative impact of the recession that began in 2008, transport companies around the world have continued to operate albeit with many changes to services, operations and staff. The identification of logistics-based leading indicators is a valuable contribution to the industry for all managers who are charged with looking into the future and creating plans for our companies.

I want to thank Issa and Charles for writing this book and I commend it to the industry and those who study the transport and logistics industry as an insightful study of the value and impact of what we do every day.

Uli Ogiermann
Chairman
The International Air Cargo Association

ACKNOWLEDGEMENTS

Our big thanks go to the following people, organizations and government bodies that played a fundamental role in making this otherwise difficult book project possible. The tremendous support and encouragement that each one of you has generously given made our journey to completing this undertaking rewarding and productive. The wheel of commerce continues to roll as the global transport logistics industry thrives—and this is all possible because of the commitment and hard work of people like you.

Editor: Kim Gazella
Designer: Beth Oldham
Logistics: Rowena Odiaman (Swift Freight International, U.A.E.)
Secretariat: Lachelle Arevalo (GSA Alliance, U.A.E.)

UNITED ARAB EMIRATES

Government:

H.H. Sheikh Ahmed bin Saeed Al-Maktoum, President, Dubai Department of Civil Aviation; Chairman, The Emirates Group

Ali Al Jallaf, Vice President, Cargo Unit, Dubai Airports Company

Marietta Morada, Senior Statistical Researcher, Dubai Chamber of Commerce

Private Sector:

Albert Alba, Former Editor, Logistics Review; Public Relations Practitioner

Lachelle Arevalo, Corporate Communications Manager, GSA Alliance

Vincent Brank, Director Sales & Operations, Dubai, Swift Freight International

John L. Dragonetti, Published Author; Business Consultant and Financial Liaison

Gregory Gottlieb, Program Manager, Lighter-Than-Air Systems

Ram Menen, Divisional Senior Vice President, Emirates SkyCargo

B. Rajagopalan, Managing Director, Swift Freight International

Ashok Thomas, Managing Director, Middle East & India, FedEx Trade Networks

SWEDEN
Robert Uggla, Managing Director, Broström AB

SWITZERLAND
Jean-Claude Delen, President, International Federation of Freight Forwarders Associations (FIATA)

BURUNDI

Government:
Libère Nahimana, Administrative Director General, Societe d' Entreposage Petrolier du Burundi
V. Narakwiye, Director Generale, Ministry of Transport, Port and Telecommunications
Consolata Ndayishimiye, President, Burundi Women Entrepreneurs Association
H.E. Elie Ntawigirira, General Consul, General Consulate, Republic of Burundi, Dubai
H.E. Dr. Masumbuko Pie, Former Prime Minister, Kingdom of Burundi; Former Representative, World Health Organization (West Africa); Honorary Consul, Republic of Burkina Faso
H.E. Dr. Yves Sahinguvu, First Vice President, Republic of Burundi

Private Sector:
Joseph Hicuburundi, Internal Audit, Interbank Burundi
Habib A. Hussein, Branch Manager, Swift Freight International
Cyprien Mbonigaba, Consultant, The World Bank
Deo Ntibibuka, Director, UTi Burundi SARL

CANADA
Christopher J. Gillespie, Chairman MTI (Multimodal Transport Institute), FIATA (International Federation of Freight Forwarders Associations) and President & CEO at Gillespie-Munro Inc.
William Gottlieb, President, David Kirsch Forwarders Ltd.; Immediate Past President, FIATA; Director, Canadian International Freight Forwarders Association (CIFFA)
Ryan Heslep, Coordinator, Braden Bury Expediting
J. Andy Hutchinson, Executive Director, Northern Frontier Visitors Association
Pete Jess, President, Jessco Logistics, Inc.
Ron Noseworthy, Operations Manager, Braden Bury Expediting

Dr. Barry Prentice, Professor,
University of Manitoba
Gary Reid, President, Braden
Bury Expediting
John Zigarlick, Chairman, Nuna
Logistics Ltd.

CHILE

Government:
H.E. Jean-Paul Tarud K.,
Ambassador of Chile, UAE

Private Sector:
Cabero Javier Figueroa, Regional
Director, Swisslog
Allen Szydlowski, Waters of
Patagonia
Ian Szydlowski, Waters of
Patagonia

ETHIOPIA

Government:
Hon. Deriba Kuma, Minister of
Transport
Haileselassie Tekie, Director
General, Ethiopian Horticulture
Development Agency

Private Sector:
Tewolde Gebremariam, COO,
Ethiopian Airlines
Tilahun Mulugeta, Secretary
General of the Ethiopian Freight
Forwarder and Shipping Agents
Association

Yeneneh Tekleyes, Director—
Advertising and Promotions,
Ethiopian Airlines
Alex Varghese, Branch Manager,
Swift Global Logistics
Girma Wake, CEO, Ethiopian
Airlines

GHANA

Government:
Hon. Mike Allen Hammah,
Minister of Transport

Private Sector:
Joseph Agbaga, First Vice
President, Ghana Institute of
Freight Forwarders (GIFF)
Carlos Kingsley Ahenkorah,
Director, Carlos King Services;
President, GIFF
Kristopher Klokkenga, Operations
Director, Africa Atlantic
Franchise Farming Ltd.
Robert Kutin, Managing Director,
All-Ship; Immediate Past
President, GIFF
David Kofi Nutakor, Managing
Director, Dock to Door
Shipping Ltd.; Vice President,
GIFF
Jon Vandenheuvel, Managing
Director, Africa Atlantic
Franchise Farming Ltd.

INDIA

Government:

Dr. Rahul Khular, Secretary, Ministry of Commerce and Industry

N.N. Kumar, Acting Chairman, Jawaharlal New Port Trust

K. Mohandas, Secretary, Ministry of Shipping

Hon. Kamal Nath, Minister of Road, Transport and Highways

Y.G. Parande, Special Secretary, Central Board of Excise & Customs, Ministry of Finance

M. Rama Rao, Secretary, Indian Revenue Service (Customs & Excise) Association

Shree Kant Singh, Deputy Chairman, Mumbai Port Trust

Rakesh Srivastava, Joint Secretary, Ministry of Shipping

Private Sector:

Shailesh Chandra, Assistant General Manager, TATA Motors Limited

K. Govindarajan, Vice President, Cargo, Mumbai International Airport Pvt. Ltd.

Virat Khular, Assistant General Manager, Nano Brand, TATA Motors Limited

Dushyant Mulani, Member Managing Committee, The Bombay Custom House Agent's Association

Dinesh Prakash, Country Head, Ayezan Logistics India Pvt. Ltd.

R. Radhakrishnan, Chairman, Clearship Forwarders Pvt. Ltd.

Nitin Seth, Head, Car Product Group, TATA Motors Limited

Yash Vardhan, Director International Marketing & Operations, Container Corporation of India Ltd.

KENYA

Government:

Alex Kabuga, Project Implementation Team Leader, National Single Window System Project

Dr. Mutule Kilonzo, Lead Advisor, Ministry of Transport

Hon. C.A. Mwakwere, Minister of Transport

Private Sector:

Hussein Baluch, Executive Director, Seithmar Marine Limited

Howard H. Crooks, Partner, H.H. Crooks & Associates

J.K. Mathenge, Regional
Executive Officer, Federation of
East African Freight Forwarders
Association

Jack Mwaura, Regional Business
Development Manager,
Barloworld Logistics

Sam Njoroge, Chief Executive,
SAMSAY International Agency

Denny Varghese, Regional Head,
Swift Global Logistics

Abbas Wazir, Branch Manager,
Swift Global Logistics

LUXEMBOURG

Lucien Schummer, Vice President
Alliances and Strategy, Cargolux
International Airlines

RWANDA

Government:

Cyrille Hategekimana, Advisor to
the Minister, Ministry of Trade
and Industry

Hon. Vincent Karega, Minister,
Ministry of Infrastructure

Hon. Monique Nsanzabaganwa,
Minister, Ministry of Trade and
Industry

Private Sector:

Thérèse Dusabe, Director
General, A.T.C, Rwanda s.a.

Jeanne Nyantaba, Operations
Manager, Select Boutique Hotel

SINGAPORE

Stanley Lim, General Manager,
Seagull Marine Services
Pte. Ltd.; Council Member,
Singapore Logistics Association
(SLA)

Thomas Sim, CEO, Topocean
Group-Singapore; First Deputy
Chairman, SLA

TAIWAN

J.P. Tseng, Chairman, King Freight
International Corp.

TANZANIA

K.I. Bwesha, President, Freight
World Limited

O.O. Igogo, Chairman & CEO,
Utegi Technical Enterprises (T)
Ltd.

Douglas Kroeker, VP of
Operations, Canadian Gas
Services International

Fredrick M. Maeda, Commercial
Assistant, Embassy of the United
States of America

K. Moses Nkanda, Power Plant
Manager, AG&P Power Ltd.

Arbogast Oiso, Government
Relations Manager, Artumas
Group

Chris Oppermann, Country
Director, Ras Al Khaimah Gas
Tanzania Ltd.

Emily Schaffer, Economic and
  Commercial Officer, Embassy of
  the United States of America
Mark Seqeira, Branch Manager,
  Swift Global Logistics

THAILAND

Suwit Ratanachinda, Managing
  Director, Profreight Group

TUNISIA

Gilbert Mbesherubusa, Director,
  Infrastructure Department,
  African Development Bank

UGANDA

Government:

Merian S. Kyomugisha, Chair,
  President's Commission of
  Technology & Transportation
  Investment

Private Sector:

Dave Carlstrom, President &
  CEO, AirServe International
Charles Kareba, Managing
  Director, Kargo International
  Ltd.
M.S. Swamy, Regional Manager,
  East and Central Africa
  Barloworld Logistics (Uganda)
  Ltd.

CONTENTS

INTRODUCTION

The relationship between transport logistics and commerce lends itself to a chicken-and-egg argument. Some might argue that without transport logistics services there would be no commerce; others would argue that without commercial activity, there would be no need for transport logistics services. Transport logistics industry veterans might argue that these two economic sectors have always been inseparable.

Those seasoned professionals repeat the same mantra: Transport logistics don't create markets—they serve them. Transport and logistics services move raw materials to places of conversion, transfer those converted raw materials to locations where components and final products are made, and then finally transport the products to distribution centers and consumers. This represents how transport logistics services facilitate the various steps that lead to the production of goods that are moved around the world in response to consumer demand.

Yet, one can argue that economic and social developments in Singapore and the United Arab Emirates have emerged because of the multimodal hub operations. This is because apart from having aggressive governments that fearlessly execute plans, these two countries also share the same pattern to success: Utilizing their transport logistics prowess to drive other economic sectors to progress.

The first book—*Transport Logistics: Past, Present and Predictions*—provided a historical illustration of the evolution of the worldwide industry of transport logistics. Now, five years after its release, that book is available in four languages and has been sold to more than 30,000 readers. Many have expressed an interest in a companion work that addresses the importance of transport logistics services to the economic and social development of the world.

Transport Logistics: The Wheel of Commerce does just that by addressing two topics. The first is the 2008 recession and the impact of the economic downturn on transport logistics services and operations. Secondly, this book describes the importance of the transport logistics industry on the economic and social fabric through a series of examples.

The first recession of the 21st century began in late 2007 and took hold around the world throughout 2008. Five years of stock market gains were wiped away. Major financial institutions closed or were forced to merge with competitors. Millions of production and service workers around the world were laid off, and transport logistics companies sidelined equipment and employees as demand for their services fell precipitously. Globalization, the engine that brought together manufacturers and consumers scattered around the world, has been adopted by other sectors of the world's economy, including finance and stock markets.

We examine from a transport logistics perspective how the recession evolved. The examination includes the identification of leading indicators—some economic and others transport focused—that foretold the recession, in some cases up to one year beforehand. This section of the book presents our thoughts regarding the nature of the recovery and how managers of transport logistics services will have to manage their companies in response.

The close relationship between commercial activity, economic and social development, and transport logistics services also is the focus of the book. Transport logistics services are provided across the face of the earth, on land, on the seas and in the air. Often, the provision of these services creates new opportunities and unintended consequences apart from the original project or focus.

The primary focus of the interplay between transport logistics services and the broader economic and social fabric is Africa, particularly East Africa. In addition to Ghana in West Africa, the authors illustrate this fundamental structure through an examination of projects and services in Burundi, Ethiopia, Kenya, Tanzania and Rwanda. External factors such as project funding and the negative impact of corruption and "extra charges" are identified and discussed.

Pushing a road into an undeveloped part of Tanzania as part of the development of a gas field now means that the inhabitants have, for the first time ever, better access to the rest of their country and the world. In

Ghana, our study focuses on a new farming strategy, combined with the development of inland water transport and the revitalization of what was once one of the largest railway systems in Africa. Ethiopia's reliance on airfreight to transport its bounty of coffee, beans and flowers illustrates the value of transport services in economic and social development. In Kenya, we look at how a local entrepreneur has developed a thriving seafood export business that employs sea-based, road haulage and airfreight services. Landlocked Burundi has the potential to become a distribution hub for countries that border Lake Tanganyika, but must deal with forces outside of its control in surrounding countries. Finally, Rwanda provides the venue for examining the negative impact of corruption, including extra charges that are levied on shipments that move from East African ports to this small landlocked country.

Outside of Africa, we examine unique transport logistics services in northern Canada, southern Chile, India, Singapore, and the United Arab Emirates. These studies illustrate the role of transport logistics services in specific environments, and in meeting various challenges and needs. Serving mines and petroleum fields in the harsh environment of northern Canada is a major challenge for transport logistics companies. In Chile, the impact of global warming has created an opportunity for a Chilean company to move vast quantities of fresh water to other parts of the world where supplies are all but exhausted or dangerously close. Quietly, the Indian transport logistics industry, in collaboration with the Excise & Customs Service, is shedding hundreds of years of bureaucracy to serve that nation's rapidly expanding economy. Singapore and the United Arab Emirates provide us with examples of the value of multimodal transport hubs that have been created by vision and action, providing significant evidence about how a government-driven strategic action plan based on the implementation of world-class transport logistics services can propel other economic sectors in these two respective countries to success.

Because knowledge acquired in one place can potentially be adapted to another situation, the lessons learned in supplying the mines and fields in the Canadian Arctic can be employed in the newly discovered oil and gas fields in East Africa. Similarly, moving large quantities of fuel to those remote mines has provided the basis for a technology to move vast quantities of water. As the former Secretary-General of the United Nations recently said, the visionary leadership of places like Singapore is needed in Africa so that the nations in the oft-called "Dark Continent" can realize their goal of taking their rightful place in the world's economy.

By creating and constantly updating efficient transport logistics systems, the developing nations of the world will be able to promote their commercial sectors. That will, in turn, lift their economic and social status.

Transport
Logistics
– the Wheel of Commerce

SECTION I
THE WHEEL: A HISTORICAL REVIEW

A round the world, the wheel comes in many forms and has many purposes. Apart from components on vehicles, the wheel exists as the basic design of major parts of engines that power trucks, trains, ships and planes. The wheel appears in manufacturing and processing equipment, and in power generation such as hydroelectric generators or wind turbines. Without the wheel, it is doubtful if world economics could have evolved to the state we know and enjoy today.

This section of the book takes a historical look at the evolution of the wheel and its applications, with a primary emphasis on transportation and logistics. The section is divided into two chapters. The first chapter, THE WHEEL: FRONTIER OF INNOVATION, takes a brief look at how the wheel emerged in various forms as far back as 3,500 B.C. This chapter also traces the development of the wheel and various transport vehicles, including automobiles, trucks, ships and planes.

Chapter Two, THE WHEEL: SOCIAL AND ECONOMIC DEVEL-OPMENT, describes industries that emerged by employing the wheel or making objects that incorporated it. The evolution of transport networks and how they have fostered and become an integral part of social and economic development is also studied.

CHAPTER 1

THE WHEEL: FRONTIER OF INNOVATION

Think trade, travel, sports or even entertainment—can you imagine these industries in the modern world without the wheel?

The world as we now know it might have been something else entirely if not for the invention of the wheel. Its contributions to mankind are both enormous and revolutionary. The wheel has facilitated and become an integral part of all aspects of human life, good and bad.

One could ponder how trade might have evolved without the wheel. Or what if the wheel did not exist, if chariots and other forms of war transportation were not developed? Think trade, travel, sports or even entertainment—can you imagine these industries in the modern world without the wheel? Harder to imagine still is the reason for the wheel's creation. Who was that person or group so many ages ago that developed the concept, and then through trial and error created what we now accept as a fundamental part of our lives? Society owes a debt of gratitude to the creator of the wheel, whoever he or she was.

From Pots to Chariots

There is no definitive account of the specific date the wheel was discovered or name ascribed to the invention. Based on archaeological reports, the wheel was first discovered around 3,500 B.C. in Mesopotamia and is believed to have been used to make pottery.

Potters had long known that circular objects were stronger than square ones. While it is doubtful

that they cared, the forces of tension and comprehension were more evenly distributed around a circular or cylindrical object than a square one. Thus if it were dropped or hit, it was less likely to be damaged or break.

With that in mind, the equipment to fashion a cylindrical object should also be a circle. The early forms of the wheel were likely made of stone or wood. They were often large blocks of stone fashioned into circular shapes, or flat wooden slabs rounded and cut with holes in the middle for an axle. These prehistoric wheels were used to spin clay for functional items, such as water containers. Thus, the invention of the wheel likely benefited manufacturing even before it did transportation.[1]

When larger items needed to be moved, tree trunks were adopted. While not perfectly cylindrical, they roll and thus a series of them could be used to move large stones or other objects from one place to another. Most archaeologists believe that rollers were essential tools employed on various ancient constriction sites, including the Egyptian pyramids and Stonehenge.

However, the main problem with this method was that many rollers were required, as was careful attention to ensure that the rollers stayed on course. One theory as to how this obstacle was overcome suggests that a platform, or a sledge, was built with crossbars fitted to the underside, thereby preventing the rollers from slipping out from under the load.[2]

Two rollers were used, with two crossbars for each roller—one in front, and the other behind. This complicated and problematic method of hauling goods probably led our early brothers to prefer walking and carrying goods on their backs instead.

It was only after 300 years, roughly in 3,200 B.C., that the functionality of the wheel for transportation was realized—for chariots.

The chariot is the earliest and simplest type of carriage used in ancient times. The chariot, driven by a charioteer, was used for warfare during the Bronze and Iron Ages.[3] More than a thousand years later, approximately in 2,000 B.C., the Egyptians came up with the spoked wheel—a significant development that gave way to the construction of lighter and swifter vehicles.[4] Eventually, the Greeks designed their version of the wheel. Around 1,000 B.C., the first iron-rimmed wheels were spotted on Celtic chariots.

Chariots continued to serve their purpose in warfare and were frequently mentioned in history, such as the Old Testament—particularly by the prophets—who referred to the vehicles as instruments of war or as symbols of power or glory. First mentioned in the story of Joseph (Genesis 50:9), "iron chariots" are noted also in Joshua (17:16, 18) and Judges (1:19, 4:3, 13) as weapons of the Canaanites. 1 Samuel 13:5 mentions chariots of the Philistines, who are sometimes identified with the Sea Peoples or early Greeks.[5]

The adoption of the wheel around the world, both as a manufacturing platform or use in transport, was sporadic until the 19th century Common Era (C.E., sometimes referred to as A.D.). In the Americas, the great native tribes, including the Inca, Aztec and Maya civilizations, reached an extremely high level of economic and social development, despite being wheel-less societies. In fact, there is no evidence that the use of the wheel existed among native people anywhere in the Western Hemisphere until well after contact with Europeans.

On the other side of the world, in Asia, the wheel was an integral part of Chinese civilization. Evidence shows that the Chinese used wheels for manufacturing, trade, travel and war.

Although wheeled chariots were present in Europe, the wheel evolved little until the beginning of the 19th century.[6]

An Essential Part of Transport

In the space of about 2,500 years, the wheel evolved from use as a manufacturing platform to use in transportation. Even with the accounted value of chariots in the early times, the optimal use of the wheel in commerce did not flourish until well into the 19th century.

In his 1975 book, *The Camel and the Wheel*, author A.D. Richard Bulliet mentioned several possible reasons why camels supplanted the wheel as the standard mode of transportation in the Middle East and northern Africa between the 2nd and 6th centuries. His reasons included the decline of roads after the fall of the Roman Empire and the invention of the camel saddle between 500 and 100 B.C.[7]

In the English version of the Qur'an by Muhsin Khan, one prominent mode of transport mentioned several times was the caravan (Surat Al-'Anfal 8:7, 42; Letter Yusuf 12:10, 19, 70, 82, 94; Surat Quraysh 106:2), which depicted the use of animals, particularly camels, in moving goods and people.

Despite abandoning the wheel for hauling purposes, Middle Eastern societies continued to use wheels for tasks such as irrigation, milling, and pottery.[8]

The Wheel Rediscovered

With the advent of the Middle Ages and Industrial Revolution, the wheel became the central component of technology. It was adapted for use in thousands of ways, in countless different mechanisms. Improvements continued to be made, leading to the use of wheels as gears during the Middle Ages.

This prompted the invention of mechanical devices such as clocks, water wheels, cogwheels and the compass, among others. Clocks permitted people to better measure and, in turn, provided a framework for conducting experiments that broadened scientific exploration and application of the results to numerous tasks and operations.

The water wheel provided a means to convert the energy in moving water into power used to grind grain in larger quantities or to run spinning machines to make textiles that began to replace homespun

fabrics. Cogwheels were created to transfer the energy from spindles and axles connected to the water and animal powered wheels to individual machines. Horse-powered lifts were developed so that vertical instead of horizontal mine shafts could be constructed to access new deposits of coal and iron. Finally, the compass, an adaptation of the sundial, along with the chronometer, a specialized clock, revolutionized ocean transport. Ship captains and navigators were able to not only better record where they had sailed, but more importantly were able to return to the same place repeatedly over long distances, which enhanced international trade.

Steam Engines, Manufacturing, Mining, Railways and Ships

The marriage of steam engines to the wheel was the essential foundation of the Industrial Revolution. Larger quantities of products could be produced with fewer people and animals. With this technological combination, more iron ore and coal was mined. Factories, once limited to waterways for

Clock at the Royal Observatory, Greenwich, England

Source: en.wikipedia.org

power, could be placed closer to demand or sources of labor. Higher quality textiles could be spun and clothes made on the basis of this marriage. Finally, with the creation of the portable steam engine in the form of the steam locomotive for railways and ships, goods and people could be moved further, faster and in greater quantities than previous technologies capacities allowed.

A mill engine from the Stott Park Bobbin Mill, Cumbria, England
Source: en.wikipedia.org

From the late 1700s through the 19th century, major changes in agriculture, manufacturing, mining, and transport had a profound effect on socioeconomic and cultural conditions—initially in the United Kingdom, and subsequently throughout Europe, North America, and eventually, the world. The onset of the Industrial Revolution marked a major turning point in human history, as almost every aspect of daily life was eventually influenced in some way.[9]

Like many other technologies, the first crude steam engines emerged some 2,000 years ago. The concept of boiling water to create a flow of pressurized air that translated into a physical motion was the first evidence of this technology. However, it was not until the 18th century that the development and adaptation of the technology began in earnest. Just like the wheel, the first steam engines were designed and operated as a source of power for manufacturing and mineral extraction.

Hero of Alexandria recorded what could be presumed to be the first rudimentary steam engine, known as the "aeolipile," in the 1st century C.E. Between then and the 16th century, other "steam engines" were experimental devices used to demonstrate the potential power of steam. In 1690, a piston steam engine, whereby a piston moved through the injection and exhaust of steam, was developed. This led to the first practical steam-powered engine, a water pump, developed in 1698 by Thomas Savery. Although the first steam engines were highly unreliable, and in some cases prone to horrific explosions when pressures exceeded the strength of the boilers, steam engines became common sites at mines where they were initially employed to remove water from the shafts or to move water into canals and aqueducts.

The first steam engines emerged as power sources for the textile mills and mines of Northern England in the 17th century. Initially highly unreliable and dangerous, they became the preferred source of power for hundreds of looms or access to deep veins of coal. Textile plants no longer had to be located alongside rivers where paddle wheels would turn vast arrays of pulleys and belts to power the looms. Natural flows of water were replaced by an engine, which produced steam that powered a machine that turned the pulleys and belts. Coal mines could now be kept drier, allowing the miners to dig deeper and extract previously unreachable seams of coal.

In 1765 the Scotsman James Watt created a working model of a relatively efficient steam engine. Although it was patented 10 years later, the first operational model was not available for another year due

Trevithick's locomotive (1804) the first successful steam locomotive

Source: en.wikipedia.org

to lack of finances. The application of steam engines paved the way for the Industrial Revolution that began in England and spread around the world on the back of expanded trade and transport.

The use of steam to power road vehicles first was attempted by yet another Scot, William Murdoch, who in 1784 developed a prototype road engine. Twenty years later, the first successful steam locomotive was invented by Richard Trevithick and began un-manned operations on a tramway at an iron works in South Wales. The age of horse-drawn carts on simple railed tracks was coming to an end. In 1829, the most famous steam locomotive, Locomotion, built by George Stephenson, began operating on the Stockton and Darlington Railway.

The steam locomotive changed the way goods were moved, first in England and then throughout Europe and in North America. Larger volumes of goods could be carried in shorter periods of time. In the case of North America, the steam engine and the railways were essential tools in the development of the United States and Canada.

Application of the steam engine to power vessels also occurred about the same time. This revolutionized that form of transport.

While technology was changing, the future of the world depended on man-made energy. The powers of nature and human physiology played the dominant role. Reliance on the wind or manpower to cross bodies of water expanded trade and development. The Phoenicians established seaborne links around the Mediterranean Sea. Arab traders sailing dhows created trade lanes from southwest India to the east African coast. The famous treasure ships of the Chinese in the 1400s and the later Portuguese and Spanish fleets explored new lands and moved vast fortunes over the Atlantic, Pacific and Indian Oceans.

While all of these efforts created trade and fortunes, and in many cases spread war and disease, they all operated at the mercy of the weather. Ship routings were dependent on ocean currents and prevailing winds. The monsoons of the Indian Ocean and the typhoons of the Pacific dictated when and where ships could sail. Major wind and ocean currents like the Roaring Forties of the southern hemisphere or the Gulf Stream of the north Atlantic could either aid or hinder seaborne trade.

In the 1780s and 1790s, John Fitch crafted the first steamboat. Further developments by Robert Fulton and Isaac Brunel in the early 1800s contributed to the creation of river and sea-going vessels. As engines grew larger and more powerful, ships also expanded in size and capacity. No longer were shippers and vessel owners subject to the weather and ocean currents—schedules could be created and maintained. The Atlantic Ocean could be crossed in as few as five days, instead of 30. These improvements spurred trade flows between Europe and North America and throughout the world.

By this time, steamships, canals, railroads, and the telegraph were up and running. They were the technological marvels of the 19th century, setting the stage for the 20th century. Yet the invention that would spark a revolution in transportation was a simple two-wheeler—the bicycle.[10]

Two-Wheeled Wonder

In 1802, the spoked wheel under-went a makeover when G.F. Bauer registered a patent for the first wire tension spoke. This wire spoke con-sisted of a length of wire threaded through the rim of the wheel and secured at both ends to the hub. Over the next few years, this wire spoke evolved into the round tension spoke we see on bicycles today.

Another major invention that came about was the pneumatic tire, which was first patented in 1845 by R.W. Thompson. His idea was further improved in 1888 by John Dunlop, a Scottish veterinarian, who also patented it. Thanks to the smooth ride, Dunlop's tire replaced the hard rubber used by all bicycles at that time.[11]

The bicycle's popularity in the 1880s and 1890s is one of many testa-ments of the wheel's significance to mankind. Nevertheless, it was another by-product of the wheel that was predestined to dominate the modern roads—the vehicle that we now call simply, the car.

The Automobile and the Truck

The word "car" came from the French word "carre" and earlier from Latin "carrus,"' which meant "wheeled vehicle." From the 16th to 19th centuries, the word was mainly used in poetry to describe any vehicle in a solemn or dignified procession, such as those concerned with pageantry, or in times of triumph or in war. The word was mainly used in relation to vehicles traveling on railways un-til it was transferred to automobiles around 1896.[12]

Benz Patent Motorwagen, first built in 1885

Source: en.wikipedia.org

According to records, more than 100,000 patents created the modern car. However, automobile aficionados insist that the birth of the modern car started with Karl Benz's 1885 Benz Patent Motorwagen. The three-wheel vehicle used bicycle-like wire wheels, which were fitted with hard rubber tires. And speaking of rubber, the first people who thought about using it for automobile purposes were André and Edouard Michelin, who later founded the famous tire company. In 1910, the B.F. Goodrich Company invented longer life tires by adding carbon to the rubber.[13]

Ironically, the next step in wheel evolution was the disc. This design bears more resemblance to the initial solid wheel designs. As with many other things in history, the change was prompted by lower cost, as the steel disc wheels were cheaper to make. The rim could be rolled out of a straight strip of metal, and the disc itself could be stamped from sheet metal in one easy motion. The two components were welded or riveted together, and the resulting wheel was one that was relatively light, stiff, resistant to damage, and could be easily fabricated in large quantities. Most importantly, it was cheaply produced.[14]

While the passenger-carrying automobile was an improvement over horse-drawn carriages, the movement of goods became the subject of study and development. A period when multiple horse-drawn wagons operated alongside steam engine powered trains and combustion engine powered automobiles came to an end during World War I. Automobiles were adapted as machines of war, including the first armored cars, vehicles of mercy, the first ambulances, and carriers of supplies.

During the interwar period, trucks were developed in Europe and the United States, and their cargo capacity increased. The tractor-trailer design, which separated the power unit from the cargo carrier, was introduced. Enclosed driving cabs for the driver emerged. By the Second World War, trucks had evolved and were adapted as an essential part of military logistics to move ever-increasing volumes of supplies and personnel.

And Now, We Fly

The wheel in the form of the engine, the propeller, the components of the jet engine and the gyroscope are elements of the latest evolution of transport technology, the airplane. The two dimensional environment

First flight of the Wright Flyer I, on December 17, 1903 with Orville piloting and Wilbur running at wingtip.
Source: en.wikipedia.org

of trucks, trains and ships has expanded to the three dimensions in which aircraft operate. While the first airplanes were rudimentary affairs susceptible to mechanical breakdowns and limited capacity, the commercial airplanes of the late 20th and early 21st centuries have become integral parts of the global transport and logistics system.

On December 17, 1903, the first powered flight occurred on the northern dunes of eastern North Carolina, swept by the winds off the Atlantic Ocean. Although prior flights had occurred using hot air balloons, this event marked the first real beginning of powered flight whereby aviators were no longer at the mercy of the winds. Just like the advent of the steamship, powered aircraft provided the foundation for the design and creation of aircraft with higher capacities, the ability to fly longer distances, and to fly at higher speeds.

Antonov AN-124
Source: en.wikipedia.org

By covering increasing distances and flying above the highest mountain ranges, airplanes have brought distant regions of the world closer together. A six-month journey by sailing ship from England to Australia can now be flown in less than one day. Specialized cargo-carrying aircraft built in the Ukraine can carry shipments with weights exceeding 200 metric tons. Aircraft operating off runways made of gravel and ice provide essential services in the Arctic regions.

Conclusion

There can be little doubt that the adoption of the wheel in transportation was key to the globalization of the world economy. If humans had been unable to overcome the limitations of animal-drawn vehicles or sail-powered vessels, trade as we know it would never have evolved to the extent that has become commonplace. As we discuss later, the development of countries such as Russia, Canada and the United States would have taken much longer to achieve.

---

[1] eHow, www.ehow.com/about_4658773_invention-wheel.html

[2] Autoevolution, www.autoevolution.com/news/history-of-the-wheel-7334.html

[3] Wikipedia, http://en.wikipedia.org/wiki/Chariot

[4] Wikipedia, http://en.wikipedia.org/wiki/Wheel

[5] Wikipedia, http://en.wikipedia.org/wiki/Chariot

[6] The Great Idea Finder, www.ideafinder.com/history/inventions/wheel.htm

[7] Smithsonian Magazine, www.smithsonianmag.com/science-nature/A-Salute-to-the-Wheel.html

[8] Ibid.

[9] Wikipedia, http://en.wikipedia.org/wiki/Industrial_Revolution

[10] About.com: Inventors, http://inventors.about.com/od/cstartinventions/a/Car_History.htm

[11] Autoevolution, www.autoevolution.com/news/history-of-the-wheel-7334.html

[12] Dictionary.com, http://dictionary1.classic.reference.com/help/faq/language/e37.html

[13] Autoevolution, www.autoevolution.com/news/history-of-the-wheel-7334.html

[14] Ibid.

CHAPTER 2

THE WHEEL: ECONOMIC AND SOCIAL DEVELOPMENT

"The Wheel of Commerce:" How major events in history have prompted the coining of this terminology

The employment of the wheel in industry and transport has had a far-ranging impact on social and economic development. It has removed physical barriers. It has brought together regions of the world that previously had limited or no connectivity. It has facilitated the spread of ideas and products, and even disease and war. In short, the wheel has been a fundamental factor in the development of human society and civilization.

The impact of wheels on the transport industry is reflected in the following story about the reduced cost and time it takes to move goods between the Kenyan Indian Ocean port of Mombasa and points in Uganda. Before the construction of the railway between Mombasa and Uganda, the cost of conveying goods to Uganda from Mombasa was about Ksh240 (US$100) per ton, using human porters. It also took the better part of a year to transport goods to Uganda. As of the mid-1990s, the average cost of carriage on the railway system was approximately US$60 per ton, and more importantly, it took only three to four days to complete the same journey. The 40-percent reduction in transport costs was overwhelmed by the 99-percent reduction in time. Obviously commerce on any scale was impossible before the construction of the railway, since so few goods could bear the transport costs. The result was that only largely non-commercial supplies for missions and administration could move. The cost-effectiveness of the railway has vastly improved trade between Kenya and Uganda, as goods can bear transport costs.[1]

From a historical perspective, the Industrial Revolution and development of the western regions of North America provide dramatic examples of the value and social and economic impact of the wheel and transportation. In the former case, the development of large-scale manufacturing was possible only through the adaptation of the wheel both as a source of power and of critically needed transport. In the latter case, the wagons of the original settlers that could carry more and penetrate lands beyond the limits of the rivers and lakes gave way to the railroads that linked the east and west coasts and opened the vast inland prairies. In the case of Canada, the nation was created on the back of the Canadian Pacific Railway, whose route was both an economic and political statement.

Many industries have been created because of the wheel, or have benefited from it. The Industrial Revolution was based on the use of the wheel. Manufacturing, mining and transport were all able to expand both geographically and in capacity through the use of the wheel. The fabrication of textiles, which began as a "cottage industry" tied to the sources of the raw material—wool—and made by either by the sheep owners or local wool makers, was industrialized with the water wheel power factories and subsequently by steam power. Basic raw materials including coal and iron could be extracted in larger volumes through the application of pumps to remove water from the mines and winding engines to lift men, equipment and materials from deeper and deeper mines. Canal boats that were pulled by men or animals were replaced by trains drawn by steam locomotives.

The wheel appears in many guises. Bicycles, ox-drawn carts, automobiles, trucks, trains and planes, machinery, construction and manufacturing equipment—the list is endless. The companies that make these products also rely on the wheel. Transportation is the industry that has benefited the most from the wheel.

A study of the Industrial Revolution that began in England between the 1700s and the 1900s provides a fascinating look at how the wheel as a manufacturing and transportation tool facilitated both the geographical spread of industry as well as the growth of production and consumption.

Between 1705 and 1780, production of cotton in England increased from approximately 1.15 million pounds per year to just under 5 million pounds per year. After the introduction of the "Crompton Mule," a wheel based spinning machine, the annual production volume rose rapidly from about 5.5 million pounds in the mid-1790s to 60 million pounds by 1805.[2] In the first 75-year period, annual production grew at a rate of about 1.5 percent per annum and in the latter phase by more than 8 percent per annum. While the annual production level leaped almost 100-fold, the use of machines did not require a similar increase in production labor. At the same time, the growth in productivity and the associated reduction in production costs reduced the price of cotton so that more people could purchase it, which in turn increased the demand level for the product that replaced wool and other textiles in everyday clothes.

An essential material in machines and transport products was iron. Before 1700, pig iron was made where charcoal was available. In forest-rich England, the source of wood that was converted to charcoal was in southeast England near Dover and in southeast Wales near Cardiff. By 1750, while the original forests were being reduced to levels unsustainable for pig iron production, other areas in the West Midlands and Scotland emerged. Total pig iron production in England in 1750 was estimated at about 21,000 tons per year. At the same time, iron imports from Sweden, Russia and North America began to replace sources in the United Kingdom.

Smelting operations continued in South Wales and developed in the West and East Midlands of England along with operations in Scotland. When coal replaced charcoal, the production of iron moved to sites close to this new source of heat and power. While the West Midlands produced an estimated 50 percent of all pig iron in 1800, it accounted for just 26 percent by 1850, while South Wales hosted an estimated 36 percent of the nation's iron production. In that same period, total iron production expanded from an estimated 150,000 tons annually to in excess of 2 million tons per annum. By 1900, as steel replaced iron as the primary industrial metal, production centers in the United Kingdom coalesced in southwest Scotland, Sheffield, Northeast England and South Wales.[3] The spread and growth of production of iron and later, steel, was supported by the adoption of the wheel in manufacturing, mining and transportation. Larger production facilities with their own internal railway systems, deeper and more extensive mines, and railways that could carry increasing volumes of coal, coke and iron ore between the mines and the mills were possible only by using the wheel.

Unlike previous transport alternatives, the railway was a significant paradigm shift. Much larger quantities of goods could be carried in a shorter period of time than were possible along stage roads or canals. Access to internal sites that were not alongside seacoasts or rivers was possible. The growth of railways in England, continental Europe and the United States between 1825 and 1844 was nothing less than spectacular. At the beginning of the period there were barely 100 total miles of railways; by 1840, the United Kingdom boasted 2,500 miles of railways. Total railway mileage in England reached an estimated 2,200 miles by 1844, while total railway mileage in continental Europe was about 1,100 miles.[4]

As production volumes increased, the demand for iron ore required larger shipments from overseas sources. The sail-powered coastal and longer-range ships were incapable of carrying the larger loads. Initial steam-powered ships were horribly inefficient. In many cases the large amounts of coal required to fuel the boilers significantly reduced cargo capacity. However, improvements were steadily made. In 1865 a steam-powered ship carrying 3,000 tons completed a non-stop journey from England to Mauritius. This voyage proved that the age of steamships was about to emerge as the dominant form of long haul transport. By 1880 it was estimated that 50 percent of seaborne cargo capacity was carried by steam-powered ships, even though steamships only accounted for about 25 percent of the number of vessels.[5] The higher capacity was a function of the higher speeds of the steamships as compared with the sailing ships.

Companies that make transport equipment have, of course, benefited from the invention of the wheel. The automotive industry is one of the largest complexes in the world. Assembly plants are linked to suppliers. Auto and truck parts move around the world from suppliers to assembly plants. Specially designed ocean-going vessels move finished vehicles to regions that lack assembly capacities. While the majority of the parts and finished vehicles move by surface—trucks, trains and ships—airplanes carry some specialty components or critical parts for manufacturing plants.

Makers of locomotives, freight cars and passenger cars all exist because of the wheel. Shipbuilders also benefit from the wheel. The engines that power these leviathans of the world's oceans and the propellers that convert the engine power to propulsion are visible examples of the wheel. But on a broader scale, manufacturing, mining and other economic activities that employ wheels create freight flows that are carried by ships around the world.

Jet engines, intricate flight instruments and other components that are derivations of the wheel are components of commercial aircraft that link distant sites around the world. The makers of the airframes, engines and instruments all exist in part because of the invention of the wheel. In all cases, the passengers and the cargo transported by airplanes are carried to the airport or away by wheeled vehicles, whether they are road vehicles or trains.

Clearly, transport networks and services have fostered social and economic development around the world. Settlement of the inland prairies of the United States was possible only with the building of the transcontinental railways. Where once small parties of settlers traveling in convoys of ox-drawn wagons had taken months to travel from St. Louis and Chicago across the Rocky Mountain and coastal mountain chains to the Pacific Ocean coast, the rail lines allowed thousands of people to cover the same distance in a matter of days. Settlements along the lines emerged as major population centers while resources became available to feed this hungry and growing nation. In Canada, the Canadian Pacific Railway was an instrument of political and economic enterprise. In order to keep British Columbia in Canada, the CPR was pushed across the plains and through some of the toughest mountain passes. That line and others became the primary routes of development for the new country.

Studies of the development of Ghana, Nigeria and East Africa illustrate the importance of transport networks. One study by Edward J. Taaffe, Richard L. Morrill and Peter R. Gould[6] focused on Ghana and Nigeria, while another study by B.S. Hoyle[7] examined seaport and internal railway links in east Africa. These two studies demonstrated a similar evolution of transport networks that spread inland from villages along the coasts and led to the development of the regions.

Based on these studies, there are four distinct phases of network development. The first phase is a series of scattered fishing villages along the Atlantic and Indian Ocean coasts. Some of the villages emerged as primary population centers, usually because of external forces. Locations such as Mombasa (Kenya), Dar es Salaam (Tanzania), Accra (Ghana), and Lagos and Port Harcourt (Nigeria) emerged as major centers because they were trading posts and/or forts. With this development, indigenous populations gathered around to seek trade or protection. A few routes from these centers following rivers or historic footpaths emerged as primary routes inland to facilitate expanding trade or, in some unfortunate instances, the movement of slaves.

The second phase of network development involves the emergence of primary routes into the interior. The studies established three primary reasons for one route becoming more important than another:

1. A link between two administrative and population centers,
2. A link from the seacoast to a mineral deposit, and
3. A link from the seacoast to a rich agricultural area.

These three reasons reflect social and economic drivers that led to the expansion of a route and the collateral development of one population center over another. The combination of lower transport costs, available labor and high marginal productivity favor one location and one route over another. On the Indian Ocean, Zanzibar emerged as the major Arab trading center. By the mid-19th century, an extensive network of routes moved slaves, ivory and other goods into modern day Uganda, Tanzania and the Congo. These pathways were replaced by railways that ran westward from Dar es Salaam to Tabora and eventually Kigoma on Lake Tanganyika, and from Mombasa to Nairobi and onward to Kampala in Uganda.

Eventually, the east African railway network incorporated a route from the Dar es Salaam-Kigoma line northward to Lake Victoria and a ferry service across the lake that linked to the rail line from Mombasa. These interconnections as well as other feeder routes represent the third phase of a transport network. In the case of North America, spur lines to agricultural and mining centers spun off from the main lines to create a web of rail linkages that furthered the development of that continent in the 1800s and early 20th century.

The network of railways that had dominated the development of inland areas was supplemented by the emergence of better vehicles and roads. Network densities, the measure of linear distances of a transport link within a specified area of land, increased with the advent of roads.

The fourth phase of development is the emergence of so-called high-priority routes. These routes serve the highest concentration of population or economic activity. The Interstate highway system in the United States, primary sea lanes from the Arabian Gulf to Africa's Indian Ocean ports, and the main air routes that span out from Changi International Airport around the world represent this fourth stage of transport network development. Major nodes such as the great ports of Rotterdam, Singapore and Hong Kong, and major air hubs such as Atlanta, Dubai and London, are both a product of the evolution of transport networks as well as enablers of the networks and the transport services. Feeder routes extend from these hubs. Those feeder routes and services collect and distribute traffic that is carried by services operating along the high-priority routes. Whether they are smaller ships or planes, they serve the same purpose. They link the smaller ports and airports into the global transport web and provide equivalent access for members of the wheel of commerce to virtually all points on the earth's surface.

The "Wheel of Commerce" can be seen in many guises throughout the world. At its most basic, the wheel of commerce is represented in the transport vehicles that carry goods from place to place. The wheels of the trucks and trains; the propellers that push container ships, very large crude carriers and other ships through the seas; the spinning discs of jet engines, and the valve wheels of the pipelines are all readily visible examples of how wheels are used to further all forms of goods transport around the world. These wheels, in their myriad forms, reflect how essential the wheel is to international trade and commerce.

Transport hubs can be considered as some of the clearest and most visible examples of the wheel of commerce. The spokes of a wheel are the transport routes that radiate from the hub. Arrayed

Transport
Logistics ——————▶ Providers of transport and logistics services

– the Wheel of Commerce ——————▶ Users of the transport and logistics services

around the hub are the various support services such as cargo terminals, customs and immigration inspection stations, customs house brokers and freight forwarders, handlers, and road haulage services. Just like the emerging seaports, these transport network nodes play an important role in transport networks. The nodes provide meeting points of transport services and users of those services, as well as the other support services that enable operations of both groups.

In 1990 a new concept was developed at the University of North Carolina at Chapel Hill by John D. Kasarda, Ph.D., then the new Director of the Kenan Flagler Institute of Private Enterprise. His concept was based on an innovative combination of transport services, logistics support, distribution, manufacturing and commercial support services at a single site. Known as the Global TransPark, the first example was established in the eastern part of the State of North Carolina in the southeastern

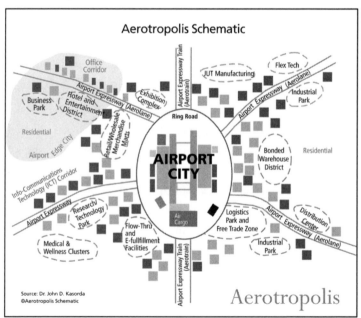

United States in the mid 1990s. A further evolution of the concept was the proposed establishment of a network of similar facilities at strategic sites around the world. An adaptation of the concept was developed at Hahn in western Germany. Hahn has become one of the busiest cargo airports in Germany.

A further evolution of the concept has emerged. It is known as Aerotopolis. This concept broadens the original idea by establishing links beyond the corporate limits of the transport node into the surrounding community. One location where this new concept is being applied is the new Al Maktoum International Airport in Dubai and the surrounding logistics facilities, including linkages to the nearby Jebel Ali port.

Dr. Kasarda has noted that "airports will shape business location and urban development in the 21st century as much as highways did in the 20th century, railroads in the 19th and seaports in the 18th."[8]

Coat of Arms of Port Coquitlam, British Columbia, Canada

Source: en.wikipedia.org

The wheel of commerce even occurs on seals and coats of arms. One example is the Coat of Arms of Port Coquitlam, British Columbia, Canada, a shield that blends the themes of native and natural heritage and the railway. The railway is highlighted through the red steam locomotive and the twin bands of gold, the color of commerce. Other transport and wheel symbols that appear in the coat of arms include the coronet, set with six anchors, three visible, which represent ships and maritime commerce and a Salish spindle whorl that honors the Stahlo People (native Canadians).

Food production and its distribution have also benefited from the wheel and improvements to transport and logistics. As long as there have been humans, there has been food production. Initially, food was available through hunting and gathering—from animals or what was found naturally growing. If the animals disappeared or if drought reduced edible plants, then famine spread and in severe cases death followed.

About 10,000 years ago, agriculture, the planned raising of food, emerged as not only a symbol of the evolution of the human species but also a necessary development to support the growing populations.

Agriculture has experienced many stages of development and evolution. A wide variety of technologies has been developed and applied to improve crop yields, minimize the effects of weather and natural pests, and expand the distribution area.

While the emergence of agriculture can be traced to such locations as the "fertile crescent" of what is now Iraq, along the banks of the Nile River in Egypt, New Guinea, parts of China, Africa and regions of North, Central and South America, the distribution of agricultural products was limited by the lack of transport. By 5,000 B.C., the Sumerians had developed some of the fundamental aspects of agriculture that are still in use today, including intensive cultivation, single crops, irrigation, and dedicated labor. The application of mechanization initially to move water to the fields increased the productive capacity.

The Harvesters. Pieter Bruegel. 1565.
Source: en.wikipedia.org

However, it was not until the last years of the 15th century that a global exchange of crops and livestock began to evolve. Christopher Columbus is credited with bringing to Europe the tomato, the potato, cocoa and tobacco. His and other voyages carried wheat, spices, coffee and sugar cane in the opposite direction. Horses for the soldiers were introduced to the New World on the voyages. Those that escaped and survived were cared for by the Native Americans, and became beasts of burden. As settlers from Europe began to take over more land in North and South America, horses provided the power to prepare the land for food production.

The availability of more and cheaper food is a critical element of the growth in the world's population. The productive capacity of farms has risen with increased mechanization. Horses and oxen replaced humans as the primary source of power and they, in turn, were replaced by mechanized equipment whose output was measured in multiples of horsepower. Wheel shaped discs replaced flat blades to open the soil. Circular implements to till the soil, place seeds, cut the weeds and harvest the crops increased the productive capacity of farms around the world. The net effect of this mechanization, irrespective of the impact of better seeds and fertilizer, was to increase crop yields and reduce the cost of food, allowing more people to eat better and thus avoid the insidious spread of famine and starvation that was a common part of life. The improved volumes of food have been accompanied by better transportation.

An example of improved transport included the use of steamships that significantly reduced transit times and had larger carrying capacities, along with the development of refrigeration that allowed perishable items such as fruits to be carried over longer distances. Bananas from Central America to North America and Europe, butter from New Zealand and beef from Argentina to England are only a few examples of improvements in transport technology that spurred the international flow of food around the world.

The application of these and other technologies was redirected in the tremendous growth of international flows of food between 1850 and 1914. At the beginning of the period, total worldwide food exports were estimated to be about 4 million tons annually. By 1850, this had grown to 18 million tons and by the beginning of World War I, the volume was an estimated 40 million tons. As of 2007, the World Bank estimated that food exports accounted for 7 percent of all merchandise exports and had a total value of US$976.7 trillion in 2007.[9]

Food that once was available only in close proximity to where it was grown is now available around the world—for example, the New Zealand kiwi fruit. Wines produced on one continent are available in distant countries. As the sun moves across the equator, the growing seasons shift. Improved transport services follow the sun and the crops. Vegetables grown during the northern summer are still available in the northern hemisphere in the winter but come from thousands of miles away.

Fruits, vegetables, seafood, wines and flowers that are raised and made on distant farms, vineyards and seas are now available in local green grocers and shops. This evolution not only benefits the consumers but also the producers. The produce raised by a farmer in northern Kenya is sold in stores in the Middle East and Europe. A wine made in Chile or New Zealand is purchased by consumers in Europe and North America. Transport has increased the reach of these farmers and wine makers.

Conclusion

According to *Encyclopedia Britannica,* one of the greatest inventions of all time is the wheel.[10] The wheel in a variety of forms is a part of most modern inventions. Some of those inventions were formulated around the wheel, while others could not function without the wheel.

The wheel represents both a technological development that is essential to transport and commerce around the world and a convenient descriptor of the relationship among a wide variety of factors and actions. Economic forecasts such as those prepared by Boeing Commercial Airplane Company have long used a symbolic wheel to graphically portray the complex interplay of economic, social, political, climatic, and logistics factors that underlie the estimate of air travel and hence the demand for commercial aircraft. A number of statistical displays borrow from the wheel to illustrate complex relationships over time.

The wheel gave us the ability to achieve mobility and freedom in transportation. Without the wheel, there would be no automobiles, no airplanes, no ships, no space launches, and no turbine engines.[11] As in the case of the example of the difference of transport from the Port of Mombasa to Uganda, the use of the wheel not only significantly reduced the transport time from months to days, but also dramatically increased the volume of goods that could be transferred to and from the seaport. This is just one of many equally striking examples around the world. The center of North America could not have been developed without the wheel, first on the oxen-drawn wagons and later on the steam engines and cars that knitted the east and west coasts of Canada and the United States together.

The paddle wheels that replaced sails on ships plying the North Atlantic have given way to massive propellers that push very large container ships and tankers on courses around the world. Without the application of the wheel, ocean trade would not have evolved to the point where the majority of the world's trade is carried by ocean-going vessels.

It is reasonable to assume if the wheel had not been applied to motors as propellers and later, in the form of jet turbine engines, there would be no aviation system. Previous propulsion systems using flexible wings, like birds, were unable to move a heavier-than-air vehicle over any distance. Even the massive dirigibles of the 1930s relied on diesel engines connected to propellers for their propulsion. With the advent of jet engines, especially in more powerful versions, both the cruising speeds and capacities of commercial airliners have increased, but the basic design can be traced to the original flights in the early 20th century.

The wheel has brought about a whole new lifestyle for mankind—we have gone from hard manual labor jobs to a more sophisticated workforce. Application of the wheel in industrial situations was key to the Industrial Revolution in the mid 1800s. The conversion of water power to spinning looms and forges through a variety of wheels provided the foundation for the industrialization and urbanization of the world. Now it is taken for granted that the wheel in many guises and forms is an inextricable part of modern life. The turntable in the microwave, the wheels of the private automobile or scooter or semi tractor-trailer, the clock or the electrical generator are but a microcosm of the examples of wheels in modern society.

Without the many forms of manufacturing, the global economy of the 21st century would not be a reality. The millions of jobs that are associated with making, distributing, transporting and selling goods around the world are all based on the use of the wheel.

The Wheel of Commerce is not just a symbol of the many elements that comprise modern day world commerce—it is also the foundation upon which the world's commerce operates.

---

[1] USAID, "Comparative Transportation Cost Analysis in East Africa, Final Report," Technical Paper No. 22, April 1997

[2] Carlo M. Cipolla, ed., *Before the Industrial Revolution,* (Fontana Press 1973), 196

[3] Cipolla, 198-199

[4] Cipolla, 208

[5] Cipolla, 211

[6] Edward J. Taaffe, Richard L. Morrill and Peter R. Gould, *Transport Expansion in Underdeveloped Countries: A Comparative Analysis,* (American Geographical Society, 1963)

[7] B.S. Hoyle, *Transport and Economic Growth in Developing Countries: The Case of East Africa,* (London: MacMillan, 1973)

[8] Aerotropolis Business Concepts, LLC™

[9] World Bank, *World Development Indicators 2009,* (World Bank, April 2009), 218

[10] Edinformatics, www.edinformatics.com/inventions_inventors/

[11] HubPages, http://hubpages.com/hub/Invention-of-the-Wheel

Transport
Logistics
– the Wheel of Commerce

SECTION II
THE WHEEL OF COMMERCE: A SYSTEM

Transport and logistics services are an integral part of economies around the world. The interplay between the members of the transport and logistics industry and the users and supporters of those activities is known as The Wheel of Commerce. This integration is not a recent development; it has been in existence for thousands of years. Facilitating trade not only within a sovereign nation or region but also on a worldwide scale is an essential component of the foundation of the world's economic growth. Even isolationist economies like those of Myanmar and North Korea participate in The Wheel of Commerce. Other countries such as The Netherlands, Singapore and the United Arab Emirates are major hubs that handle shares of international trade far in excess of their domestic production capacities.

In this section, Chapter 3, TRANSPORT NETWORKS, examines the development of networks and their impact on social and economic development. Chapter 4, LOGISTICS SYSTEMS, is an overview of transport and logistics system that play an integral role in the movement of goods and wealth around the world.

CHAPTER 3

TRANSPORT NETWORKS

While each element of a network is important individually, it is the coordination among them that provides the power of the logistics industry to move goods around a region or around the world.

Trade became part of the economic landscape as soon as specialization in economic enterprises emerged. Once people began to focus on one element of economic output, such as farming instead of raising sheep or spinning wool or making fabrics or making clothes, the need for trade evolved. Those making clothes or fabrics or wool required food. Whether through barter or the use of coins, goods were exchanged. Once the agreement was confirmed, the goods needed to be moved from place of production to point of consumption. What were originally local and regional flows of goods have expanded into global flows of goods that link diverse parts of the world.

From earliest times, trade and commerce has been a fundamental impetus for economic and social development. The exchange of goods has also meant the exchange of ideas and concepts. The Phoenicians who pioneered trade around the Mediterranean spread language and culture in addition to their loads of pottery, wine and textiles. Arab traders sailing dhows from the Arabian Gulf opened trade routes around the Indian Ocean from Mombasa to Goa in southwestern India. In order to boost their business in east Africa, traders created a common language that borrowed words and phrases from Arabic and some native African languages. That language, Swahili, is now spoken by an estimated 200 million people in Africa and on the Arabian Peninsula.

The Chinese treasure fleets that operated from China to Africa established trade routes that promoted the seaborne movement of goods and people over thousands of miles. In addition to the trade of goods, people and their cultures spread between the various points along the routes including Malacca (Malaysia) and Calicut (India). On land, Chinese and

Arab traders developed the Silk Road that brought spices and silks to the west where Venetian traders then carried them into Europe. The travels of Marco Polo exemplified the interchange between different cultures almost halfway around the world from each other.

From an economic perspective, trade is a natural result of the search for increased wealth. "Gains from trade occur because goods move from where their relative prices are low (in the absence of trade) to where they are high."[1] The movement of goods or the shifting of production is a response to differing value judgments, costs of operation, and levels of demand.

In his seminal treatise on political economies, Adam Smith noted that "Plano Carpino, a monk sent as ambassador from the king of France to one of the sons of the famous Genghis Khan, says that the Tartars used frequently to ask him if there was plenty of sheep and oxen in the kingdom of France...They wanted to know if the country was rich enough to be worth the conquering." The Tartars spoke of sheep and cattle because they were the instruments of wealth and commerce. Even then the concept of international trade, albeit from the perspective of conquering and capture, was readily understood.

By the 17th century, the concept of international trade was better known, understood and pursued. Trade across the Mediterranean, along the Silk Road and elsewhere, was an accepted form of economic activity. In 1630 Thomas Mun, a successful merchant and member of the East India Company, wrote a book entitled "England's Treasure by Foreign Trade." Mun was a "mercantilist," a term applied to people who were convinced that "England's prosperity was bound up in the possibilities of foreign commerce or merchandising." In his book, Mun argued that it was in England's self interest to participate in and promote trade with foreign lands. In the beginning of the book, he argued that "the ordinary means therefore to increase our wealth and treasure is by Foreign Trade, wherein we must ever observe this rule: to sell more to strangers yearly than we consume of theirs in value."[2] That argument is no less valid in the 21st century than it was in the 17th century. Some countries in the 21st century, like the United States, appear to have forgotten this basic economic precept. Trade deficits have been a constant reminder that the United States no longer makes all of the products that it consumes, especially consumer goods. However, this situation did spur and support the emergence of global supply chains as products once made in North America were made in more distant locations, primarily China and Southeast Asia.

Transport networks come in many shapes and designs.

Networks, the arrangement by which the various members of the logistics chain work or are physically tied together, are an important part of the puzzle. Physical networks such as roads, sealanes or airways function alongside other networks composed of data lines or satellite links, financial arrangements, insurance policies or personal relationships. While each of the networks is important individually, it is the coordination among them that provides the power of the logistics industry to move goods around a region or around the world.

The study, design, construction and operation of transportation networks are important steps in creating a visible tool for economic development. A principal characteristic of a transport network is to merge different flows so that they move over a common link.[3] In other words, instead of building specific links between discrete origins and destinations for separate traffic flows, the effectiveness and utility of a transport network is optimized by combining different flows on a common link that maximize the utility of the transport network. This increases the efficiency of the network and reduces the transport cost.

A network can be examined from five perspectives:[4]

1. A network is a set of interconnected nodes that reflects a trade-off between efficiency and stability.
2. The connection between the nodes is not random; they reflect the interplay between demand and the desire of the nodes to increase value by increasing the number of connections.
3. A hub's efficiency is based on achieving economies of scale.
4. The emergence of dominant hubs reflects a "winner takes all" approach to economic development.
5. Networks are scale free and not static; they are continually responding to internal forces and external demands and requirements.

The evolution of a market is the response to four types of arbitrage, all with the goal of seeking the lowest cost or risk. Markets and their constituent members are constantly addressing inputs related to costs, information, taxation and regulations. As the outcomes of the arbitrage analysis emerge, a network will also change. Sites that can demonstrate lower costs, improved information flows and lower taxes, and have fewer regulations, will be preferred over others. In response, transport networks and services will realign to link those sites into the overall network. The capacity of the links is increased and the services levels improved in response to expanding traffic flows on the links to these emerging locations.

There are many varieties of transport networks, as the following diagrams illustrate. Each of these network models incorporate benefits and costs for the builders and the transport companies that use the network. Selecting the network option is a mix of the influence of the regional geography, such as the location of large bodies of water, bridges and mountainous terrain, the location of the origin and destination nodes, the traffic volumes both current and predicted, and the density of population and commercial activities.

A transport network is composed of two primary elements: The nodes, represented by the blocks in the diagrams, and the links, which are represented by the lines that connect the nodes. The nodes can be thought of as individual street addresses, railways stations, seaports or airports. The links can be both physical elements such as roads or rail lines or simply as paths followed by ships through oceans or air routes used by aircraft. Regardless of the transport mode, all networks, at their most basic elemental structure, are a combination of nodes and links.

The composition of the nodes and links and the general arrangement as illustrated by the five basic alternatives in the following diagram reflect a combination of complexity, flexibility and influence of physical, political and social factors. The design of the transport network can simply be based on decisions by the transport companies as to where they want to operate and provide services. In other cases, the transport network can be the result of political or regulatory influences. While the former is preferable, the latter is usually the reality. The impact of political

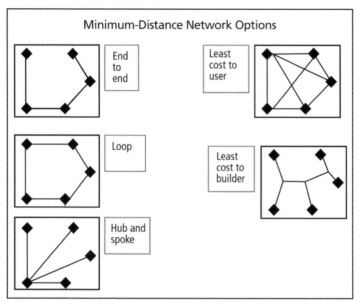

Source: W. Bunge, "Theoretical geography, Land studies in Geography," Series C, General and Mathematical Geography, 1962, pg. 183-189.

and/or regulatory influences can affect the operational efficiency of the transport network. If these factors are too onerous, the transport network can fail and the much-needed services are unavailable to the passengers or shippers.

A failure or dilution of the efficiency or effectiveness of the transport network and the associated service levels can lead to broader economic and social impacts. The response to those impacts can either redress the situation or exacerbate the negative impacts. There are many instances where political and/or regulatory impacts have negatively affected a transport network and/or associated service. While a totally "free" environment is not necessarily feasible, especially in the case of maintaining safe and secure operations, the removal of the political factor is usually highly desirable.

Each of the five basic network designs represents the combined influence of many factors. For the purposes of this discussion, we focus on the operational efficiencies and by relation the likely operating costs associated with each alternative.

The "end to end" network is a basic system that is reasonably efficient for the operator and the user except for traffic that moves from one end to the other and has to pass through all of the nodes. Such a network creates undue pressure (loading) on each link and collaterally on each node. Each link, except for the two on the ends, has to carry both traffic between the adjacent nodes and transit traffic that is passing through to nodes beyond. If we think of this network as a railway, where the two outer links might be single tracks, the intermediate links might be double or even triple tracked. The heavier traffic carried either by longer trains or more services on the intermediate links may require more investment and thus higher fixed and possibly operating costs. Therefore, while this network is simple in concept, it can result in either lower operating efficiencies or higher operating costs, or a combination of the two.

The "loop" network relieves some of the pressure of the "end to end" network. Traffic from what were the two end points can transit a direct link between them. This added link can also permit traffic from beyond the two former end points to be routed over it, providing alternate paths for the traffic and the transport services. This network is sometimes referred to as the "delivery" network. It is so called because it allows the delivery driver to return to his origin without having to retrace his route. This is more efficient and thus can be operated at a lower cost. That lower operating cost can be conferred to users through lower rates or preserved by the operator in the form of higher contributions to overhead and profit.

The "hub and spoke" network reflects the desire of the operator to control the services through a central node or hub. Many airline operations are designed this way. FedEx made the hub concept a reality when it started operating at Memphis Airport in the early 1970s. The hub was adopted by passenger airlines in the U.S. at Charlotte, North Carolina, by Piedmont Airlines and at Atlanta, Georgia, by Eastern Air Lines. Now almost every airline in the world has one or more hubs in its network.

This network design has a number of associated benefits and risks. Because of the limited number of links or spokes from the hub, control of the operations is focused on few alternatives. Transport units all pass through the hub where maintenance, support and operating crews can be concentrated. Because all passenger and/or cargo traffic pass through the hub, it is easier to shift them from one spoke to another. As there are only a limited number of spokes from the hub, the investment in the infrastructure is also limited.

The primary risk associated with this type of transport network is the impact to the entire system if the hub ceases to operate for any reason. Because all transport services arrive and depart at the hub, when the hub is closed, there are no services to any of the other nodes. Selection of the hub, especially in a small network where there is only one hub, is very important. If weather is a controlling factor, especially for airlines, then a location that is free of bad weather, such as fog or heavy snowfalls, is desirable. Another risk related to the hub is its capacity. If traffic growth results in volumes exceeding the capacity of the hub, the hub becomes a bottleneck instead of a traffic facilitator. The economic costs of the hub overcome the inherent economic efficiencies of the "hub and spoke" network, resulting in diminished returns both to the service provider and users of the service.

The "hub and spoke" network concept has been adopted by other transport modes. Steamship companies have established key ports where their largest vessels call. Shipments are transferred between the larger ships and the "feeder" vessels. These smaller vessels carry shipments to/from smaller ports that have lower volumes. "Hub and spoke" networks also bring together different transport modes to a single point of transfer. In almost all cases, a shipment, especially of manufactured goods, will be carried by two or more transport modes. The locations where the shipments move from one mode to another can occur at a hub. With similar economic and operational benefits of a single-mode hub, a multimodal hub benefits different transport operators and modes, and better uses the infrastructure and related support services.

The "least cost to user" network provides the most routing possibilities for the transport provider. Because every node is linked directly to every other node, the service provider enjoys an environment of maximum flexibility in routing. This can be accentuated when services can be adjusted to reflect changing demand. If a particular link is not required because of a lack of demand, then the service operator does not need to operate over that particular link. This network form presumes that there are no physical, social, political or regulatory impediments. If the network is based on a physical system of linkages, such as in the case of a road or rail network, this network will have the highest fixed costs, related to construction and maintenance. If, however, the network is for an ocean or aviation operation, the existence of the various links is of little consequence so long as the political or regulations do not require operations over every link regardless of the traffic load.

The final basic network form, the "least cost to builder" reduces the number of links. However, it relies on a central spine, much like the human body. As in the case of the "hub and spoke" network, operations in this environment are subject to problems that can arise on the links that comprise the central spine of the network. If any of those links fail or are closed, then at least a portion of the network will be cut off from the rest of the system. Unlike the "hub and spoke" network, services can still be provided to at least some portion of the network that is not possible if the hub is closed. This network is particularly appropriate for transport operations that employ a physical system of links like a road system, railway or pipeline. By using the spine, each node is directly linked to a central spine, only a limited number of links may need to have expanded capacity, there are alternative routes for the traffic, and there is, to some extent, alternate routes if a link is put out of service.

Transport networks have evolved into more complex structures. One driver of the complexity has been the mixing of transport modes. In some cases the different modes are directly connected to each other such as on-dock rail at a seaport or road transport with air service at an airport. With this evolution has come a new hub and spoke design that is illustrated by the following diagram.

The links between the four primary transport modes reflect the typical connections. As an example, shipments are regularly moved by a combination of road or rail to/from seaports and by sea services between ports. In some instances, shipments that have been carried by an ocean service are transferred to air. The only intermodal connection that does not commonly exist is between air and rail. While there have been a number of attempts to create and maintain this connection, especially within Europe, the projects have not been sustained.

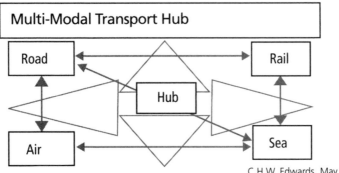

C.H.W. Edwards, May 2010

In the case of intermodal connections, the hub becomes more than a simple facility in which the transfer occurs. Additional value-added services occur at the hub. These services can range from simple transfer of shipments from one transport container to another, or can include relabeling or repackaging. In some instances, a physical link can be as important as a hub. An example is the Panama Canal, which is a very important link in the worldwide network of ocean routes.

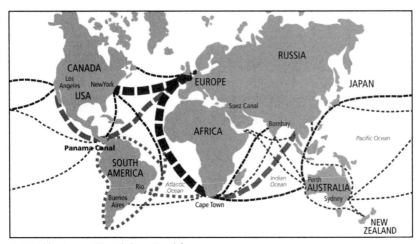

Adapted by C.H.W. Edwards (May 2010) from:
www.wired.com/wiredscience/2010/01/global-shipping-map/#ixzz0sd2saZu7

The Canal, which opened in 1914, handled 298,313 PC/UMS in the 2009 fiscal year. (PC/UMS is the tonnage measurement system used for the Panama Canal tolls assessment. This amount also includes the PC/UMS tonnage for full containership and passenger vessels that transited

Trade Route	PC/ UMS	% of Total	Trade Route	PC/ UMS	% of Total
East Coast U.S-Asia	119,513	40.1	Europe-West Coast U.S./Canada	6,781	2.3
East Coast U.S-W.C. South America	30,852	10.3	Europe-Asia	5,773	1.9
Europe-West Coast South America	20,463	6.9	East Coast U.S./Canada-Oceania	3,458	1.2
U.S. Intercoastal (including Alaska and Hawaii)	14,048	4.7	E.C. South America-West Coast U.S./Canada	3,158	1.1
South America Intercoastal	14,043	4.7	Round-the-World	542	0.2
East Coast U.S. -W.C. Central America	10,317	3.5	Sub Total	236,606	79.3
West Indies -W.C. Central America	7,658	2.6	All Others Routes	61,707	20.7
			Total	298,313	

Source: Panama Canal Authority, www.pancanal.com, 2010

the Panama Canal.) As the table shows, the single largest trade route is between Asia and the east coast of the United States. This trade lane accounted for 40 percent of the total volume in 2009. Until 1999, when the canal was transferred to the Republic of Panama, it was owned by the United States.

Source: Panama Canal Authority (Multimedia) www.acp.gob.pa

As one of the world's two primary canals, the other being the Suez Canal in Egypt between the Red and Mediterranean seas, the Panama Canal is key to the world's ocean trade network. The Panama Canal can be likened to a central spine link in a "least cost to builder" network. Physically, the canal provides a shortcut for ships moving between the Atlantic and Pacific Oceans that once had to travel to the southern end of South America. However, because of its age, the canal has become a bottleneck. The width and length of the locks that lift or lower the ships across the spine of Central America cannot accommodate many of the vessels that now ply the trade routes. In addition, because of the growth of trade, the total capacity of the canal is unable to handle the number of ships that might use this route.

In response to these demands, the Panama Canal Authority has embarked on a US$5.25-billion expansion that will add a set of longer, wider locks to allow ships with capacities up to 12,000 TEU, instead of the current limit of 4,500 TEU, to transit this vital trade route. The Panama Canal has become more than just a series of locks. The Colon Free Zone, near the Atlantic entrance, has become the world's second largest re-export center, just behind Hong Kong. In 2008, an estimated US$9.1 billion worth of goods was unloaded, relabeled and repackaged before being re-exported.[5] These services would not have evolved without the Panama Canal.

Transport networks are not static. New roads are built and existing roads are expanded, as are transport hubs, whether they are rail yards, airports or seaports. On a broader scale, the shift of industrial activity can create new demands for new or additional transport networks and services. The developments in Asia reflect these changes. Internal transport modes, including pipelines, roads and rail lines, are overtaking the once dominant seaborne trade. In December 2009, a 7,000-kilometer (4,400 miles) pipeline was inaugurated between Turkmenistan and China. Where once the Mekong River was the transport route in Southeast China, a network of roads, some linked to those in China, are being built to handle growing trade flows. As of 2009, China now hosts the world's most extensive high-speed railway network, including a Maglev route between Pudong Airport and Shanghai. From a security perspective, which can influence both the design and operation of a transport network, these internal routes are no longer under the watchful eye of the United States Navy. The inland transport routes have to be protected by the Asian countries through which they run.[6]

Conclusion

A transport network is the fundamental structure within which transport and logistics services operate. There are many versions, but the common objective of all of them is to create an arrangement in which different flows of goods move efficiently between the different origins and destinations. Transport networks are always in a constant state of flux as the traffic changes with respect to volume, direction or by virtue of changes in the configuration. New origins and destinations can emerge and either add to the complexity of the network or replace other nodes that decline in importance. The multimodal hub represents the evolution of transport and logistics services. Shippers want choices and the transport networks have responded by creating linkages between different modes that were once considered as barriers. Sea to air or vice versa links are an example of this evolution.

The final design of the network can be influenced by a wide variety of factors—both physical and non-physical. Mountains, large bodies of water, swamps and other geographical features can force diversions from the most direct route. National borders also can force diversion of a route. As transport technologies change, the impact of physical and non-physical barriers change. Airways are not affected by surface features such as mountains or oceans, but they can be affected by noise reduction zones or national controls on flight operations. Similarly, non-tariff barriers such as extra charges and low-maintenance spending can force transport companies to use alternate routes that are not necessarily the most efficient or least costly.

While the "least cost to user" provides the maximum number of optional routes for service providers, the construction and maintenance costs of such a network are the highest. The "end to end" network is missing a single link and thus can lead to congestion and added travel time and related operating costs, especially if goods and passengers have to move between the two end nodes. The "hub and spoke" network is efficient in terms of a limited number of links between the nodes. However, this transport network can create severe congestion at the hub node and also requires additional travel back and forth along the links. The final option, the "least cost to builder," creates a central spine link from which branch links connect all of the nodes. While the "least cost to builder" is much cheaper to build and maintain, it does add to the operating costs of the transport services in comparison with the "least cost to user" network alternative. Similarly, the "least cost to builder" option reduces hub-related congestion costs as there is no hub and also reduces the travel time between the end points. That is the case of the "end to end" network alternative. The critical link in the "least cost to user" network is the central spine, which has to carry all traffic between most of the nodes in this simplistic network.

---

[1] Richard E. Caves, Ronald W. Jones, *World Trade and Payments: An Introduction,* (Boston: Little, Brown, 1977), 160

[2] Leonard D. Abbott, ed., *Masterworks of Economics,* Vol. 1, (Garden City, NY: Doubleday, 1946), 6

[3] Peter Haggett, Richard J. Chorley, *Network Analysis in Geography,* (London: Edward Arnold, 1969), 111

[4] Andrew Sheng, "Financial Crisis and Global Governance: A Network Analysis," Globalization and Growth, (Washington, DC, World Bank, 2010), 72-75

[5] "Briefing: The Panama Canal, A Plan to Unlock Prosperity," *The Economist,* December 5, 2009, 45-47

[6] "New Silk Roads: Roads, railways and pipelines are redefining what we mean by Asia," *The Economist,* April 10, 2010, 48

CHAPTER 4

LOGISTICS SYSTEMS

The transport and logistics industry is truly the "The Wheel of Commerce" as it strengthens and expands economic growth and development.

The role of logistics is pervasive in the world's economy. Companies in this industry haul goods from point to point; handle myriad paperwork that governs the flow of raw materials, components and finished goods; package and warehouse the products, and manage the flows within countries and across borders. Without the actions of the many members of the national and worldwide logistics chains, the newest cell phone would not be on the market, fresh vegetables and fruit would not be available in the depths of winter, and the latest fashions would not be ready for eager consumers.

The economic impact of transport and logistics companies is multi-fold. In addition to their essential role in moving and handling products as they are transformed from a raw material to a finished consumer good, logistics and transport companies employ millions of people around the world. An efficient logistics system is essential for the economic growth of a country.

As discussed later, it is the transport and logistics industry that links all of the actors within the supply chain together. Whether this involves the physical movement of goods, the processing of paper-based or electronic orders, clearing goods across national borders or financing the various steps, the logistics chain involves a variety of flows and myriad activities. The transport and logistics industry is truly the "The Wheel of Commerce" as it strengthens and expands economic growth and development.

One of the most important aspects of doing business is the ability to understand the impediments and incorporate those issues into the operations of the business. It is often said that not knowing the unknown is the scariest part of life. If a businessman does not know what he does not know, then it is almost impossible to create or implement a plan. Therefore, it is of vital importance that businesses are able to understand all of the hurdles and challenges that they must deal with in the normal and usual conduct of their business.

The emergence of globalization, by which goods and services are exchanged not just across adjacent borders but around the world, has brought both benefits and costs. Globalization has given rise to manufacturing centers in Asia. The Pearl River Delta region of China has rapidly changed from quiet backwater to a region dotted by new cities and thousands of manufacturing and processing facilities that are serving the needs of people all over the world. The rise of globalization in the 1990s tightened the relationship between transportation and trade and the economic growth of the world. As we have already argued, transportation and logistics have always been inextricably tied to economic development; globalization was possible only through the complete integration of transport and logistics parties and activities into all elements of the supply chain. This activity has only expanded as globalization has become an accepted part and, some might say, an essential aspect, of the world's economy.

The old "silos," in which a product or shipment was handed off from one company to another as it progressed from origin to destination, have been torn down. Barriers between companies have been eliminated or weakened. Traditional freight forwarders like Kuehne and Nagel, Schenkers, Panalpina and others have spread their nets beyond the traditional services of freight forwarding, groupage/consolidations, and customs house brokerage into "new" business opportunities, including warehousing, distribution, reverse logistics, procurement and even in some cases trade finance.

In the not too distant past, steamships operated on a schedule that was not fixed. Now, similar to the integrated air carriers like FedEx and UPS that base their operations on precise timekeeping, steamship companies operate their vessels according to tight timetables. Vessel calls at ports are measured in terms of hours instead of days. The faster handling is of course due to the dominant use of containers that permit faster loading and discharge of shipments. As a result, shippers and consignees can now rely on this dependable schedule to use the vessels as moving warehouses. Safety stocks, that extra, very expensive inventory that is maintained for potential delays in the transport process, have been whittled down, if not eliminated. The savings have been significant, as this additional component of inventory has been replaced by the goods that are in transit.

Classic boundaries and separation of responsibility have been brushed away. New business models, some introduced by innovative companies like Federal Express, United Parcel Service, TNT Express and Deutche Poste Worldwide Network, have been copied by companies large and small in the transportation and logistics field.

The net effect of these changes has served to fully integrate the transport and logistics services into the global supply chain. In some cases it is difficult to know where the transport and logistics services end or begin. Famous guitar makers use logistics companies not only to move their products to retailers and consumers, but also to complete the production, inspection and packaging process. Hospital supplies are stored and dispatched not by the makers of the products but by third-party companies that are adept at sourcing from a variety of manufacturers, and then packaging and delivering the needed supplies not just to the hospital receiving dock but in many instances specifically to the nurses' station where the supplies are needed.

The logistics chain is composed of many players whose combined actions move goods through the various steps from origin to final destination, from producer to consumer. In addition to the value of the output of the raw material suppliers, manufacturers and consumers, the activities of these various players of the logistics chain also contribute significantly to the country's economy.

The following diagram illustrates the many companies that touch a product as it is transformed from a raw material to a consumer product and moves through the supply chain. The companies along each step comprise the transport and logistics chain. Those include transport companies like long-distance and local truck haulage, railways, airlines, river barges, and lake and ocean carriers. The list of non-transport members of the

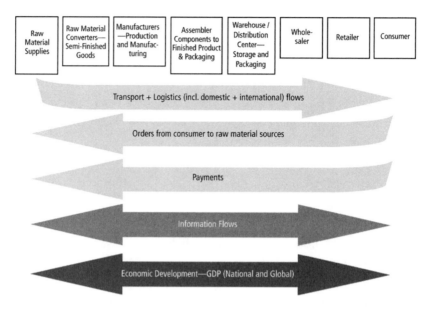

logistics chain includes a wide variety of companies such as freight forwarders, customs house brokers, warehouse and distribution center operators, stevedores, communications companies, insurance companies and banks. Government agencies, including customs inspectors, scale operators and others, also are involved in the flow of products. As the product undergoes its transformation from a raw material to a consumer good, it passes through the hands of each of these companies, either physically or in the form of paper or electronically delivered bills of lading or invoices.

The following diagram shows the integration of the "The Wheel of Commerce" within the broader economic activity of the world. It illustrates the interplay between all elements of the economic process. The wheel symbolizes the transportation, distribution and logistics industries that comprise the physical and non-physical elements of the supply chain. The wheel is constantly turning. Its turning reflects the continual movement of products along the supply chain from raw material to component through work-in-progress to the finished good that is sold (and sometimes, returned unsold or as damaged or refused goods). Along the wheel pass volumes of data and information about orders, proposals, shipment status, tracking reports and the general exchange of

Transport
Logistics
– the Wheel of Commerce

information that makes the supply chain function. Additionally, flows of funds also pass along the wheel and make it turn. Payments for the mined ores, the manufacturing, the transport and the distribution processes, and the finished goods power the wheel.

Arrayed around the wheel are the various players who through their combined efforts conceive, develop, design, make and sell goods. The shipment of soft drinks might move just a hundred kilometers from the bottling plant to the retail shop, but the action of acquiring the raw materials, the empty bottles or cans, and transporting the finished beverage to the shop are all part and parcel of the broad transport and logistics wheel.

Like a wheel, many component parts must work together. Just as a bicycle wheel will fall apart if the spokes detach from the rim or the hub, so too, the highly integrated systems of today's transportation and logistics systems will fail if any one of the member parties abandons his role or duty. Orders might not be placed, shipments may become lost or damaged, or payments could fail to be transferred. If these or the innumerable other processes fail to function, then the supply chain seizes up. A major failure imperils not a single shipment but tens of thousands that pass through the logistics system. If a major transport hub like the Port of Jebel Ali in the United Arab Emirates or Changi International Airport in Singapore stops operating or experiences reductions in productivity, those impacts spread out not as mere ripples on a pond but like a tsunami that washes up in ports and airports around the world.

The operational, legal, financial and procedural complexities of making sure that the right product arrives at the right place at the right time require a multifaceted group of companies and individuals. The complexity increases when shipments cross national borders.

The outside elements of the logo represent those companies and individuals that rely on the transportation and logistics wheel. The coffee farmer in Burundi, the diamond miner in the Canadian Arctic, the automotive supplier in India, and the shopper at the Sarit Centre in Nairobi exemplify the diverse populations that directly or indirectly rely on and use the services of the transport and logistics wheel. The farmer relies on the Tanzanian railway to move his precious container of coffee without delay to the seaport at Dar es Salaam. The miner expects the winter road trucker to haul in the much needed drill tool to keep the mine working. The factory manager needs to know that the truck carrying the parts will arrive at the assembly plant on time. The shopper wants to see the latest fashions on the racks in her favorite store.

But globalization also has become an avenue that accelerates the spread of downturns and economic slowdowns on a broader scale than was previously the case. The old saying, "If the United States gets a cold… Canada gets the flu" is still valid, but the links are not just across a single border as in that simple example. Rather, they now involve supply chains that encircle the globe. When major consuming regions like the United States or the European Union lose their appetites for imported goods, manufacturers in Asia lose valuable sales. As the World Bank has noted, whereas in the 1960s and 1970s, a 1-percent change in the world's combined output (GDP) would create a two-percentage change in the volume of trade, that ratio as of the 1990s had increased to 1:3.4. That 70-percent increase in the ratio reflects the growth of trade around the world. According to the World Trade Organization, merchandise trade not only moves in tandem with world gross domestic product, as illustrated by the ratio above, but in fact export growth exceeds the growth of GDP.[1]

The expansion of worldwide trade has many outcomes. One of those outcomes is that an economic reversal in one part of the world quickly spreads. As the ratio of trade to output increases so, too, the impact of downturns and slowdowns becomes magnified and dramatically spreads geographically. The first 21st century economic downturn, which started in the United States, led to dropping consumption levels that affected producers all over the world. Unlike past recessions in the latter part of the 20th century, no part of the world has escaped unscathed. Granted, while some economies in Asia and elsewhere have been able to rebound quickly from the initial downturn, the effects of this economic reversal are not yet known and may not be for many years.

But, in spite of this, the wheel of commerce has not stopped turning. Rather, the load has lightened as volumes declined. Transport companies have pulled assets such as ships, planes and trucks from the market and millions of people have lost their jobs or are working for less pay or for fewer hours. The demand for goods has fallen, but not evaporated. In some cases, trade has been diverted from higher cost and faster transport modes to slower, cheaper alternatives.

The response of transport and logistics companies to the 2007 recession has varied. Almost every company has laid off managers and staff, idled equipment and sought out cost-saving opportunities. In many cases, the actions were a reaction to customers dramatically reducing demand. By early 2010, anticipating the recession lasting into 2013, companies had looked at their systems, organizations and market presence, and prepared themselves for the eventual recovery. Those companies that have taken a deliberate but realistic look at their operations will most likely be very successful in the next economic phase of recovery.

One example of a response to the "new normal" is a slower rate of hiring in response to market growth. New management systems are being installed. Their focus is to better use the human and physical assets of the acquiring company. If more traffic can be carried or processed with fewer people, then when the next downturn occurs, the layoffs may not be as dramatic. However, this also means that many former employees might never be rehired. Because many believe that the new normal will be reflected in lower levels of consumption, particularly in the developed nations, the number of product variants, expressed as stock keeping units (SKU), will be lower. This in turn will ease the burden of tracking so many different products, but will also reduce workloads of warehousing and distribution centers. Lastly, in an effort to seek better ways to perform tasks, many companies are finally willing to confront and reject old taboos. Fresh ideas, "thinking outside the box," and looking to other industries for ideas and concepts are being embraced aggressively and with relish.

As the number of SKUs is reduced and the demand for goods has declined, products are shifting from one transport mode to another. This modal shift occurs naturally during a product's life cycle. As a product moves from a high margin innovative or unique state to that of a commodity, the profit margin declines. With lower profit margins and a slowing of demand growth, the ability to pay for a higher cost transport alternative or to need a faster, usually higher cost, transport mode dissipates. As a consequence, the shipper and/or consignee will change transport buying decisions to select a deferred and consequently lower cost transport service.

This modal shift became more pronounced and, some would say, accelerated during the 2007 recession. An analysis of modal shifts by the Seabury Group Cargo Advisory Unit noted the air share of containerized international trade fell from 2.8 percent to 1.8 percent in terms of weight between 2000 and 2008.[2] Seabury also identified three drivers that contributed to the shift:

1. Trade lanes dominated by air grew at a slower pace than those lanes dominated by ocean services;
2. Volumes of goods usually moved by air grew slower than those that usually moved by ocean; and
3. Many goods, such as LCD screens and laptops that typically moved by air, were in fact shifted to sea services.

In a time-series analysis of the situation, Seabury identified a significant shift of international trade volume from air to sea from April 2008 to January 2009. The curve—that is, the shift from air to sea—reversed in February 2009. It is believed that while the too-high inventory levels contributed to the shift away from air because the sales were slowing and hence new product was not needed quickly on the store shelves in 2008, the combination of stock-outs and very low air freight rates supported a return of some products back to air cargo services. If the "new normal" economic environment becomes a fact, then there is a high likelihood that the shift of some goods from air service to ocean will be permanent.

Apart from the response of transport and logistics companies to the

2007 recession, logistics systems are always evolving. An example of this is the adoption of what emerged as air service factors and qualities by ocean services.

Crowley Maritime, a U.S. marine company that began operations in 1892, exemplifies how one transport mode can borrow operational and service qualities from another mode. Crowley's liner services, which connect the United States and Canada with services to most of the Caribbean including Puerto Rico, the Bahamas, the U.S. Virgin Islands, the eastern and western Caribbean and points in Central America from Honduras to Panama, carry many perishable products. The shipping company has introduced multiple weekly sailings so that the dwell time of perishable products is reduced.

Crowley assigns the term "perishable product" to any product that is time sensitive. In addition to fruits and vegetables, apparel is treated by Crowley as a perishable product that demands fast and prompt service from the manufacturing locations in the Caribbean and Central America to the markets in North America. Where once a shipping line would have provided a service level that efficiently used its assets, steamship lines like Crowley and others are more customer-focused. By adapting their services to shipper and consignee requirements, they are better positioned to capture and keep business in the face of stiff competition.

Conclusion

The symbol adopted to represent the concept of *Transport Logistics: The Wheel of Commerce* incorporates the basic element of transport, the wheel, as well as the many spinoffs and related activities that combine to create economic growth and development. From a raw material extracted from the earth to a high technology product demanded by consumers around the world, the transport and logistics industry facilitates the flow of goods. Boundaries between the many members of the transport and logistics industry are being blurred or completely removed. The interplay between production, distribution and consumption and the transport and logistics services demands a close relationship between what used to be distinct. Innovations created in one transport sector are being adopted and adapted by other transport modes. As reliability levels have achieved parity across the many transport modes, shippers are adopting true multimodal approaches to moving their products.

---

[1] World Trade Organization, "International Trade Statistics 2009," 1

[2] Gert-Jan Jansen, "Air to ocean shift—the facts behind the hype," *Air Cargo News,* April 5, 2010, 15

Transport
Logistics
– the Wheel of Commerce

SECTION III
THE WHEEL OF COMMERCE: AN ECONOMIC INDICATOR

This section of the book examines how elements of The Wheel of Commerce herald or represent changes in the broader economy. The primary focus is the first recession of the 21st century, which began in late 2007 and quickly spread around the world. This discussion is not an economics analysis of the development and effects of the recession. Rather, it is an examination of the recession from the perspective of transportation and logistics.

As the discussion highlights, many traditional economic and financial indicators confirm the existence of an economic slowdown. These include falling industrial capacity, declining levels of inventory, rising unemployment, falling interest rates, and dropping stock market indices. But another set of indicators reflects the transport and logistics industries. Such factors as the number of commercial aircraft and ships in storage, the number of empty warehouses, falling ocean freight and air freight price indices, the decline of freight traffic volumes or the shift of freight volumes from higher to lower priced modes all reflect the impact of a recession or economic slowdown on the operating elements of the wheel of commerce.

This is not a mathematically based econometric analysis. Rather the objective of this section of the book is to identify those relationships and illustrate them through examples.

The section is divided into three chapters. The first chapter, ECO-NOMIC PHASES, develops a foundation for the discussion of the 2008 recession. It defines basic economic terms and provides an overview of the role of recessions and economic slowdowns on economic development and growth. This chapter also introduces the concept of logistics-based indicators and defines selected indicators.

The second chapter, The 2008 RECESSION, examines the 2008 recession based on financial, economic and logistics indicators. This chapter looks at the different impacts of the recession in various countries and regions through the use of accepted economic and financial indicators, including gross domestic product, merchandise flows, unemployment, and interest rates. The movements of the logistics-based indicators are compared with those of the standard economic and financial indicators.

The final chapter of this section, ROAD TO RECOVERY, looks at possible indicators that can herald both the economic trough as well as the recovery, also known as expansion, phase of the economic cycle. We will focus most of our attention on logistics-based indicators. The examination also looks at the shift of freight traffic between modes. This review discusses whether those shifts are permanent based on likely economic recovery scenarios and forecasts.

CHAPTER 5

ECONOMIC PHASES

Economic cycles are natural progressions of developed and developing economies as they experience periods of growth, followed by a cooling off period, followed by renewed growth.

Transport and logistics systems are crucial factors of economic development and activity, as discussed in Chapter 4. The objective of this chapter is to identify and define those transport and logistics-related indicators that herald an economic downturn.

Economic cycles are natural progressions of developed and developing economies as they experience periods of growth, followed by a cooling off period, followed by renewed growth. Typically, recessions occur every five or so years in a developed economy and, when graphed, are variations around the overall growth rate.

Economic cycles are man-made; they reflect the basic human spirit. Humans are positive. We believe in a better tomorrow. While the current environment might be difficult or demanding, we universally believe that things will get better and that we will enjoy the benefits of the better days. It is that "belief" and drive to achieve success that contributes to economic cycles. Many times we are haunted by history—usually because we fail to look backward and digest what happened before blindly moving forward into unstable territory. Other times, we just believe that we are smarter and do not take into account the natural order that can pull us up short. But, even in the midst of a recession or at the bottom of an economic trough, there is a belief that the future will be better. This optimism drives humans and, in turn, is reflected in the cycles of economic growth and development.

A complete economic cycle is composed of four phases:

    1. **Expansion**. During this phase inventories are used up,

which leads to production speeding up to meet demand. Unemployment declines as workers are hired to meet expanding demand. This in turn increases consumption, which supports higher rates of production. Profits begin to grow, generating excess cash that is converted into investment in various forms of productive capacity.

2. **Peak**. At a certain point, demand growth slows and then stops. The demand for investment funds pushes interest rates to levels that lead to a decline in the demand for the investment funds, because the returns on new project investments do not exceed the cost of the funds. At the peak, the level of unemployment is so low that there are no more workers to hire and thus the growth of consumer based demand stops.

3. **Recession**. Demand for investment falls. Stock market indices fall, which in turn removes available investment capital. The makers of capital equipment and durable goods begin to lay off employees as orders decline. This growth in unemployment reduces confidence in the economy and consumption declines as people either become unemployed and can purchase only essential goods and services, or those who are still employed focus on cash conservation to protect themselves financially against a possible loss of income. Additionally, inventories are drawn down as manufacturers generate cash through sales of existing products and not through increased sales of new products. Interest rates fall as demand for investment funds also declines.

4. **Trough**. Declines in output of capital and consumer goods eventually will reach a minimum sustainable level that matches demand from employed and unemployed people in the case of essential consumer goods and services or the need for replacement machinery in the case of capital goods. The lower interest rates attract demand for investment funds from those individuals and companies that have avoided the worst of the recession. With access to more investment funds, the level of demand for consumer and capital goods and services will

stabilize and begin to rise, which will eventually lead back to
the first phase of expansion.

Therefore, a recession is just a phase in an economic cycle. A recession
is a business cycle contraction during which there is a slowdown in the
expansion of the economy over some period of time, and is part of the
economic landscape. There have been four significant global downturns
in the last three decades of the 20th century. The following table provides
a summary of recessions in the United States between 1970 and 1999.

United States Recessions

Year Decline	GDP Decline	Year	GDP Decline	Year	GDP
Dec 1969-Nov 1970	-0.6 %	Nov 1973-Mar 1975	-3.2%	Jan-Jul 1980	-2.2%
Jul 1981-Nov 1982	-2.7%	Jul 1990-Mar 1991	-1.4%		

Source: The National Bureau of Economic Research, www.nber.org

But when are we in a recession? That depends on the definition of a
recession, and there is no universal definition. In the United States, a
recession is a significant decline in economic activity spread across the
economy, lasting more than a few months and normally visible in real
GDP, real income, employment, industrial production, and wholesale-
retail sales.[1] Another definition is to measure the year-on-year change of
the nation's economic output. If the year-on-year measurement indicates
a decline, then the economy is deemed to be in a recession. Another
definition is to define a "growth recession," whereby the growth of the
country's GDP falls below that country's long-term productive potential.[2] Not surprisingly, these definitions have a common theme in that
they are a retrospective look at economic data. The data have to be
compiled and reviewed before a "recession" is identified and announced.
While the U.S. approach is the fastest, requiring just two quarters, or six
months, of decline to confirm the existence of a recession, the primary
alternative definition of a recession is based on at least one year's data.

The first recession of the 21st century, which began in late 2007, has
been touted as the worst worldwide economic reversal since the Great
Depression of the 1930s. While many "experts" argue the causes of the

reversal and when and how the recovery will occur, business continues to be transacted. Raw materials are extracted, refined and converted into products; shipments move from one location to another, and products are purchased and consumed.

The effect of the recession on supply chains varies, but they have been changed. Many would argue that the fundamentals that were once accepted as the norm are no longer applicable.

Changes to the world gross domestic product and merchandise trade generally move in tandem. When changes in GDP and merchandise trade are compared, the latter changes are more volatile. The rises and the declines are larger for merchandise trade than the changes in GDP levels. One of the reasons for this situation is that merchandise trade not only includes the flow of finished goods for sale, but also the export and import of intermediate products. Thus, the flow of raw materials to a processor or the movements of sub-components to a final assembly factory are part of the merchandise trade. As the World Trade Organization (WTO) notes, the emergence of international supply chains has increased this phenomenon.[3]

Exports of manufactured goods react more significantly to changes in income than the more general measure of merchandise trade. Manufactured exports have higher income elasticity. In other words, as changes in income occur, the trade of manufactured goods will rise faster and fall further than that of general merchandise. The WTO analysis calculated income elasticity of merchandise trade at 1.7 while the income elasticity for manufactured goods was 2.1. The higher level of elasticity means that a change in income will be magnified in terms of the flow of manufactured goods.

As a result, the impact of an economic recession on supply chains is felt throughout the system. Decline in the demand for goods reduces the need for transport, warehouse, and processing services. As the flow of goods across international borders slows, the need for customs house brokerage services falls off. In addition to employee layoffs or more drastic closure of companies, transport assets such as trucks, rail cars and engines, ships and planes are taken out of service. Warehouses and distribution centers operate at lower levels or are closed down. As demand declines, prices for services also drop. Suppliers and vendors increasingly compete for less traffic. Profit margins are whittled down or sometimes eliminated in search of positive cash flows that will sustain a company through the recession and trough phases of the economic cycle. Those companies that created flexible, variable cost-driven operations and/or built up a hoard of cash will survive the worst of a recession and trough, especially if the decline is severe and the trough is extended.

One of the outcomes of globalization is the creation of a complex network linking all parts of the world together. This network helps spread economic wealth around the world and also facilitates the geographic spread of an economic downturn.

These changes in economic activity, including transport and logistics services, are reflected in general economic and specific logistics- and transport-related indicators. Because of the importance of trade in the world economy, indicators that measure trade and transport services are likely to respond earlier to any downturn or any recovery. As soon as demand begins to weaken, manufacturers will slow both production and shipments. As the decline increases, manufacturing plants will experience either reduced hours or complete shutdown. In either case, the transport and logistics services that count on the shipments from those plants will see immediate reductions in demand for their services. The result of the decline in traffic can vary, but will likely include temporary layoffs of staff, taking vehicles out of service, lowering freight rates and ancillary charges, or even going out of business. Because of the nature of their business, any economic indicator that follows transport and logistics services is likely to herald downturns or upticks of economic activity.

There are literally hundreds of macroeconomic and microeconomic indicators. Among them are 11 indices that reflect both the demand for transport services and the services themselves. The first four indices, Gross Domestic Product, Inventory Levels, Factory/Production Utilization, and Merchandise Trade Flows, present information about the economic activity of a country or region. The remaining seven indices reflect the actions of the transport and logistics providers to the macroeconomic information presented by the first four indices.

1. **Gross domestic product**. This indicator measures the

sum of value added by all producers in an economy. "Value added" is the value of the gross output of producers less the value of intermediate goods and services that are consumed in production before taking into account the consumption of fixed capital. That is to say, the value of the raw materials and/or sub-components that are used to make a finished product are deleted from the calculation of the economy's gross domestic product on the presumption that the value of the finished good implicitly incorporates the value of everything that has gone into its manufacture. This measure of economic activity does not reflect the ownership of the productive assets. As an example, if a Canadian firm owns a factory in Tanzania, the output of that factory would be included in the GDP of Tanzania and not of Canada, even though the productive assets were owned by a Canadian.

2. **Inventory levels**. Inventories reflect the unsold goods that have been produced. They can be for capital, durable and consumer goods.

3. **Factory/productive utilization**. This measure indicates how much of the theoretical productive capacity of a nation's economy is being used.

4. **Merchandise trade flows**. This indicator measures the flow of goods across national borders. It is the sum of both imports and exports of goods. The trade is based on "Free On Board" valuation. Thus the value of the goods does not include the cost of international transportation charges and fees.

5. **Number of aircraft in storage**. This indicator identifies by category those commercial aircraft that are not in service. Commercial aircraft in storage are reported in three basic categories—regional, narrow-body and wide-body. Regional aircraft are smaller planes with capacities typically between 35 and 90 passengers. Examples of regional aircraft include the Saab 340, Canadair regional jets and those made by Embraer. Narrow-body aircraft have a single center aisle. The majority of narrow-body aircraft are made by Airbus Industrie and Boeing.

Examples of these aircraft include the A320 and the B737. Wide-body aircraft have two aisles and include the Airbus A330 and the Boeing B747 among others.

6. **Number of ships out of service.** This indicator is similar to the aircraft indicator, reporting those ships that are in storage or not in service.

7. **Air freight price indices.** This index monitors the price of air freight services, typically for general cargo over time. A downward shift indicates a softening of pricing, usually because of a drop in demand.

8. **Sea freight price indices.** This index functions exactly the same as the air freight price index.

9. **OECD System of Composite Leading Indicators.** This is a set of macroeconomic indicators that is published on a monthly basis by the OECD. The primary focus of the indicators is the constituent member countries of the OECD. The indicators include selected manufacturing variables such as product deliveries, the level of domestic trade and international trade activity.

10. **Baltic Dry Index.** This daily index tracks worldwide shipping prices of various dry bulk cargoes such as coal, grain and iron ore. Marginal increases or decreases in demand for ships to carry these and other commodities can drive the index rapidly upward or downward as the supply of vessels are both tight and inelastic. The index is issued by the Baltic Exchange in London.

11. **HARPEX.** This weekly index tracks worldwide shipping rates for container ships. It reflects the volume, prices and length for charters of container vessels across eight classes of ships as well as composite picture. The index is prepared by Harper Petersen & Co. (GmbH & Cie. KG), a shipbroking services company with offices in Hamburg and London.

Conclusion

Economic recessions are a naturally occurring phase. They occur when economies have become overheated and need to "cool off" before continuing to grow. Basically, a recession is a period of review. Businesses review their organization, their costs, and their revenue streams. They search for better and more efficient and effective ways to conduct their business. Countries also conduct similar analyses, although those examinations are influenced by politics.

Identifying a recession is a retrospective process. While that may be acceptable for politicians, business leaders and individuals are keen to know in advance about an impending recession, regardless of its duration and scale. As this chapter illustrates, there are certain transport- and logistics-related indices that do herald a recession. Monitoring those indices and relating them to the operations of the company or individual requires constant attention.

---

[1] The National Bureau of Economic Research

[2] "Guide to Economic Indicators—Making Sense of Economics," *The Economist*, 2007, 55

[3] World Trade Organization, "International Trade Statistics—2009," 1

CHAPTER 6

THE 2008 RECESSION

This chapter examines the first recession of the 21st century, which began in late 2007. This discussion is not an econometric analysis of the development and effects of the recession. Rather, it is an examination of the recession from the perspective of transportation and logistics.

As identified in the previous chapter, transport and logistics services are some of the first activities to be affected by any change in production and trade volumes. Indices like the Baltic Dry Index and the HARPEX tend to herald the changes and experience significant changes in their values as a result of changes in the underlying volume of trade and demand for the transport services. That being said, it is of course all but impossible to separate transport and logistics activities from economic activity. As previously stated, most economists agree that the first recession of the 21st century began in late 2007 or early 2008. For the purposes of our examination, we have decided to simplify the argument and name this economic slowdown "the 2008 recession."

The 2008 recession is very different from most recent economic declines. First, this economic decline has affected countries around the world, in contrast to meltdowns that have affected only specific regions or countries. Second, the decline that began in the over-heated financial sector created ripples throughout the world economy as access to credit dried up and consumption fell precipitously, leading to a dramatic slowdown in production. Additionally, underlying asset values, such as U.S. housing stock and financial instruments, have experienced significant losses.

Globalization is typically associated with the production and movement of consumer goods from Asia to North America and Europe. However, it is part of all aspects of the world's economic and financial fabric. The creation of the worldwide financial network based on the emergence of reliable international communications technologies has created opportunities for investors and those seeking capital to find returns and financial support in markets many time zones distant.

The downside to financial globalization, which can be argued as a factor in the worldwide spread of the 2008 recession, was noted by John Authers of the *Financial Times* in March 2007, who wrote that he realized "that two of the world's markets held each other in a tightly and deadly embrace."[1] In one day the Shanghai market lost 9 percent of its value, immediately followed by other stock market declines, ending up with a 2-percent decline in the Dow Jones Industrial Average (DJIA). A confusing and troubling indicator of the embrace was that the simultaneous movements of the U.S. Dollar-Japanese Yen exchange rate (USD-JPY) and the Standard & Poor's 500 (S&P 500) stock index. While the former reflects the movement of funds between the world's two largest economies, the latter represents the valuation of 500 companies in the world's largest economy, the United States.

The similar movements of these two highly liquid indices were initially regarded as being "unnatural," because they were traded by different people and therefore should act independently of each other. In fact, analysis after the so-called "Shanghai Surprise" showed that any change in the S&P 500 explained 40 percent of the USD-JPY exchange rate change. This particular observation was one of many that illustrated how the world's financial markets had become intertwined and thus if one became overheated, other markets would react in a similar way. That development meant that the bursting of asset bubbles in the U.S. quickly spread and affected the rest of the world in a relatively short span of time.

The investment bubble that burst in 2007 and 2008, initially in the United States and then around the world, is but one in a long line of similar events. While psychologists and sociologists might debate the root causes, the similar actions of many individuals reflect a common human desire to act together for protection—in this case from unknown financial threats.

The belief that investment values will rise both constantly and endlessly has created a long series of "bubbles." Investors poured their life savings into purchasing tulip bulbs in the 17th century or building railways in the United Kingdom in the 19th century. More recently, the price of gold rose and then fell dramatically in 1980, followed by Mexican and Latin American debt in 1982 and 1984, respectively. Bursting investment bubbles continued through the 1980s and 1990s, including the collapse of the Japanese stock market in 1990, the crash of stocks in Southeast Asia among the so-called "Tiger" economies in 1997 and the "dot-com" bubble of 2000.

In all those cases, up to 2008, the impact of the decline was relatively limited to either individual investors or a specific world region. But because of the success of globalization in the financial sector, the 2008 recession changed all that. The rise of U.S. residential property valuations fueled an increase in consumption, which in turn supported the expansion of production facilities and the supporting transport and logistics services around the world. With the dramatic unwinding of segments of the U.S. financial system, including banks, investment banks, and mortgage and insurance companies, followed by massive layoffs and bankruptcies of companies in all sectors, the ability of the United States to continue as the world's largest consuming nation came to a screeching halt. The ripple effect spread throughout the world like a tsunami. It brought an abrupt end to the continued rise of consumption, production and transportation that was based on debt incurred by individuals who believed that U.S. housing prices would continue to rise.

The recession did not begin equally in all countries. In fact, some countries in developing economies never experienced an economic decline. The following table provides a pictorial timeline of when the recession was reported to affect different countries. The "√" denotes the quarter in which the recession was announced.

Transport and logistics services and companies have felt the brunt of this worldwide retrenchment. Ships, aircraft, railway rolling stock and trucks have been taken out of service. Rates have fallen as operators have

Selected Country's Recession Announcement

Country	2007 4Q	2008 1Q	2Q	3Q	4Q	2009 1Q
Denmark[2]			√			
Estonia[3]				√		
Latvia[4]				√		
Ireland[5]				√		
Singapore					√	
Germany[6]					√	
Italy[7]					√	
Hong Kong[8]					√	
Euro area[9]					√	
Japan[10]					√	
Sweden[11]					√	
United States[12]					√	
United Kingdom[13]						√

Notes: √ announcement

■ initial recession period

discarded the notion of profit for simply enough cash flow to keep the wheels turning and the doors open. Hundreds of thousands of workers in transportation and logistics have joined their neighbors from the manufacturing and commercial sectors in the unemployment lines. An estimated 940 narrow-body aircraft and 400 wide-body aircraft were in storage as of January 2010.[14]

One of the most widely watched transport indices is the Baltic Dry Index (BDI). This index monitors the charter activity of bulk carrying vessels. The following chart illustrates the relationship between the Baltic Dry Index and the S&P 500 index. While the BDI provides a look at one segment of the international transport industry, the S&P 500 index reflects the valuation of 500 U.S. corporations.

Another index, the HARPEX, is maintained by Harper Petersen & Co., a shipbroking company with offices in Hamburg and London. That index monitors charters of container vessels.

As the chart shows, the HARPEX index began falling in late 2006. It then rose above the long run average through early 2008, before its fall

Baltic Exchange Dry Index (BDI) & SP500 (green)

Chart created with NeoTicker EOD© 1998-2007 TickQuest, Inc.

to 317 in late April 2010, some 1,100 points below the peak recorded in February 2008.

From an air freight perspective, the Drewry Air Freight Price Index recorded a decline in the movement of worldwide air cargo. As of November 2008, the index stood at 100. By January 2009, it had declined below 90 and fluctuated between 80 and 90 through September 2009. Then through November-December 2009, it rapidly rose to 145-150 in response to the traditional peak season, before declining to about 120 in January 2010. One explanation of the rapid rise was that many manufactur-

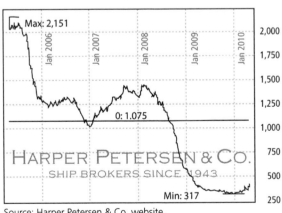

Source: Harper Petersen & Co. website,
www.harperpetersen.com, 29 April 2010

ers engaged in restocking the retail shops in anticipation of the traditional holiday shopping season after very low production for most of 2009
that had left the shop shelves relatively bare.

In early 2010, the International Air Transport Association (IATA)
reported that despite a glimpse of an upturn in the final couple of months,
global air freight volumes ended 2009 down by 10.1 percent and with an
average load factor of 49.1 percent. "In terms of demand, 2009 goes into the history books as the worst year the industry has ever seen. We
have permanently lost 2.5 years of growth in passenger markets and 3.5
years of growth in the freight business," said Giovanni Bisignani, IATA's
director general and CEO.

Yet another index, the European Freight Forwarding Index-Airfreight
(EFFI-A) prepared by Danske Markets Equities, recorded a continued
contraction in the activities of European freight forwarder activity
through the first eight months of 2009 (a reading below 50 identifies
contraction, while a reading above 50 identifies expansion). Just as the
Drewry Air Freight Price Index climbed during the last three months of
2009 as air freight volumes grew during the traditional peak season, the
EFFI-A started climbing in August as the freight forwarders began their
work to arrange for the shipments that actually started moving a month
later. Similarly, while the peak of the Drewry Air Freight Price Index
was achieved in December 2009, the EFFI-A index recorded an earlier
decline, reflecting the fact that the work of the freight forwarders was
complete.

As of early 2010, macroeconomic and transport and logistics indicators record a picture of a continued economic slowdown in many regions
of the world as well as in various transport modes.

In an August 2009 report, "Global Air Freight: Demand Outlook and
its Implications," MergeGlobal, Inc., noted that "there has been a migra-
tion of traffic from air to ocean in recent years, driven by increasing
fuel costs, higher ocean service reliability and declining commodity unit
values." They identified four primary drivers for this shift:

1. Shippers making modal choices based on total distribution
   costs at the commodity level—a combination of transport and
   inventory related costs;

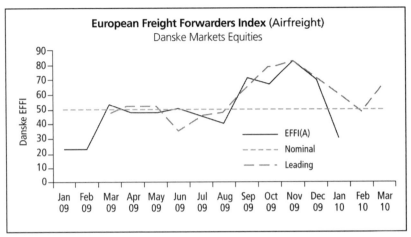

Created by C.H.W. Edwards, May 2010—from www.oecd.org April 2010 and information published by MergeGlobal, Inc. based on information from Danske Market Equities

2. The increasing expense of air freight due to rising fuel prices;

3. A decline in unit values of many products, which caused managers to increasingly focus on transport cost reduction; and

4. The emergence of a viable ocean-truck alternative through reduced door-to-door transit times, higher reliability, and better freight visibility (better tracking).

The following chart illustrates the general decline in total weight of the top 1,000 products typically carried by air on the Asia-U.S. trade lane. It is highly likely that this trend will continue, especially if long-

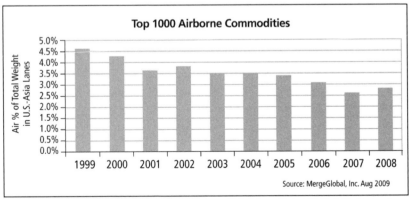

Adapted by C.H.W. Edwards (May 2010) from: MergeGlobal, Inc., Global Air Freight: Demand Outlook and its Implications, August 2009, pg. 11

term effects of the 2008 recession persist. Consumption rates could continue to fall or at least not return to pre-crisis levels as savings are directed to household debt reduction and unemployment rates remain relatively high due to a slow recovery.

Conclusion

The 2008 recession brought an abrupt and dramatic end to the economic growth of the last three decades of the 20th century. The financial crisis created a significant decline in consumption in the developed countries, which in turn has led to significant production reductions around the world. Globalization throughout all sectors of the world's economy, which bolstered rising incomes and social benefits in most regions, also contributed to the quick spread of the negative impacts of the economic downturn.

The transport and logistics industry has been hard hit as demand for its myriad services has declined with falling trade volumes. Many assets and employees in the worldwide logistics industry have been removed from service. Some may never return.

As the analysis of the Asia-U.S. trade lane suggests, the shift of products from air to sea freight could become a fixture in the future as lower unit costs and prices lead to permanent shifts from higher cost transport modes to lower cost modes. As consumption rates remain low, more products will be moved by ocean services (this becomes a part of the inventory chain) with air freight used for new product introduction or to meet spikes in demand, such as during traditional peak periods.

---

[1] John Authers, "Market Forces," *Financial Times*, May 22, 2010, Life & Arts 1-2

[2] "Denmark in recession after first quarter contraction," *EU business*, www.eubusiness.com (July 1, 2008)

[3] Mike Collier, "Recession arrives in Estonia," *The Baltic Times*, ww.baltictimes.com/news/articles/21072/(August 13, 2008)

[4] "Crash landing for Latvia's housing market, *Global Property Guide*, www.globalpropertyguide.com/Europe/Latvia (January 26, 2009)

[5] Julia Kollewe, "Ireland falls into recession," *guardian.co.uk*, www.guardian.co.uk/business/2008/sep/25/recession.ireland (September 25, 2008)

[6] "German economy officially in recession," *FRANCE 24,* www.france24.com/en/20081113-german-economy-officially-recession-financial-crisis-europe (November 13, 2008)

[7] Wikipedia, http://en.wikipedia.org/wiki/Timeline_of_the_late_2000s_recession

[8] "Hong Kong slides into recession," *BBC News,* http://news.bbc.co.uk/2/hi/business/7729652.stm (November 14, 2008)

[9] "Eurozone officially in recession," *BBC News,* http://news.bbc.co.uk/2/hi/business/7729018.stm (November 14, 2008) and Jan Strupczewski, "Euro zone recession confirmed," *Reuters,* www.reuters.com/article/idUKTRE4B32JK20081204 (December 4, 2008)

[10] Harry Wallop, "Japan joins growing list of countries to fall into recession," *Telegraph.co.uk,* www.telegraph.co.uk/news/worldnews/asia/japan/3472608/Japan-joins-growing-list-of-countries-to-fall-into-recession.html, (November 17, 2008)

[11] "Sweden stumbles into recession," *The Local,* www.thelocal.se/15998/20081128/ (November 28, 2008)

[12] Neil Irwin, "NBER: U.S. In Recession That Began Last December," *The Washington Post,* www.washingtonpost.com/wp-dyn/content/article/2008/12/01/AR2008120101365.html (December 1, 2008)

[13] "UK economy 'Weakest in 30 Years,'" BBC News, http://news.bbc.co.uk/1/hi/business/8015704.stm (April 24, 2009)

[14] SpeedNews, www.speednews.com, January 2010

CHAPTER 7

ROAD TO RECOVERY

The road to recovery will not be a single path nor likely easily identifiable at first. It will be fraught with many barriers—some technical, some physical, some fiscal, some brought on by suspicion and greed, some caused by government policy. Recovery will be different for each country, for each industry, and for each consumer group.

The combination of these barriers and differences will create volatility in the marketplace. It is in this disparate environment that the members of the transport and logistics industries will have to operate. No single business model will work. In fact, it is highly disputable whether the business models of the past will have any value in this new economic environment. As one transport leader recently observed, the current recession has convinced almost everyone that one cannot plan for the future by looking in the rear view mirror. In truth, because of the many variables, an inflexible plan could be worse than no plan at all.

As Viktoriya Sadlovska, a researcher with the Aberdeen Group, noted in March 2010, "Economic volatility has been the cause for the majority of supply chain disruptions in 2008-2009, forcing companies to put an increased emphasis on supply chain management."

The paper notes that unstable prices for commodities, fuel and raw materials had led to economic volatility. This causes companies to 1) reduce inventory at all levels; 2) shift focus from strategic to more tactical, short-term improvement projects, and 3) restructure their supply chain organization to increase efficiencies. The author notes that in order to participate in this new environment, improvements in the supply chain infrastructure have to include enhanced visibility and integration and a higher level of responsiveness, and incorporate supply chain risk management.[1]

But a barrier for one person is an opportunity for another. Economic activity does not stop in a recession; it slows down and changes. A recession is a period when the "norm" is questioned, when the old ways of doing business are shaken up or thrown out. There is an argument that a recession is valuable to economic growth and development because of this period of change. A fresh look associated with an innovative approach to business is most likely the outcome of this period of economic change.

Weaknesses are exposed, whether they are found in the organizational structure, staffing levels, the level of innovation or production techniques. Strengths are rewarded—companies that are nimble will find new opportunities. Lazy habits and outdated business models are killed off, usually with accompanying dislocation of employees.[2]

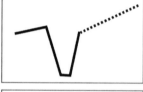

"V" economic recession—This scenario is identified by a steep decline in economic activity that is followed by a fast recovery after a very short period at the bottom of the economic decline. The recovery after the recession and initial recovery may be at a rate faster than the growth rate prior to the recessionary period.

"U" economic recession—This scenario is identified by steep or gradual decline in economic activity that is followed by a relatively long period of neutral economic growth. The recovery tends to be more gradual, and then the final stage of growth replicates the growth rate prior to the crisis.

"W" economic recession—This scenario is identified as a short-term "false" recovery followed by a second trough that precedes the final recovery periods.

"L" economic recession—The initial phases of the recession are similar to the "W" scenario. However, because of such factors as systemic unemployment, tight credit, reduced consumption, higher commodity prices and high inflation, the recovery rate is slower over an extended period of time.

A diagram of a recessionary period can assume different shapes. There are four general versions, with three scenarios known as "V," "U" and "W" usually mentioned. The fourth, "L," is another likely option. The first version, "V," represents a short and sharp downturn in economic activity that is followed by a sharp upturn back to the economic level before the recession. The "U" diagram represents a recession with a more gradual slowdown in economic activity as compared with the "V" scenario. Similarly, the recovery is slower and more gradual than the "V" alternative. The third scenario, symbolized by the "W," incorporates a sharp decline, followed by a brief recovery, a second smaller decline and then either a sharp or gradual recovery. The fourth scenario, the "L," begins with a sharp decline in economic activity followed by a very slow and gradual rise in economic growth through an extended recovery period. The preceding diagrams depict these four scenarios.

While these four scenarios are simple representations, the reality is that the economic environment of the 21st century is affected by such forces as credit tightening, globalization, changes in consumer tastes, and growing economic dominance of countries such as Brazil, China and India, as well as lower savings rates and massive deficit overhangs. They all combine to cloud the perspective and confuse those who are charged with forecasting the future. With a wide variety of economic conditions around the world, it is highly likely that when economists study this recession, they will observe a variety of scenarios and not just one simple model.

As of mid 2010, almost two years after the recession began, there is evidence of recovery in select sectors and world regions. The World Bank estimates that real growth of Gross Domestic Product on a worldwide basis will average 2.7 percent for 2010. By comparison, in 2007, the worldwide GDP growth was 3.9 percent. The World Bank's estimate for 2011 is 3.2 percent, still below the pre-recession rate.[3] While the economic growth among the high-income nations will average 1.8 percent, the developing country economies will experience an average of 5.2 percent. East Asian and Pacific economies, which include China, are expected to grow 8.1 percent and 8.2 percent in 2010 and 2011, respectively. South Asia, which is dominated by India, is predicted to experience annual economic growth of 6.9 percent and 7.4 percent for 2010 and 2011, respectively.

As noted by the World Bank, fiscal programs around the world have stimulated economic growth. The bailout of automobile makers in the

U.S., incentives to purchase energy-efficient consumer white goods, special programs to purchase new cars and dispose of less efficient vehicles, and provision of significant funds for infrastructure construction are some of the many examples of government interventions around the world to stimulate economic growth.

However, while these programs have slowed the economic decline and even—in discrete economic sectors and countries—stimulated growth, they cannot replace real economic growth that is based on increased consumption rates, available credit, and higher production rates spurred initially by inventory replacement and then by growing demand. Of real concern is the additional sovereign debt that is being used to pay for the stimulus packages. Rising government debt can crowd corporate debt out of the market. Then, as interest rates rise, taxes must follow, which in turn drag down consumption levels as households have less disposable income.

One outcome of the 2008 recession is the increase in the number of very poor people. The World Bank estimates that by the end of 2010, an additional 64 million people will be living on US$1.25 per day than would have been the case if the recession had not occurred.[4] This development means that consumption levels in some countries will remain depressed until income levels rise to lift people out of poverty.

Another outcome of this recession is substantial changes to the economic order that preceded the downturn. One country that could experience a major transformation is the United States. For decades, the U.S. has been the world's primary consumer. While most of its consumer manufacturing capacity shifted initially to Mexico and subsequently to Asia, consumers using increasing levels of debt and reduced savings rates continued to increase their rates of consumption. That evolution was the foundation of emergence of global systems of manufacturing and distribution. Fleets of large container vessels moved finished goods from the factories in Asia to the distribution centers on the west and east coasts of the United States. Vast complexes of distribution centers were constructed in southern California and elsewhere to receive and ship out the imported goods to stores across the nation.

Economists now assert that the old model of the U.S. economy is no longer sustainable. Debt-fueled consumption must be replaced by savings and exports. It is estimated that U.S. households have seen their wealth shrink by 18 percent, or US$12 trillion, since 2007.[5] This loss can only be replaced through savings.

While it is impossible to conceive that the U.S. economy will make such a change easily and quickly after so many decades, the simple fact is that fundamental changes will force a new economic order. Very few experts expect that the very low levels of unemployment that Americans were used to will be seen for many years, and perhaps not for a decade after the recovery begins. As a result, consumption levels will naturally decline. Consequently, the international transport and logistics systems that were focused on moving finished goods to the U.S. will have to be re-configured. At the same time, as consumption rates decline in the U.S., the Chinese export industries that were focused on North America will have to realign themselves to other markets, including an expanding domestic demand.

It is interesting to note that in the early years of the 21st century, the discount giant Walmart shifted its purchasing department from its headquarters in the United States to China. Ostensibly this was so the purchasing staff would be closer to the suppliers. But quite possibly, if consumption levels in the U.S. do fall, Walmart could be well placed to buy Chinese products for its expanding chain of stores in China.

A shift away from a consumer-led economy will be difficult for the United States. Since the 1950s, household consumption has ranged between 66 percent and 76 percent of U.S. GDP. While the effect of the 2008 recession will eventually wear off, it is likely that household spending—which, in the last decade before the recession grew faster than household income—will grow at a rate below income growth. The difference will be in the form of savings. A higher savings rate will be necessary as households attempt to rebuild their retirement pools.

The macroeconomic goal of expanding export industries will be a challenge for the U.S., given the current situation. Professor Matthew J. Slaughter of Dartmouth College has determined that only 4 percent of all U.S. firms and 15 percent of U.S. manufacturers export. In fact, 80 percent of the U.S. exports are controlled by just 1 percent of American companies.[6] Unlike Germany or China, the United States does not have an export focus or a base upon which to develop this economic sector. According to the Economist Intelligence Unit, exports of goods and services in 2009 accounted for 40 percent of German GDP, and almost 30 percent of China's and the U.K.'s GDP. In contrast, they equaled just 10.8 percent of the U.S. GDP.

If the U.S. is successful in reviving its export industries, it will have to face the cold reality that many industries, such as furniture, consumer electronics, and textiles that so many years ago moved to lower-cost countries, are unlikely to return. New industries, which the U.S. generally is very good at creating, will have to be developed. This will require significant levels of investment, a challenge if the nation's debt continues to grow. A high proportion of the investment will be for retraining older employees or educating new employees. Another possible barrier to this development is the low level of students who are enrolled in engineering and science.

An initial policy initiative to stimulate export growth in the United States, The National Export Initiative, is a presidential-level, government-wide export promotion strategy to help put Americans back to work and put the United States on a path to sustainable economic growth. In support of this effort, Ex-Im Bank is expanding its outreach efforts and working to make its financing products accessible to more exporters. In the first quarter of 2010, U.S. exports recorded a year-on-year growth rate of 16.7 percent.[7]

While the United States seeks to rebalance its economy, developing economies will continue to grow. China, which has an unbalanced economy—too much savings and little consumption—can afford to restructure its economy without accumulating a crippling level of sovereign debt.[8] As the Chinese economy continues to grow and mature, rising consumption levels will attract commodity imports from countries including Australia, Brazil and Canada and finished goods from other Asian countries that are already developing their manufacturing sectors based on low labor rates. Under this scenario, transport and logistics systems will need to be reconfigured to accommodate these new flows, especially as the volumes increase.

In mid-2010, an area of concern that could delay the recovery, especially in high-income nations, is governmental policy decisions. Questions are emerging as to how Greece, Spain and other countries in Europe will deal with their debt crises. Additionally, concerns focus on how China will deal with a possible property bubble, the actions in the United States to tackle financial regulation and reform, the impact on developing countries of inflation and commodity asset price rises, and the impact of the ending of stimulus packages. As a result, it is impossible to definitely forecast the economic future. In spite of these many variables, the Organization for Economic Co-Operation and Development (OECD) published a forecast of its Composite Leading Indicators on April 12, 2010. As the following chart shows, the trend from October 2009 through February 2010 was upward, indicating gradual improvement among the OECD member countries.

OECD Composite Leading Indicator Estimate—April 2010

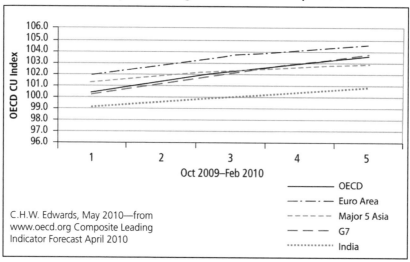

On May 26, 2010, the OECD reported that economic activity in OECD countries was picking up faster than expected. However, they cautioned that volatile sovereign debt markets and overheating in emerging-market economies were presenting increasing risks to the recovery. The Economic Outlook projected gross domestic product (GDP) across OECD countries to rise by 2.7 percent this year and by 2.8 percent in

2011. These were upward revisions from the November 2009 forecasts of OECD-wide GDP growth of 1.9 percent in 2010 and 2.5 percent in 2011. The following chart graphically presents the forecasts for the OECD, the Euro area, the U.S., and Japan.

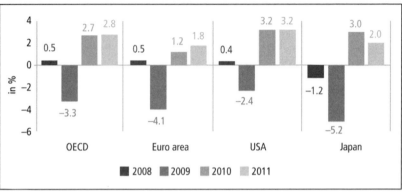

GDP Projections (% change from previous year)

Source: www.oecd.org May 25, 2010 "Economics: Growth rising faster than expected but risks increasing too, says OECD Economic Outlook"

Trade flows are rising again. Strong growth in China and other emerging markets is helping to pull other countries out of recession. But at the same time, the risk of overheating and inflation is growing in emerging markets. A boom-bust scenario cannot be ruled out, requiring a further tightening in countries such as China and India. The knock-on effect would be slower growth in other regions. Exchange rate flexibility could ease some of the pressure on Chinese monetary policy and provide more scope for addressing domestic inflation, says the OECD.[9]

A slow recovery, especially in the United States and Europe, appears to be the most likely scenario for the post-recession recovery period. Economies in Asia, especially China and India, will slowly increase their growth rates, but possibly not at the same levels as experienced before the recession. Structural changes to economies around the world are likely, but whether and to what extent they occur will depend on the appetite and commitment of politicians to do what is right instead of what is expedient for them to remain in power.

In an effort to forecast the likely structure of the world's transport and logistics industry, two economic scenarios have been created for the post-recession recovery period. The analysis presents a number of macroeconomic and trade-related factors that have been shown to influence the demand for transport and logistics services. The economic analysis is presented for the entire world as well as for the United States, China, Euro area, the United Kingdom, India and Sub-Saharan Africa. One scenario, "Major Restructure," presents our interpretation of the policies that the subject countries and regions need to undertake in order to adjust to the new post-recession environment. The other scenario, "Likely Situation," presents a more probable outcome of politically palatable decisions that address the various fiscal and economic challenges.

Post Recession—Economic and Transport Forecast

Country/ Region	Pre-Crisis Situation	Major Restructure Post Recession	Likely Situation Post Recession
Economic Analysis			
World	• Rising commodity prices • Rising asset values • Debt driven consumption • Increasing consumer goods production in Asia • GDP growth rate 3.9 percent (2007)	• Moderating commodity prices • Falling or stable asset values • Consumption rates in line with household incomes	• Slow recovery due to lower foreign direct investment in developing countries • Weak international financial system • More expensive capital • Continued high unemployment levels • Higher levels of poverty in developing nations • Uncertainty of government policies regarding financial regulation and fiscal stimulus packages • Reduced consumption levels • World merchandise trade growth 4.3 percent (2010) amd 6.2 percent (2011)
United States	• Highly leveraged economy • Historically high household consumption rates (76 percent of GDP) • Import most consumer goods from Asia	• Reduce household debt levels • Increase taxes to reduce government debt to limit consumption • Reduce household consumption rate to average levels (70 percent)	• Some increase in household savings rates • High government debt levels remain • Reliance on imports for consumer goods • Slight increase of export activity

Post Recession—Economic and Transport Forecast *(continued)*

Country/ Region	Pre-Crisis Situation	Major Restructure Post Recession	Likely Situation Post Recession
Economic Analysis *(continued)*			
United States *(continued)*	• 1 percent of U.S. firms account for 80 percent of exports • GDP growth rate 2.1 percent (2007)	• Significant increase in export activity	• GDP growth rates 3.2 percent (2010 and 2011)
China	• Very high household savings rate • Export focus to US and Europe • Major commodity consumer • GDP growth rate 13 percent (2007)	• Increasing household consumption • Reduced savings rate • Reduced exports as products are made for domestic market • Exports to rest of Asia	• Some increase in household consumption that may be reduced by bursting of housing bubble • Above average savings rate • Exports to U.S. and rest of Asia • Major commodity consumer • GDP growth rates 8.1 percent (2010) and 8.2 percent (2011)
Euro area	• Imports from Asia • Germany and France are major economies • High growth in Spain and Ireland stimulate consumption • Germany is leading exporter	• Major restructuring of sovereign debts in many countries • Weakening Euro • Increased exports based on lower Euro rates • Consumption rates decline	• Isolated economic restructuring—Greece and Spain • German exports expand based on low Euro • General decline in consumption • GDP growth rates 1.2 percent (2010) and 1.8 percent (2011)
United Kingdom	• Imports from Asia • Increasing household consumption levels • Increasing government and household debt levels • Rising asset values • GDP growth rate 3.0 percent (2007)	• Dramatic reduction of government debt through taxes and/or reduced services • Reduced consumption levels if taxes rise	• Gradual reduction of government debt • Moderately lower consumption rates • GDP growth rates 1.3 percent (2010) and 1.8 percent (2011)
India	• Major increase in domestic demand • Opening of export and import markets • Continued bureaucratic barriers	• Expansion of exports by domestic producers • Higher imports from expanding middle class • Improved internal transport systems	• Moderate growth of exports • Moderate growth of imports • Bureaucratic barriers are slowly reduced

Post Recession—Economic and Transport Forecast *(continued)*

Country/ Region	Pre-Crisis Situation	Major Restructure Post Recession	Likely Situation Post Recession
Economic Analysis *(continued)*			
India *(continued)*	• GDP growth rate 9.1 percent (2007)	• Reduced bureaucracy	• Improved international transport • GDP growth rates 7.6 percent (2010) and 8.0 percent (2011)
Sub-Saharan Africa	• Reduce percentage of population in poverty • Increasing development of natural resources • Limited reduction of corruption • Some improvements to regional and local transport systems • GDP growth rate 6.5 percent (2007)	• Aid-focus on reducing poverty • Continued development of natural resources with transparent returns to national economies • Aggressive reduction of corruption • Implementation of major improvements to regional and local transport systems	• Increased percentage of population in poverty • Moderate development of natural resources • Varied contribution of natural resource development to national economies • Limited reduction of corruption • Some improvements to regional and local transport systems • GDP growth rates 3.8 percent (2010) and 4.6 percent (2011)
Transport and Logistics Forecast			
World	• Major trade lanes Asia to North America and Europe • Global dispersion of manufacturing with increasing importance of Asia and other lower labor cost countries • Rising fuel prices did not stifle transport services • Declining inventory: sales ratio (1.5 in 2005/06) supported increased use of faster transport services • Shift to ocean services as consumer goods become commoditized	• Lower consumption rates will reinforce shift of consumer goods to cheaper ocean services • Air freight for emergency, demand spikes and new product introduction • Possible directional shift as U.S. increases exports • Cheaper Euro supports European exports growth at cost to U.S. export growth • Higher Asian consumption rates will command more transport capacity in region	• As consumer products are commoditized they will continue to shift to reliable ocean services • Intra-Asia ocean services will increase to meet higher consumption levels • Air freight services for emergency, demand spikes and new product introduction • Slower growth rates than pre-crisis which will delay recover to pre-crisis traffic levels • Average annual world air cargo growth rate 5.4 percent (2008-2028) • Average annual intra-Asia air cargo growth rate 8.1 percent (2008-2028)

Post Recession—Economic and Transport Forecast *(continued)*

Country/ Region	Pre-Crisis Situation	Major Restructure Post Recession	Likely Situation Post Recession
Transport and Logistics Forecast *(continued)*			
World *(continued)*	• Average annual air cargo growth rate of 5.1 percent		

Sources: Boeing Commercial Airplanes, Emirates SkyCargo, Organization for Economic Co-Operation and Development, International Monetary Fund, The Economist, and World Bank.

A more subdued economic outlook has replaced the last couple of "go-go" decades of the 20th century. As has always been the case, the economic landscape will eventually return to an overheated state, but it is highly likely—given the degree of the economic shock associated with the 2008 recession—that the recovery period may be a very long process. In some ways, the 2008 recession is similar to the Great Depression of the 1930s. In looking at that economic cycle, many economic elements did not return to the pre-Depression levels of the 1920s for almost 20 years, until the 1940s and 1950s. While this scenario has not been considered, we believe it is reasonable to assume that the economic shock of the first decade of the 21st century will impact economies around the world for five to 10 years before the world returns to a growth stage.

In the intervening period, one can presume that an overriding effect of the 2008 recession will be for individuals, companies and countries to live within their means. Consumption levels will be based on income levels instead of anticipated asset value appreciation. Countries with low sovereign debt levels will be rewarded, while those nations that continue to maintain high levels of debt will suffer.

Based on the presumption that the majority will at least attempt to live within their means, it is reasonable to expect that commodity prices will not experience dramatic rises. As resources are more efficiently used, demand will moderate, and prices, other than related to speculation, will rise based on general inflation trends.

Access to credit and capital, both of which have been either impossible to secure or at least highly expensive, will ease. However, if country debt levels remain high, individual and company access to debt could be crowded out of the market. If this situation emerges and is not managed through fiscal policies or the actions of central banks, consumption rates could remain low. Low consumption levels will have a ripple—or more accurately, a tsunami—effect on production and transport. We believe that it is safe to presume that legislators and central bankers will enact to one degree or another policies that concurrently address the need to reduce the level of sovereign debt and ensure access to credit for companies and individuals.

A very likely outfall of the 2008 recession is that the plethora and frequency of new products will diminish. Just as those who lived through the Great Depression learned how to live with less, a similar approach to consumption is likely to continue after the economic recovery period. Recent observations that "house" brands are growing at the expense of "brand-name" products suggests that this transition is already underway. As consumers seek a lower priced value option, the demand for higher priced brand names that were used to announce an individual's economic achievement will moderate. That is not to say that brand named products will disappear. Rather, as the emerging middle classes in India, China and elsewhere increase their disposable income, it is likely that they will seek out products based on a lower price-value proposition.

We expect that growth rates of transport and logistics services will take time to recover to the pre-crisis, but some regions will likely experience a faster and stronger recovery than others. Those regions are Asia, especially China, and India in South Asia. Many of the sub-Saharan African nations also will be a source of transport demand related to the extraction of natural resources, including oil, gas and minerals. However, continued fiscal problems among developed nations are expected to moderate growth rates and hence the demand for transport and logistics services.

The shift of products from higher-priced transport and logistics services to lower-priced alternatives is expected to continue. This situation will be based on a combination of factors, including demand for lower priced products whose margins are smaller and thus less able to pay for higher priced transport services, and fewer new products that require faster, higher priced services to speed their introduction. Also, the overall lower and more stable demand levels lend themselves to the use of slower transport services, such as ocean instead of air freight. We expect that this will support a faster recovery of ocean freight services. Air freight services will revive, but the operators will have to seek out new products and services.

Conclusion

The 2008 recession has affected the worldwide transport and logistics industry in many ways. Trade routes and volumes have been disrupted as traditional sources of demand, primarily in Europe and the United States, declined rapidly. Demand for air and ocean freight services has fallen. Accepted growth rates of merchandise trade and associated transport services have been discarded. Hundreds of commercial aircraft, ships, trucks and railway rolling stock have been sidelined along with transport, logistics and manufacturing employees.

After two years in the recessionary period, the outlook for a recovery is patchy at best, not to mention confusing. Some regions, especially in East and South Asia, have weathered the economic storm, while the high-income economies are dealing with higher-than-normal unemployment levels, rising government debt resulting from aggressive fiscal stimulus programs, and post-stimulus declines. What was accepted as normal in the last half of the 20th century—continued economic growth, emerging globalization, rising asset values, and reduction of world population in poverty—is no longer valid. The once dominant economies of the United States, Japan and Europe are being challenged by those of Brazil, China and India.

These changes will alter the world's transport and logistics industry. More flexible multimodal systems will emerge to be able to respond quickly and efficiently to shifting levels and areas of demand. Ocean services will carry an increasing percentage of consumer products that previously were carried by air freight. All of these changes will occur within a changed macroeconomic environment.

The challenge then becomes how to plan and predict the future. The following are suggested forecasting tools for transport and logistics managers in the 21st century:

1. The OECD Composite Leading Economic Indicators—This index is published on a monthly basis and provides a proven picture of short-term economic trends;
2. Merchandise trade statistics—there is high correlation between this index and the demand for transport services;
3. Crude oil prices—as the price increases, rising transport costs can force a shift of products from higher priced services to cheaper alternatives (i.e., from air freight to ocean freight). A cautionary note is to identify and discount speculation effects on rise changes; and
4. Comparative currency values—the key exchange rates, until the Chinese yuan is allowed to float, are the US$-Euro, US$-British Pound, and US$-Japanese Yen. These exchange rates reflect the relative attractiveness of the major economic regions.

Finally, all managers must be willing to be highly flexible and focus on short—and medium—term plans. A state of an ever-rising growth road has been replaced by a bumpy, ever changing path. Forecasting the future based on past performance and experience is no longer valid. In an environment of variability, only those who are aware of changes and willing to adapt to changes will survive.

---

[1] Viktoriya Sadlovska, "Global Supply Chain Management: Demand-Supply Networks: Success Factors in 2010," *Global Supply Chain Management,* March 18, 2010

[2] "Thriving on Adversity—Some Companies are Finding Opportunities in the Recession," *The Economist,* October 3, 2009, 82

[3] World Bank, "Global Economic Prospects—Crisis, Finance and Growth 2010," Washington, DC, Table O.1, 3

[4] Ibid, 3-4

[5] "Time to Rebalance—A Special Report on America's Economy," *The Economist,* April 3, 2010, 3

[6] Ibid, 9

[7] U.S. Department of Commerce press release, May 18, 2010

[8] Robin Bew, "Not So Fast," *The Economist,* January 2010

[9] Organization for Economic Cooperation and Development, "Economics: Growth Rising Faster Than Expected but Risks Increasing, Too," OECD Economic Outlook, May 25, 2010

Transport
Logistics
– the Wheel of Commerce

SECTION IV
ROLE OF LOGISTICS IN THE WORLD: COUNTRY STUDIES

This section comprises a series of country studies. Each study examines unique transport and logistics solutions that facilitate trade. The country studies are divided into two groups, arranged alphabetically. The first group studies logistics and transport operations in six African countries, while the second group studies five countries in Asia, the Middle East, and North and South America.

Chapter 8, TRANSPORT LOGISTICS: PERFORMANCE AMONG STUDY COUNTRIES examines the countries from the perspectives of the World Bank Logistics Performance Index and the World Bank's Doing Business analysis.

Chapter 9, AFRICA, presents an overview of the African continent as well as the individual country studies. Each study focuses on a unique aspect of transport and logistics, whether a key to economic growth and development or a search for a solution to facilitate higher levels of trade and economic prosperity.

The final chapter, OTHER COUNTRIES, presents the non-African country studies. As in the previous chapter, unique transport and logistics systems are presented. Each of these stories illustrates how members of the transport and logistics industry create unique systems to manage trade in harsh weather conditions, move specialty goods to far-reaching countries or act as major conduits and hubs that link world regions around the world.

The complexity of the world's logistics systems cannot be adequately covered in one book. That is not the intent of this effort. Rather, our goal is to illustrate the challenges and opportunities that are associated with providing logistics services or creating transport systems in 11 countries in Africa, North America, South America, Asia and the Middle East. The authors' research has focused on specific logistics operations or the development of transport systems that are unique or essential for the economic development of the respective nations.

The primary focus of the country studies is Africa. We believe that this large part of the world generally is not well known, and that significant opportunities exist for those who are willing to put their toe into the waters. As the studies identify, many challenges and potential barriers also must be addressed. But as many entrepreneurs say: "Where there is a challenge, there is an opportunity for success!" It is a matter of looking at the glass as being either half full or half empty. In any business venture, "unknown elements" arise from nowhere and give the business owner pause as how to proceed.

CHAPTER 8

TRANSPORT LOGISTICS:
PERFORMANCE AMONG STUDY COUNTRIES

Logistics is pervasive. It touches each of us and affects our lives in many ways each day. But for many, it remains an unknown force. The food in the store, soft drinks in the vending machine, cell phones in the store, cement for the construction site—these and almost everything else comes to the point of use through the integrated operation of the many members of the transport and logistics industry.

The performance of the logistics systems is a function of a multitude of members of the logistics community. A worldwide assessment of logistics systems conducted by the World Bank provides a window into this element of the world's economy. Begun in 2007 and reported again in 2010, the World Bank's Logistic Performance Index (LPI) provides a side-by-side comparison of the efficiencies of logistic systems in some 155 countries. Logistics encompasses an arc of essential activities including all modes of transport (road, rail, air, and ocean), express services, warehousing and distribution, cargo handling and consolidation, and an array of border clearance processes that involve various public and private agents. An efficiently operating network is the backbone of international trade. Many developing countries have not yet benefited from the productivity gains of logistics modernization and internationalization implemented over the last 20 years in more advanced economies.

The role of logistics as an economic development factor has become more widespread since the emergence of globalization. The value of efficient logistics services has increasingly become recognized as a major factor that supports the economic development of a region or country. Evidence from the World Bank analysis of LPIs in 2007 and 2010 indicates that, for countries at the same level of per capita income, those with the best logistics performance experience additional growth: 1 percent in gross domestic product and 2 percent in trade. These findings are especially relevant today, as developing countries need to invest in better trade logistics to boost recovery from the current economic crisis and emerge in a stronger and more competitive position.

The World Bank LPI is a multi-dimensional assessment of logistics performance, rated on a scale from one (worst) to five (best). It uses more than 5,000 individual country assessments made by nearly 1,000 international freight forwarders to compare the trade logistics profiles of 155 countries.

There is a significant logistics gap between high- and low-income countries. The LPI scores of advanced economies and some emerging and transition economies are relatively high due to their well-developed infrastructure and trade facilitation programs. But many countries are still in the process of addressing their performance bottlenecks. Although small differences in scores and rankings of individual countries should be interpreted with caution, especially for countries in the intermediate group of performers, the countries that have the worst performance, which are primarily least developed countries, are hampered by severe capacity constraints that are usually sustained because of low levels of maintenance and inadequate planning to add capacity. This makes sustained progress difficult.

It is naïve to simply focus on the country's income level, its GDP, because it is not the only determinant of its logistics environment. Even in low-income countries, policy makers can do much to boost performance. Liberalizing logistics services markets, for example, can encourage local service providers to increase service quality and price those services on a competitive basis. This is particularly important in sectors such as trucking and customs brokerage that are essential to efficient service delivery of imported goods. Also, countries with low LPI scores tend to have higher-than-average import or export times. But it is important to keep these delays in perspective. Lead times reported by international forwarders are generally much shorter than shipping times.

Landlocked countries, many of which are located in Africa, including those examined in the next chapter, face geographic-based and operationally related challenges. These countries are at a disadvantage because they cannot control transport and logistics shipping conditions outside their borders. The state of the roads in the coastal countries, the efficiency of the ports, the existence of non-operational barriers such as repetitive inspections of transit trucks, all combine to typically make the transit a week longer than for its coastal neighbors. As in any case, times can vary widely, especially in Africa.

Even more than time and cost, logistics performance depends on the reliability and predictability of the supply chain. The level of logistics service available in the best performing countries is about double that of the lowest performing countries. Unreliability of logistics in low performance countries can take many shapes. Excessive physical inspection or inappropriate reliance on the discretion of the inspector can cause large variations in clearance times, and multiple inspections are frequent. Increasingly strict safety and security measures impair service provision in all but the top ranking countries. In the lowest performing countries, importers and exporters incur extra costs as a result of the need to mitigate the effects of unreliable supply chains. These include increasing inventory to hedge against failed deliveries or simply losing sales as needed shipments either are lost or damaged en route.

With the exception of Burundi, the 2010 LPIs are available for the countries that have been studied by the authors. The Logistics Performance Indices of the study countries range from 4.09 for Singapore to 2.04 for Rwanda. Three of the countries, Singapore, Canada and the United Arab Emirates, belong to the highest ranking. Two countries, Chile and Uganda, belong to the upper-middle range of countries. Tanzania and Kenya belong to the lower-middle range of countries, while the remaining three countries, Ghana, Ethiopia and Rwanda, have been classified in the lowest range. Burundi was graded in 2007, but it was not graded in the 2010 report.

The top four scoring—and coincidentally, the most developed—countries saw their composite scores decline between 2007 and 2010. The composite Logistics Performance Indices declined by between 1.3 percent (Canada) and 4.9 percent (Chile). In contrast, the emerging countries recorded significant improvements in their Logistics Performance Indices ranging from 1.6 percent (India) to 25 percent (Tanzania).

World Bank—Logistics Performance Index

Int. LPI Rank	Country	LPI	Customs	Infrastruc-ture	International Shipments	Logistics Competence	Tracking & Tracing	Timeli-ness	LPI 2007	2007-2010 Change
2	Singapore	4.09	4.02	4.22	3.86	4.12	4.15	4.23	**4.19**	-2.4%
14	Canada	3.87	3.71	4.03	3.24	3.99	4.01	4.41	**3.92**	-1.3%
24	United Arab Emirates	3.63	3.49	3.81	3.48	3.53	3.58	3.94	**3.73**	-2.7%
47	India	3.12	2.70	2.91	3.13	3.16	3.14	3.61	**3.07**	1.6%
49	Chile	3.09	2.93	2.86	2.74	2.94	3.33	3.80	**3.25**	-4.9%
66	Uganda	2.82	2.84	2.35	3.02	2.59	2.45	3.52	**2.49**	13.3%
95	Tanzania	2.60	2.42	2.00	2.78	2.38	2.56	3.33	**2.08**	25.0%
99	Kenya	2.59	2.23	2.14	2.84	2.28	2.89	3.06	**2.52**	2.8%
117	Ghana	2.47	2.35	2.52	2.38	2.42	2.51	2.67	**2.16**	14.4%
123	Ethiopia	2.41	2.13	1.77	2.76	2.14	2.89	2.65	**2.33**	3.4%
151	Rwanda	2.04	1.63	1.63	2.88	1.85	1.99	2.05	**1.77**	15.3%
	Sub-Saharan Africa	2.42	2.18	2.05	2.51	2.28	2.49	2.94		
	Lower middle income	2.59	2.23	2.27	2.66	2.48	2.58	3.24		
	Low income	2.43	2.19	2.06	2.54	2.25	2.47	2.98		
	Burundi	No information in 2010							**2.29**	N/A

The World Bank's study of "Doing Business 2010" provides another detailed and interesting perspective on the study countries. This study compiles information about 38 factors in 10 categories that reflect various aspects of doing business in 183 countries. The 10 categories of activity surveyed in the study include: starting a business, dealing with construction permits, employing workers, registering property, getting credit, protecting investors, paying taxes, trading across borders (which is the category presented here), enforcing contracts, and closing a business.

The study noted that in "2008/09 more governments implemented regulatory reforms aimed at making it easier to do business than in any year since 2004." One of the leading reforming countries was Rwanda, which will be considered in greater detail later. As a result of those reforms, the World Bank ranking of Rwanda rose dramatically from the previous year's score, to 67 from 143. That score placed Rwanda among the most open and easiest countries in which to do business in the world.

The following table summarizes that information, which uses seven factors that reflect logistics and trade activities for the study countries. The countries are arranged from the best to the worst in terms of overall doing business ranking, with Singapore being the best (rank of 1) and Burundi being the worst (rank of 176).

World Bank "Doing Business 2010"
Trading Across Borders

Country	Overall 2010 Doing Business Rank	LPI Rank	Trading Across Borders Rank	Documents to Export Goods (no.)	Time to Export (days)	Cost to Export ($ per TEU)	Documents to Import Goods (no.)	Time to Import (days)	Cost to Import ($ per TEU)
Singapore	1	2	1	4	5	456	4	3	439
USA	4	15	18	4	6	1,050	5	5	1,315
Canada	8	14	38	3	7	1.610	4	11	1,660
UAE	33	24	5	4	8	593	5	9	579
Chile	49	49	56	6	21	745	7	21	795
Rwanda	67	151	170	9	38	3,275	9	35	5,070
Ghana	92	117	83	6	19	1,013	7	29	1,203
Kenya	95	99	147	9	27	2,055	8	25	2,190
Ethiopia	107	123	159	8	49	1,940	8	45	2,993
Uganda	112	66	145	6	37	3,190	7	34	3,390
Tanzania	131	95	108	5	24	1,262	7	31	1,475
India	133	47	94	8	17	945	9	20	960
Burundi	176	N/R-	175	9	47	2,747	10	71	4,285

Source: The World Bank, "Doing Business 2010—Reforming through Difficult Times," 2009

The two most important indicators in the preceding chart are the costs of handling export and import containers. The costs recorded in the World Bank analysis are solely related to any official fees associated with completing procedures to export or import goods on the basis of standard 20-foot (TEU) ocean containers. The fees include preparing documents, administrative fees for customs clearance and associated technical inspections, customs brokerage fees, terminal handling charges, and inland transportation. The costs do not include customs tariffs and duties or the cost of international air or ocean transport.

The fees associated with the landlocked, inland countries—Burundi,

Ethiopia, Rwanda and Uganda—are significantly higher than for the coastal countries. The total cost for export for these four countries averages $2,788 per container, while import costs average $3,935 per TEU. In contrast, the average costs for the other countries are $1,081 per export TEU and $1,080 per import container. A major impediment to economic development is the time it takes to export or import goods. The average number of days to export shipments from the four land-locked countries is 43 days; the average time to import shipments is 46 days. In contrast, averages for the other countries, including Ghana, Kenya and Tanzania, are 15 and 17 days, respectively.

Not surprisingly, those countries with better LPI scores have much lower average processing costs and shorter periods of time. The additional costs and the significant extra time to process and handle export and import shipments is a major drag on the individual country economies. These added costs stunt the growth of business and industry. Vital supplies are delayed and revenue-generating products run the risk of spoilage before they are loaded on vessels or airplanes for export. Additionally, but not reported, is the added risk of theft associated with the longer processing times. As the shipments sit in trucks or warehouses or on docks, the likelihood of part or all of the shipments being diverted increases exponentially. This is yet another cost that diminishes the contribution of trade to the individual national economies.

Many factors add to the costs. They include the capacity and maintenance condition of the roads and rail networks that link the landlocked country to ports, the service levels of road haulage and rail, the additional charges in the coastal countries, and the lower level of air services with consequent higher costs in the landlocked countries. Of increasing concern are the transit procedures that make the movement of goods impossible without payment of duties or excessive control in the transit country. As an example, there are 18 weighbridges (weigh scales) on the main road that links the major Kenyan port of Mombasa to the Kenya-Uganda border. Trucks transiting from Mombasa inland to Uganda, Rwanda, Ethiopia or Sudan must stop at each weighbridge where "charges" are levied and delays incurred.

In some cases, as exemplified by Uganda, facilitation efforts by the landlocked countries may almost eliminate this handicap. For example, landlocked Uganda is the third best performing low-income country in the entire sample (66th place), doing better than even its transit country Kenya (99th). Uganda's story is closely related to successful ongoing regional integration efforts with neighboring countries, and trade logistics and facilitation projects supported by the World Bank Group and a number of international donors and development agencies.

According to the World Bank, Africa's infrastructure "has been responsible for more than half of recent growth performance and has the potential to contribute even more in the future." Difficult economic geography, including small economies, a low overall population density, low levels of urbanization, and a relatively large number of landlocked countries are significant impediments to the development of the much needed infrastructure improvements. As a result, the overall infrastructure of Africa lags most of the rest of the world.

If the number of "unknown elements" can be minimized and the "comfort level" achieved, then the negative impact of dealing with unexpected issues and challenges can be lessened. These issues and challenges can be accommodated within a flexible and robust business environment. However, if more and more unknown issues, challenges and costs emerge, then even the most robust business owner can become demoralized and seek "greener" pastures by moving elsewhere. If that happens, ripples will be felt throughout the local and even global economy. Local employees could lose their jobs, banks could end up holding non-performing assets and suppliers could lose orders, which, in turn, can have a deleterious effect on their businesses.

Thus the short-term impact of the "special charge," "extra charge" or "delay" can have a long-term effect on a broader array of economic and business activities.

With some possible exceptions such as Egypt, Kenya, Nigeria and South Africa, many business people are not aware of the opportunities within the "Dark Continent." Just as mapmakers in the 19th century colored the interior of the vast continent because of their lack of knowledge, many business owners look at Africa with apprehension and ignorance.

The 11 countries selected for inclusion in this book represent a wide spectrum in terms of population size, per capita income, gross domestic product, exports and imports, and other key economic and other statistics. It is important not to focus too much on the statistics themselves. This book is not intended to be a definitive economic analysis of the selected countries. Rather, the selected economic indicators represent what the authors presume to be important to understanding the relationship between the logistics and broader economic activity.

The indicators' value is that they illustrate the wide range of economic and social development among the study countries and relate the economic state to the logistics systems in each country. We use the economic statistics to explain the impact of the transport and logistics industry on the economic well-being of the country, or in the case of other indicators such as mean weighted import tariffs, level of corruption, and extent of paved roads and railways, to highlight the barriers to economic growth and development.

Indicators for 13 countries have been included in this overview. The countries include Burundi, Canada, Chile, Ethiopia, Ghana, India, Kenya, Rwanda, Singapore, Tanzania, Uganda, United Arab Emirates and the United States. Seven of these are located in Africa, which is the primary focus of the book. The remaining six are located in North America, South America, Asia and the Middle East. Statistics for Uganda and the United States have been included for comparison purposes only.

The selection of the study countries was based on a few key factors. The following table lists the selection factors and the representative countries. Obviously, the individual countries fit into more than one selection criteria. Two continents, Europe and Australia, are not represented in the study.

The second table presents a few key statistics for the entire group of countries. According to the World Bank, these 13 countries had a total population of 1.7 billion (25.9 percent of the world's population) and generated a combined GDP of US$16.9 trillion (30.9 percent of the world's total).[1] Not surprisingly, the population of India dominated the group, accounting for 66 percent of the group's total. The group's GDP was dominated by the U.S., which accounted for 82 percent of the total. The group's average per capita gross national income purchasing

Study Countries

Selection Criteria	Country
Continent/Region	Africa—Burundi, Ethiopia, Ghana, Kenya, Rwanda, Tanzania Asia—India, Singapore Middle East—United Arab Emirates North America—Canada South America—Chile
Landlocked Nations	Burundi, Ethiopia, Rwanda
Unique Operating Conditions	Canada—Arctic, Chile—Glaciers
Oil, Gas and Mining Industries	Canada, Uganda, Tanzania
Perishable Products	Chile, Ethiopia, Ghana, Kenya
Transport Hubs	Ethiopia, Kenya, Singapore, Tanzania, United Arab Emirates
Developed Economies	Canada, Chile, Singapore, United Arab Emirates
High-Performance National Logistics Systems	Canada, Chile, Singapore, United Arab Emirates
Mid- and Low-Performance National Logistics Systems	Burundi, Ethiopia, Ghana, India, Kenya, Rwanda, Tanzania

power (PPP GNI) was US$12,519. Only Canada, Singapore and the U.S. recorded PPP GNI levels above the average. The average PPP GNI for the seven African countries was US$1,011, or about 8 percent of the group's average. This is reflected in the broad range of the group's PPP GNI world rank according to the World Bank's analysis.

The average annual growth rate in GDP for the group was 5.4 percent. The economies of the developed nations, particularly Canada and the United States, experienced GDP growth rates that were 50 percent of the group's average. When compared with the other African countries, the GDP growth rate of Burundi was significantly lower.

With the exception of Singapore and the UAE, the percentage of GDP derived from merchandise trade averaged 46.3 percent. The high levels for Singapore and the UAE reflect their role in world trade as transit hubs rather than major centers of manufacturing.

Conclusion

The selected countries portray a wide range of economic activity. Expressed by the nation's GDP, the economic activity ranges from that of the U.S., which dominates the world, to Burundi, which is less

Country	Population (millions)	Per Capita PPP GNI (USD)	PPP GNI World Rank	Total Labour Force (millions)	GDP (billions USD)	Avg. Ann. GDP Growth	Merchandise Trade as % of GDP
Burundi	8	330	206	4.2	0.97	2.7	39.2
Canada	33	35,500	25	18.5	1,239.89	2.7	60.8
Chile	17	12,330	82	7.0	163.91	4.5	70.4
Ethiopia	72	780	196	37.9	19.40	7.5	34.4
Ghana	23	1,320	178	10.5	15.15	5.5	80.9
India	1,125	2,740	153	447.7	1,176.89	7.8	30.8
Kenya	38	1,550	176	17.4	24.19	4.4	54.0
Rwanda	10	860	195	4.4	3.34	5.8	27.4
Singapore	5	47,950	10	2.4	161.35	5.8	348.6
Tanzania	40	1,200	182	19.9	16.18	6.7	45.5
Uganda	31	1,040	189	13.5	11.77	7.1	43.2
UAE	4	54,607	N/R	2.7	163.30	7.7	150.4
USA	302	45,840	11	156.6	13,751.40	2.6	23.1

Notes: N/R—Not Reported

than US$1 billion. The developing nations recorded GDP growth rates in 2007 that were almost double those of the developed economies in this sample, with the startling exception of Burundi. Merchandise trade includes flows of food, agricultural raw materials, fuels, ores and minerals and manufactured goods. The lowest percentage of GDP for this flow was recorded by the United States. Merchandise trade among the African nations accounted for less than 50 percent of the national GDP, with the exception of Ghana and Kenya.

Each nation's Gross National Income is converted to the Purchasing Power Parity (PPP) by applying PPP rates to eliminate differences in individual countries and to create a comparable estimate of the GNI across all nations on the basis of an international currency that is based on the U.S. dollar. Three of the nations (Uganda, Burundi and Rwanda) have a PPP GNI that is the equivalent of $1.00 or less per day. In contrast, the three top countries in the sample (Singapore, United States and Canada) have a PPP GNI range between $97 and $131 per person per day. This tremendous range indicates the diversity among the national economies and their relative states of development.

As previously stated, the economic and related social indicators have been reviewed to provide a sense of what is happening in each of the countries and to show how they relate to each other in terms of the economic indicators. The following table is a combination of numerical and graphical presentations of six selected logistics and economic indicators. The sources of the information are the World Bank "World Development Indicators 2009," the World Bank "Doing Business 2010" and the World Bank "Connecting to Compete—Trade Logistics in the Global Economy 2010."

The countries are listed from high to low according to the 2009 World Bank PPP GNI world ranking. The scores of the individual countries have been divided into quartiles. The assignment of the countries into quartiles is based on all World Bank study country reports in the case of PPP GNI, LPI indicators and corruption. The derivation of the quartiles for the remaining indicators is for the study countries along with Uganda and the U.S.

Countries Sorted by 2009 World Bank PPP GNI World Rank	PPP GNI World Rank	LPI	Avg. Ann. GDP Growth	Merchandise Trade as % of GDP	Wtd. Mean Tariff	Corruption
Top Quartile						
UAE	<3					N/R
Singapore	10				N/R	N/R
USA	11					N/R
Canada	25					N/R
2nd Quartile						
Chile	82					N/R
3rd Quartile						
India	153					
Bottom Quartile						
Kenya	176					
Ghana	178					
Tanzania	182					
Uganda	189					
Ethiopia	196					
Rwanda	195					
Burundi	206					

Quartile

Top		2nd	
3rd		Bottom	

N/R—signifies not reported information by the World Bank.

The individual country ranking of Logistics Performance Index and the Doing Business are very similar. With the exception of Average Annual GDP Growth and Merchandise Trade as a percent of GDP, the countries in the top quartile of PPP GNI generally have scores for the other economic indicators in the top two quartiles. The lower scores for the U.S. and Canada, in the case of average annual growth of GDP and the percentage of GDP accounted by merchandise trade, reflect that these economies are more balanced and more developed than other economies in the sample. Chile, which based on the PPP GNI is the only country in this sample that is in the second quartile of all nations and territories studied by the World Bank, has scores for the other indicators in the top, 2nd and 3rd quartiles. The top five countries in the sample have no reported corruption issues, according to the World Bank.

India is the only study country in the 3rd quartile based on the PPP GNI. The LPI score for India places it in the 2nd quartile of that 2010 comparative analysis. With the exception of average annual GDP growth, the rest of the economic markers for India are in the respective bottom quartiles. The low scores for these other economic markers are reflected in the lower PPP GNI for one of the world's largest countries. As the chart shows, the low LPI scores for Kenya and Tanzania are in the 3rd quartile. The rest of the countries are in the bottom quartile of the 2010 Logistics Performance Index.

The remaining seven countries of the study group, which are all located in Africa, are ranked by the World Bank according to their PPP GNI in the bottom quartile. With the exception of Uganda, their Logistics Performance Indices are in the 3rd and 4th quartiles. The bottom three countries, Ethiopia, Rwanda and Burundi, are in the lowest quartile grouping in the case of PPP GNI, LPI scores, merchandise trade as a percentage of GDP, and the weighted mean tariff levels for imported goods. Their respective world rank of levels of lack of transparency and corruption are in the 2nd and 3rd quartiles. The average annual growth rate of GDP of the bottom seven countries varies widely from top quartile for Ethiopia to the bottom quartile for Burundi.

Economic growth and development is generally lower for those countries where "Doing Business" or the "Logistics Performance Index" is low.

The impediment to doing business in general and moving goods is directly transferable into lower economy growth. The impact of higher weighted mean import tariffs and a higher level of corruption also combine to limit economic activity. The study countries that exhibit this relationship have lower levels of per capital purchasing power, parity gross national income and the percentage of GDP associated with merchandise trade.

Addressing the impediments to trade, be they structural, operational, legal or illegal, is essential in order to get the economy moving.

---

[1] World Bank, *World Development Indicators 2009,* (World Bank, April 2009)

CHAPTER 9

AFRICA

In the 19th century, Africa was first called the "Dark Continent."
The expression was applied by mapmakers to the continent, especially
the sub-Saharan portion, except South Africa, simply because little
was known about the continent's interior geography. As a result
mapmakers would often leave this portion of their maps dark to show
they did not know what lay in the interior of the vast continent.

The term still remains in active use, not because the continent has remained unexplored, but simply because of a lack of interest, a lack of education about the continent, or an absence of desire to find out more about what is the world's second largest continent, in terms of both area and population.

The business opportunities in Africa are increasing. Countries such as Rwanda are tackling the issue of governance and administration of the collection of taxes and fees across the country. This has resulted in a reported 40-percent increase of revenues to Rwanda on a year-by-year basis, which effectively has enabled the government to meet its operating needs. Rwanda also has instituted a program to employ the public-private partnership model to accelerate its economic growth. While there are many challenges, they can be converted into opportunities by entrepreneurs and businesspersons who understand and are willing to incorporate the risks into their business plans.

As the following satellite pictures show, Africa is larger in size than North America and Asia.

Africa covers an estimated 30.2 million square kilometers (11.7 million square miles) including adjacent islands. That area equals 6 percent of the Earth's total surface area and 20.4 percent of the total land area. With a population of a billion people in 61 territories, it accounts for about 14.7 percent of the world's human population. Africa, particularly

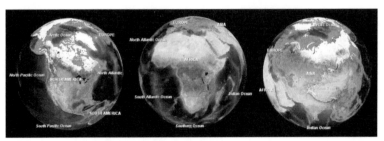

Source: en.wikipedia.org

central eastern Africa, is widely regarded to be the origin of humans. The diversity of Africa is greater than any other continent. The distance from the most northerly point at Ras ben Sakka in Tunisia to the most southerly point, Cape Agulhas in South Africa, is approximately 8,000 km (5,000 miles). Ras Hafun in Somalia is about 7,400 km (4,600 miles) east of Cape Verde, which marks the most westerly part of the continent.

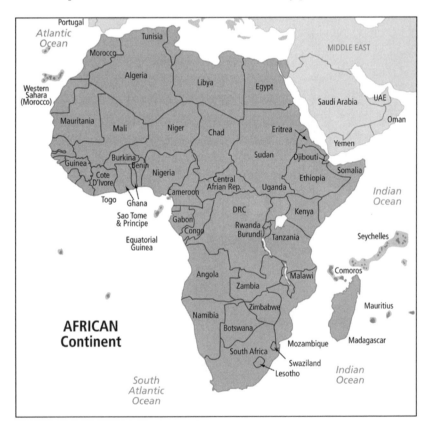

Six of the study countries are located in Africa. Ghana is located in western Africa, while the remaining five are located in east Africa. With the exception of Ethiopia, the remaining east African countries are members of the East African Community (EAC).

Africa is a study in contrasts. With respect to natural resources it is one of the richest in the world. In terms of per capita income it is the poorest. The reasons for this disparity are legion. They include violence that has stifled economic growth, the impact of different levels of integrity, and a general lack of interest by much of the rest of the world. Most of these issues are home grown. Until the collapse of the world economy, many countries within the African continent were in fact exhibiting world leading GDP growth rates.

One measure of progress in Africa is the Mo Ibrahim Index of African Governance (www.moibrahimfoundation.org). Begun by a successful Sudanese telecommunications entrepreneur, the index examines a variety of economic and governance related indicators that are important to the development of all countries. The index is composed of four primary sub-indices. Each of these sub-indices is composed of a group of indicators. All of the indicators are scaled for each country from "0" to "100,"where "100" is the best possible score. The following provides a brief description of each of the sub-indices.

Safety and rule of law: This sub-index assesses the basic rights of citizens to personal safety, access to a lawful and independent judiciary, the level of accountability of public leaders, the extent of corruption and the extent of national security including such issues as domestic security, international threats, the level of civilian-focused deaths and threats, and the number of refugees.

Participation and human rights: This sub-index focuses on civilian participation in the country's political process and free and fair elections, the extent and protection of all rights (human, freedom of expression, freedom of association, freedom of the press, civil liberties and ratification of international conventions of freedoms), and all gender and ethnicity related issues including ability of girls and women to go to school, to vote, to participate in government, and the equal access of men and women to all forms of support and resources.

Sustainable economic opportunity: This sub-index looks at a wide variety of economic and infrastructure indicators. Such issues as economic management, the existence and protection of a vibrant private sector, the quality level of the transport, electrical and water infrastructure, protection of the environment and support for rural areas and their economy are all covered in this sub-index.

Human development: This final sub-index assesses each country in terms of the access to and quality of health services by both genders, the extent of HIV/AIDS, child mortality levels, pervasiveness of vaccinations against normal childhood diseases, education programs, the level of primary, secondary and tertiary enrollment, and primary and secondary completion rates.

The following table presents summary information for seven African nations between 2000 and 2008. As of 2007/08, four countries have composite scores that are above 50 (i.e., average): Ghana, 66.0, Tanzania, 59.2, Kenya, 53.7 and Uganda 53.6. During the eight-year period, while the composite score for Ghana improved by 4.2 points (7 percent), Burundi's composite score improved by 10.2 points (29 percent). An important sub-index is "Sustainable Economic Opportunity." This sub-index comprises a series of economic indicators, as described above, of each nation's economic structure. As of 2007/08, four of the study countries had scores above 50, but none of the scores were above 52. This suggests that there is significant room for improvement to develop and sustain continued economic development.

Rwanda, which has been identified by the World Bank as implementing the largest number of reforms, had the second lowest score of the study countries. Burundi, which has the smallest economy and one of the lowest rates of GDP growth in the world had, not surprisingly, the lowest overall composite score and the lowest economic score of the study nations.

This brief survey suggests that while there is progress, at least for the seven countries in this study, much work remains to raise the levels of these countries so that their citizens can benefit. As the economic index suggests, even Tanzania, which narrowly edged out Ethiopia with the highest score, can be graded as only halfway to its objective. By way

Mo Ibrahim Index of African Governance

Country	2000/ 2001	2001/ 2002	2002/ 2003	2003/ 2004	2004/ 2005	2005/ 2006	2006/ 2007	2007/ 2008	2007/2008 Sustainable Economic Opportunity
Burundi	35.1	36.2	36.3	37.2	29.3	41.4	44.4	45.3	35.77
Ethiopia	43.9	45.4	44.4	45.5	45.8	46.0	45.9	45.6	51.16
Ghana	61.8	62.7	62.9	62.8	61.9	63.1	64.1	66.0	49.65
Kenya	52.5	53.1	53.0	53.4	53.2	54.2	54.0	53.7	50.49
Rwanda	44.0	44.1	45.1	46.5	47.1	47.9	47.9	48.5	47.08
Tanzania	53.5	53.1	53.1	52.4	53.8	55.9	57.0	59.2	51.46
Uganda	49.2	50.2	50.0	49.8	50.1	51.1	53.1	53.6	50.85

Source: www.moibrahimfoundation.org

of comparison, according to the 2007/08 composite index scores, the top five African nations plus Ghana had the following overall scores and economic scores.

Top African Nations—2007/08

Country	Overall Score	Economic Score
Mauritius	82.83	80.47
Cape Verde	78.01	68.05
Seychelles	77.13	64.51
Botswana	73.59	68.34
South Africa	69.44	62.09
Ghana	65.96	49.65

Source: www.moibrahimfoundation.org

The economic scores of the top countries range from a high of 80.5 to 62.1. These are significantly better than the study countries and demonstrate that the goals are achievable.

Transport and Logistics Infrastructure in Africa

In 2010, the World Bank published an extensive study entitled "Africa's Infrastructure—A Time for Transformation." That study included detailed analyses of all of the primary infrastructure sectors, including transport. Among the main findings of the study were:

* Infrastructure has been responsible for more than half of

Africa's recent improved growth performance;

- Africa's infrastructure networks increasingly lag behind other developing nations and are characterized by missing regional links;
- Africa's difficult economic geography is a particular challenge for development; and
- Africa's infrastructure services are twice as expensive as elsewhere, reflecting the diseconomies of scale arising from the small economic base and population and high profit margins.[1]

The direct economic value of an efficient transport and logistics system and associated infrastructure is undeniable. The policy makers and engineers in Africa face many problems in improving the continent's infrastructure. But the fact remains that this critical sector of the continent's and member nations' economies must be addressed in order to assist in economic development.

As the following brief overview illustrates, the deficiencies within the road, rail, ports and air transport systems in Africa are not uniform. They are well documented. With the exception of the air system, funding for capital and maintenance is lacking.

The road systems in the low-income Sub-Saharan African nations are significantly behind other low-income nations from a number of perspectives. As an example, paved-road density (km of road per 100 square km of arable land) at 31 in the Sub-Saharan nations is only 23 percent of other low-income nations. Total road density of low-income Sub-Saharan countries at 137 is 65 percent of other low-income nations.[2] This statistic is influenced by a relative low population density, populations that are less urban, a higher number of landlocked countries like Burundi, Rwanda and Uganda in east Africa, and the fact that many of the economies, as measured by population and GDP, are small. The effect is to limit access and thus economic growth. In particular, rural populations are cut off.

The report noted that in Africa "because of their geographic isolation, landlocked countries in particular suffer from the lack of regional connectivity." High road tariffs have more to do with high profit margins than high costs, according to the study.[3] Especially in West Africa, profit margins can range as high as 60 to 160 percent. Those levels are not seen in the developed world. The study summarized the capital investment and operating and maintenance required for the Sub-Saharan Africa's infrastructure to meet the demand levels. It estimated that transport would require $8 billion per year in capital expenditure and a further $9.4 billion annually for maintenance and operations.[4]

The study identified six policy changes necessary to address the deficiencies of the African road system:

1. Complete institutional reforms, such as ensuring that fuel taxes go directly to the road fund;
2. Increase rural accessibility because of the immediate benefits to a major part of the population and improvement in moving agricultural goods for export. By allocating at least $0.015 of fuel duties to roads, there is 1.5 times higher probability that the rural roads will be in good condition;[5]
3. Develop urban transport services to improve the quality of life of the urban population;
4. Liberalize road freight transport, including eliminating highly restrictive regulations and encouraging competition, and eliminating national protection schemes;
5. Deal with escalating costs regarding road construction; and
6. Improve road safety through better, more transparent enforcement.

While most of the railways in Africa are liberalized, few are able to generate the funds required for investment. The needed investment usually comes from bilateral and multilateral donors.[6] The majority of the systems are characterized by low axle-loadings; low-speed, small-scale, manual signaling; and undercapitalization.[7] With the exception of some routes in South and East Africa, African rail systems are domestic in scope.

Average traffic density is much lower than for developed nations. Average freight rates range from $0.03 to $0.05 per net tonne-kilometer, which are similar to rates in comparable countries.[8] Even though the rail rates are below those of road haulage, only 20-50 percent of a typical African corridor's traffic is handled by rail. The report notes that railways have been slow to adjust their operations and thus have lost market share.

African rail systems lack suitable infrastructure (high-speed operations are not required), discipline within the operating departments to
maintain schedules, and enforceable commercial arrangements whereby
both parties—shippers and the railways—live up to their contractual
responsibilities.[9] Many of the rail lines, such as those in Kenya, Uganda
and Tanzania, are based on the meter-gauge, instead of the international
standard, which is 1.435 m (4 feet 8.5 inches). The broader gauge has
many benefits, including higher stability, higher load capacity, better
ability to carry standard ocean containers, and access to a wider array of
locomotives and rolling stock. An average speed of 40 kph is more than
adequate for freight transport, so long as the schedules are maintained.
This lower operating speed regime is cheaper to build, maintain, equip
and operate.

Overall, the costs of the African railway systems are high and the rates
too low. In the case of infrastructure maintenance, a rate of $0.08 per
net tonne-kilometer is required. However the average charged rate is
only $0.05. Additionally, even using second-hand engines and other roll-
ing stock that are generally suitable for most applications requires $0.04
per net tonne-kilometer in cost. With some of the lowest rates of labor
productivity, African railways experience another set of higher costs that
should be avoidable. The combination of these costs and the depressed
rail rates means that the probability of improving the rail infrastructure
in Africa is low.

According to the World Bank, the port system of Africa in general is
operating at 80 percent of its estimated capacity.[10] Many ports are poorly
equipped and maintained, port charges are much higher than elsewhere,
and the container handling rates are well below international norms.[11]
Container transport is at an early stage of development outside of South
Africa. In east Africa, Mombasa and Dar es Salaam compete directly.
While the former is owned and operated by the Kenya Ports Authority,
Hutchinson Port Holdings manages the latter. Charges at African ports
in West and East Africa are significantly higher than elsewhere as the
following table illustrates.

These higher costs, along with longer truck cycle and container dwell

Typical Gateway Container and General Cargo Handling Charges in World Markets (USD)

Region	Container handling from ship to gate	General Cargo over the quay per ton
East Africa	135-275	6.00-15.00
West Africa	100-320	8.00-15.00
South Africa	110-243	11.00-15.00
Southeast Asia	80	8.00
Middle East/South Asia	96	7.00
Northern Europe	110	7.50

"Africa Infrastructure—A Time for Transition" Table 12.5, pg. 255

times at African ports, add extra costs for exporters and importers and disrupt the transport and logistics supply chain.

An estimated 120,000 people are directly employed in African air transport. Twenty percent of tourists travel by air. Between 1997 and 2006, traffic saw an average annual rate of growth of 6 percent.[12] While capacity is not stretched and fleets are becoming more modern, liberalization and safety are impediments to the industry's development.

Countries including Ethiopia, Kenya and South Africa have highly efficient, safe, state-owned airlines. In Sub-Sahara, three airlines—Ethiopian Airlines, Kenya Airways and South African Airways—handle 57 percent of the traffic.[13] The remaining African countries with national carriers have generally weak and highly subsidized airlines that operate in much protected markets.

Air safety and aviation security issues are being addressed at different levels in Africa. An example of proactive efforts to address air safety comes from the East African Community (EAC). The EAC has established a centralized civil aviation authority. The intent of this authority, which is still in its formative stages, is to supplement the member states' aviation authorities though support provided by the U.S. Department of Transportation's Safe Skies for Africa program.[14] This supra-national body will be able to leverage larger resources to assist member agencies to improve their air safety systems and programs. The approach is similar to the Joint Aviation Regulatory system that was in place in the European Union during the transition from individual to the single common European Air Safety Agency.

As in every case, the transport infrastructure of Africa is a combination of different rates of development and successes. The most pressing and most challenging barrier to improvement that policy makers and engineers face is adequate funding and setting and implementing clear and transparent priorities and goals. As described in the next chapter, multi-national efforts are underway in the East African Community. But even there, the lack of adequate funding and, in many cases, the continuing high levels of corruption, are delaying progress.

In spite of the capacity constraints, demand continues to grow. Freight railway services that have better operational and commercial management can begin to attract traffic from road haulage. This in turn will increase revenues that can be employed to upgrade infrastructure, acquire newer and more reliable locomotives and rolling stock, and pay workers. Road funds that are not diverted but are used as intended, along with stricter enforcement of the traffic laws, will lead to better and safer roads. A better-paid traffic police force that enforces vehicle weight limits, rather than collecting Chai Kidogo, will reduce maintenance requirements. No one can argue that maintained roads will increase the available traffic capacity without the immediate need for more construction.

While the lower end of port charges are at world levels, they can be significantly above. The major ports such as Mombasa and Dar es Salaam must address the issues of long truck cycle times and container dwell times. Those ports that are operated at higher productivity rates will address many issues that exporters and importers face in terms of moving products through the facilities. The port that offers more consistent and faster transit times will attract more traffic. The higher traffic rates will lead to higher revenues, which can be reinvested in facilities.

Infrastructure investment is always a challenging subject, whether in Africa or elsewhere in the world. The fixed assets, such as quays, rail track, roads, runways and structures, have long-term horizons. At the same time, the rolling stock—airplanes, locomotives or trucks— have shorter life spans. Finally, the operators, even those that are state-owned, face financial and commercial demands that can be measured in months. Combining these different expectations as measured by return on investment suggests that a public-private financing and operating model is the preferred option. Such a model will work and succeed only in an environment of openness and transparency. The collection and use of funds must be clearly noted and recorded. "Special charges" or perceived corruption will only poison the arrangement. Regardless of the approach, the simple fact remains that until individual African nations or communities such as the East African Community address this critical element and sector, the long-term economic development of Africa will be stunted, if not stifled.

THE EAST AFRICAN COMMUNITY

With origins that can be traced back to 1917, the East African Community (EAC) is the regional intergovernmental organization of the Republics of Kenya, Uganda, the United Republic of Tanzania, Republic of Rwanda and Republic of Burundi. The headquarters of the EAC is in Arusha, Tanzania. The Treaty for the Establishment of the East African Community was signed in Arusha on November 30, 1999, and took effect on July 7, 2000.

In the past, Kenya, Tanzania and Uganda enjoyed a long history of cooperation under successive regional integration arrangements. These have included the Customs Union between Kenya and Uganda in 1917, which the then Tanganyika joined in 1927; the East African High Commission, 1948-1961; the East African Common Services Organization, 1961-1967; the East African Community, 1967-1977, and the East African Cooperation, 1993-2000. Following the dissolution of the former East African Community in 1977, the Member States negotiated a Mediation Agreement for the Division of Assets and Liabilities, which they signed in 1984.

However, as one of the provisions of the Mediation Agreement, the three States agreed to explore areas of future cooperation and to make concrete arrangements for such cooperation. Subsequent meetings of the three Heads of State led to the signing of the Agreement for the Establishment of the Permanent Tripartite Commission for East African Cooperation on November 30, 1993. Full East African Cooperation operations started on March 14, 1996, when the Secretariat of the

Permanent Tripartite Commission was launched at the Headquarters of the EAC in Arusha, Tanzania. The East African Heads of State, at their second summit in Arusha on April 29, 1997, directed the Permanent Tripartite Commission to start the process of upgrading the agreement establishing the Permanent Tripartite Commission for East African Cooperation into a treaty.

The member states of the EAC cover 1.82 million square kilometers, and have a population of 126.6 million, a combined GDP of US$73 billion and an average per capita GDP of US$506. The EAC covers an area just slightly smaller than Mexico and has a population just smaller than that of Japan. In terms of its economy, the Mexican economy is 14 times larger and the per capita GDP of Japan is 68 times larger. The EAC is one of the poorest areas of the world but has tremendous potential, given the vast untouched natural resources, relatively young population, and high literacy rate. However, its potential is being suppressed by corruption. While the levels of corruption vary widely within the community, they are pervasive enough to stifle development.

The importance of trade within the East African Community is reflected in a variety of initiatives and programs that have as their primary objective reduction of barriers to trade both within the community as well as between the EAC and/or member countries and other major trading areas in the world. Internally, the establishment of the East African Community Customs Union (EACCU) is just one of the most visible indicators of this effort. In March 2004, the Republic of Uganda, the Republic of Kenya and the United Republic of Tanzania (the Partner States) signed a protocol to establish a Customs Union.[15] A series of key objectives are identified in the document, including:

- The Partner States resolved to reduce existing imbalances in the comparative advantage on trade in some commodities and to foster the accelerated development of the East African Community;
- The Partner States resolved to deepen and strengthen trade among the Partner States by abolishing tariff and non-tariff barriers and to create a favorable environment for regional trade;

- The Partner States recognize that a customs union will enhance economic growth.[16]

The Partner States have aggressively attacked the issue of tariffs between them. At the inception of the EACCU, the highest duty rate levied by Uganda on Kenyan imported goods was 10 percent. The Tanzanian rate on Kenyan imports was 15 percent prior to the formation of the Customs Union. As of 2010, goods between Uganda and Tanzania and those moving from Uganda and Tanzania to Kenya are treated on a duty-free basis.[17] This significant reduction in duties has reduced a significant cost of trade within at least three members of the EAC. The EAC has also addressed the duties levied on imported goods, creating a Common External Tariff (CET) system for all goods entering the community. The CET was initially issued in 2005, and was updated in 2007. The rates range between 0 and 25 percent. As of 2007, a significant number of commodities were assessed the highest rate of 25 percent.[18]

Other initiatives supported by the EAC to promote trade include:[19]

- Trade facilitation—Simplify, standardize and harmonize trade information and documentation to facilitate trade in goods.
- Anti-dumping measures—Develop anti-dumping regulations.
- Competition policy and law—Implement the EAC Competition Policy and Law currently to deter any practice that adversely affects free trade within the Community.
- Re-export of goods—Re-exports are to be exempt from the payment of import or export duties.
- Non-tariff barriers to trade—The EAC Partner States have agreed to remove all existing non-tariff barriers to trade and not to impose any new ones.
- Standards and measures—Promote trade, investment and consumer protection though a series of common practices.

Other programs include:

- Burundi, Rwanda, Tanzania and Uganda are covered by the EU's Everything But Arms (EBA) initiative, under which all products from LDCs except arms and ammunitions have preferential access to the EU market.
- Together with other Sub-Saharan African countries, the EAC

Partner States also qualify for duty-free access to the U.S. market under the African Growth and Opportunity Act.

- Products from EAC countries can access various markets in the developed world through the Generalized System of Preferences (GSP), which offers preferential treatment to a wide range of products originating in developing countries.
- Membership in the African, Caribbean and Pacific States and the GSP enables products from Partner States to qualify for preferential tariffs on exports to member countries.
- Burundi is also a member of the Economic Community of Central African States, which aims to establish a Central African Common Market.

The contributions of these initiatives and programs are subject to the limitations of individual countries to fully implement the elements, to train and monitor their customs and other officials to follow the new regime, and to aggressively reduce barriers. Additionally, an efficient transport system is critical to the development of trade within the EAC as well to and from the Community.

The EAC Development Strategy recognizes that regional infrastructure intervention—that is, improving the EAC transport infrastructure—is essential to attracting investment into the region, improving competitiveness, and promoting trade.

The infrastructure and support services sub-sector covers roads, railways, civil aviation, maritime transport and ports, multimodal transport, freight administration and management. A number of Tripartite Agreements have been reached in the field of infrastructure, including Road Transport and Inland Waterway Transport aimed at providing a facilitative instrument to regulate inland waterways transport, particularly across Lake Victoria.

The transport system in Tanzania and Kenya, in addition to supporting national economic development, acts as a vital transit network for the neighboring landlocked countries of the Lake Victoria Basin Region of Uganda, Rwanda, Burundi, Ethiopia, southern Sudan and the Democratic Republic of Congo (DRC). The Partner States have implemented sector reforms aimed at efficient provision of services, with the ultimate goal of substantially reducing the current high cost of transport in the region. These reforms include the formation of regulatory authorities and operational agencies and privatization of operations.

Since the 1990s, African countries have been addressing deficiencies in their road systems. On average, 80 percent of the main roads are in good to fair condition. The World Bank estimates the current value of the national road networks is at least 70 percent of their potential. Among the countries of the EAC, Tanzania and Kenya rank the highest in terms of reforms to their road funds, which converts into better roads. Rwanda is not far behind. In terms of estimated annual dollars spent for maintenance per kilometer within the EAC, Uganda spends almost US$18,000 per km, followed by Tanzania at US$15,000, Rwanda at US$10,000, and Kenya at approximately US$9,000. In spite of the high expenditure, only 15 percent of the roads in Uganda are assessed to be "good" while Kenya has achieved a level of 50 percent while spending half as much per kilometer.[20]

Relative Road Quality—Main Network Only

Country	% Good	% Fair	% Poor
Kenya	50	20	30
Tanzania	33	52	15
Rwanda	20	30	50
Uganda	15	75	10

These conditions affect the movement of commerce and the respective economic development. The lower the ratio of "good" roads, the harder it is to achieve positive economic development.

The EAC has identified five main corridors within the Community (a total length of about 12,000 km), which constitute a strategic priority and require rehabilitation and upgrading to complete the road network in the Community. The Northern Corridor from Mombasa to Bujumbura is part of the Transport African Highway (Mombasa-Lagos) while the Tunduma-Moyale road is part of the Cape to Cairo Highway. Insufficient financial resources have hampered development of the regional network. The EAC, in collaboration with member countries, has initiated a development partner-coordinated assistance in order to mobilize funds to develop the corridors.

Under the High Level Standing Committee on the East African Road Network, the EAC has facilitated sector reforms that include the formation of Roads Boards/Agencies, participation of the private sector, harmonization of regional policies, and axle load controls in the road sub-sector. All the Partner States have road fund boards and road agencies.

Two transit corridors facilitate import/export activities in the region. The Northern Corridor (1,700 km long) commences from the port of Mombasa and serves Kenya, Uganda, Rwanda, Burundi and Eastern DRC, while the Central Corridor (1,300 km) begins at the port of Dar es Salaam and serves Tanzania, Zambia, Rwanda, Burundi and Eastern DRC.

The EAC also has identified five main corridors within the Community (a total length of about 12,000 km), which constitute a strategic priority and require rehabilitation and upgrading to complete the road network in the Community. These corridors are:

- Mombasa (Kenya-Malaba (Uganda-Kigali (Rwanda-Bujumbura (Burundi)
- Dar es Salaam-Rusumo with branches to Kigali, Bujumbura and Masaka
- Biharamulo-Sirari-Lodwar-Lokichogio
- Nyakanazi-Kasulu-Tunduma with a branch to Bujumbura
- Tunduma-Dodoma-Namanga-Isiolo-Moyale

In addition to the road corridors, the Community has identified critical rail routes. The EAC recognizes the need to rationalize rail development within the region and to harmonize road and rail transport operations along the main corridors, and has prepared an East African Railways Master Plan to guide the future development of railway services in the region.

Railway transport is the second most important mode of transport after road, and is critical for long-distance freight along the main transport corridors in both Tanzania and Kenya. Tanzania has a total of 3,676 km of railway lines operated by two railway systems, Tanzania Railways Corporation (TRC) and Tanzania-Zambia Railways (TAZARA). Due to poor conditions of tracks and aging rolling stock and locomotives, tonnage freight volumes and passenger numbers have continued to fall every year (from 60 percent of port cargo in the 1970s and 1980s to 7 percent currently).

The World Bank, together with the ADB, has committed funds for infrastructure development. In order to alleviate the problems of the sub-sector, the government has brought in public/private sector partnerships (PPP) while retaining public ownership of the infrastructure and regulation.

One bright light among the rail system is Kenya. That country has a rail network of 2,778 km of lines. The main line connects the Mombasa port to Nairobi and to the Kenya/Uganda border at Malaba. The network carried 4.5 million tons of freight per year in the early 1980s but that load declined to 2.0 million in 2005. However, passenger traffic has been increasing steadily, from 1.8 million in 1971 to 4.8 million in 2005, but represented only 5 percent of total revenue in 2005. Even though the freight performance has continued to decline, it still plays a critical role in the transport of export and import goods, which account for about 35 percent of the long haul freight traffic handled at the port of Mombasa. Operations are hampered by the poor condition of tracks and aging rolling stock and locomotives.

The operations of the Kenya and Uganda Railways networks are currently under concession.

With the poor performance and falling service levels of the railway transport system, the road transport has taken a large proportion of the freight and passenger services in the region.

We turn our attention now to each of the countries in Africa. They are arranged in alphabetical order. Each country study focuses on a particular aspect of the interplay of transport and logistics and economic development as presented in the following summary table.

Country	Focus
Burundi	Multi-national transport planning and cooperation
Ghana	Creating a new form of farming and the need for transport improvements

Table continued from previous page

Country	Focus
Ethiopia	Developing an air-based perishables distribution operation
Kenya	Importance of high performance in perishable product handling
Rwanda	Fighting corruption
Tanzania	Leveraging off the demand for logistics support by developers of natural resources

AFRICAN NATIONS

Republic of Burundi

Bushes full of frangipani blossoms greet visitors stepping off an airplane at the Bujumbura Airport. This lush and beautiful nation is situated on the western edge of East Africa. The vast Lake Tanganyika separates the Republic of Burundi from the Democratic Republic of Congo (DRC) to the west. Wracked by ethnic violence for many years, the nation is struggling to rebuild its economic foundation. Long considered the end of the roads that stretch eastward to the great Indian Ocean seaports of Mombasa (Kenya) and Dar es Salaam (Tanzania), Burundi is at the doorstep of one of the richest parts of Africa, the DRC. Its location between its larger neighbors, Tanzania to the east and the Democratic Republic of Congo to the west, provides a foundation for the country's recovery from years of violence and economic isolation. Lake Tanganyika has for centuries been a transport route within this part of Africa, but its full potential and that of Bujumbura have not been realized. The hills of central and eastern Burundi facilitate hydroelectric power, support an expanding coffee industry, and contain rich deposits of minerals.

This chapter examines the challenges of developing a transport and logistics infrastructure that relies on investment outside of the country. Burundi's and, specifically, Bujumbura's, fate is held not only in the hands of Burundians, but by those in the other countries of the East African Community, particularly Tanzania. Rail lines and roads to the Indian Ocean ports traverse one or more countries. Coordination and cooperation are key elements to the economic recovery of Burundi. To the west, the potential of Lake Tanganyika as a waterborne route of commerce is vast, but it requires the creation of a service-focused lake transport operation that will take advantage of the lake. Again, only through cooperation and the involvement of private enterprises can Bujumbura and Burundi realize their potential of becoming a center of commerce and not the stop at the end of the road.

In the morning, the breeze rolls down the slopes of Mumirwa, one of the natural regions. The afternoon breezes that sweep down the hills of the Democratic Republic of Congo and cross Lake Tanganyika to the Burundian capital of Bujumbura gently moved the curtains in the non-air conditioned office of Mr. Narakwiye, Director General of the Ministry of Transport, Ports and Telecommunications. As he cast one last look at the traffic below him that maneuvered around the many potholes in the main road from the airport, he turned to his visitors and exclaimed, "J'ai un rêve pour le système de transport au Burundi!"—"I have a dream for transport system in Burundi!"

For the last 14 years, Mr. Narakwiye has diligently pursued his dream of an improved transport system for Burundi. He hopes the better system will change his country from being viewed as at the end of the road or rail line to that of a distribution center for Africa. He wants to establish Burundi as the center of a transport and logistics network that serves the needs of the four countries. The central focus of this network will be Lake Tanganyika linked to the Indian Ocean by a network of rail line through Tanzania and roads via Tanzania, Rwanda, Uganda and Kenya to the Port of Mombasa.

Burundi is a small and beautiful landlocked country at the crossroads of East and Central Africa, straddling the crest of the Nile-Congo watershed. Sandwiched between Rwanda, the Democratic Republic of Congo and Tanzania, Burundi has magnificent views over Lake Tanganyika, which provides much of its western border. The country is dominated by hills and mountains, with considerable altitude variation. The lowest point in the country is 772 meters at the Lake Tanganyika, while the highest soars to 2,670 meters above sea level at the tip of Mount Heha.

Bujumbura, the capital, is located on the northwest coast of Lake Tan-

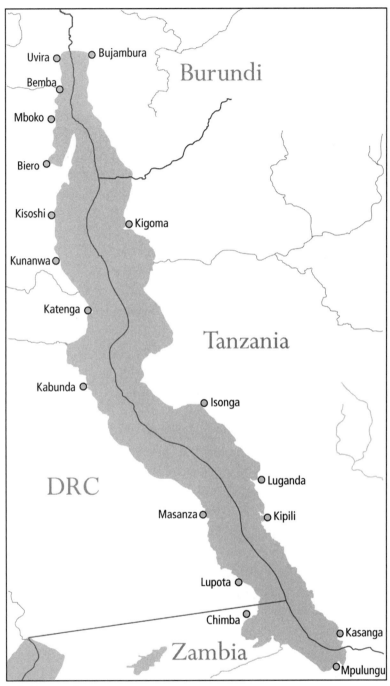

Lake Tanganyika

ganyika, the world's sixth largest lake at 12,700 square miles (32,893 square km). Lake Tanganyika has a maximum length of 420 miles (676 km) from north to south, and is the deepest after Lake Baikal in Russia.[21]

The lake is surrounded by four countries—Tanzania and Burundi along the western shore and Zambia and the DRC on the eastern shore. The primary access to the lake is via rail line from Tanzanian Indian Ocean port of Dar es Salaam to the Tanzanian lake port of Kigoma through the center of Tanzania or along roads that traverse Tanzania from Dar es Salaam and then through Burundi to Bujumbura. The transit time from Dar es Salaam can range from nine days by road up to 29 days by rail. The combination of extended transit times and high costs means that the final cost of goods is much higher inland. While the transit times to Bujumbura are long, those beyond to the DRC and Zambia are even longer, especially if the final stage is via the infrequent service of the lake freighters.

Kigoma used to be part of Burundi. In 1921, Great Britain and Belgium—then the colonial powers of Tanzania (known as Tanganyika) and Burundi, respectively—agreed to transfer a strip of land along Lake Tanganyika from Burundi to Tanganyika. Within the transferred land was the port city of Kigoma. Kigoma, then as now, was the end of the rail line from Dar es Salaam.

Burundi is a small (27,834 square km) landlocked country, and depends on neighboring countries for its access to the sea. Three available options are:

- The Northern Corridor from the Kenyan Indian Ocean port of Mombasa through Uganda and Rwanda to Burundi. It is 2,000 km long, and access is either purely road transport or road to Kampala and then rail from Kampala to Mombasa.
- The Central Corridor is through Tanzania from the Indian Ocean port at Dar es Salaam to the Tanzania lake port of Kigoma and then to the Port of Bujumbura. Traffic on this 1,400-km route travels by road or rail to Kigoma and then via lake vessel to the Port of Bujumbura.
- The last option is the Deep South route, through Zambia,

Zimbabwe and South Africa. This corridor uses lake transport on the Lake Tanganyika to Mpulungu in Zambia, and then road transport, or a mix of rail and road transport, to Durban in South Africa.

The existing corridors have many deficiencies that increase costs and lead to the diversion of traffic around Burundi.

Among the many challenges faced by Mr. Narakwiye is the fact that he must rely on transport and logistics improvements outside of Burundi. As a landlocked country, Burundi is subject to the decisions and actions made in coastal countries, especially Tanzania.

While Mr. Narakwiye has a dream that will benefit his homeland, he can only realize the dream if there is a broader multi-national agreement to improve the domestic and international transport and logistics systems. The fact that the EAC has agreed to a number of transnational projects that will directly benefit Burundi is very encouraging. They include three road corridors: 1) Mombasa (Kenya)-Malaba (Uganda)-Kigali (Rwanda)-Bujumbura (Burundi); 2) Dar es Salaam-Rusumo with branches to Kigali, Bujumbura and Masaka; and 3) Nyakanazi-Kasulu-Tunduma with a branch to Bujumbura; and two rail corridors: 1) Dar es Salaam-Kigali/Gitega (Burundi) and 2) Dar es Salaam-Dodomo-Kigoma (Tanzania). Though the origins of some of these projects can be traced back to the late 1990s, progress on many is hampered by a lack of funds to either conduct the planning or construct the links. Until they are completed, Burundi's economic fate and the dream of Mr. Narakwiye will be unrealized.

The following map presents the existing and proposed rail systems in the EAC. All of them are planned to improve the critical access of internal locations to the two major ports at Mombasa and Dar es Salaam.

Two routes are especially critical to Burundi. One is the Dar es Salaam-Dodoma-Tabora-Kigoma line, which is the most direct route between the Indian Ocean and Lake Tanganyika. The other is a multi-national route that has been studied by Deutsche Bahn Consulting on behalf of the East African Community. The latter takes the same route from Dar es Salaam to Tabora and then turns north to Isaka. While the main line turns northwest toward Keza, a branch line heads north to the

EAC Current Network with Proposed New Lines

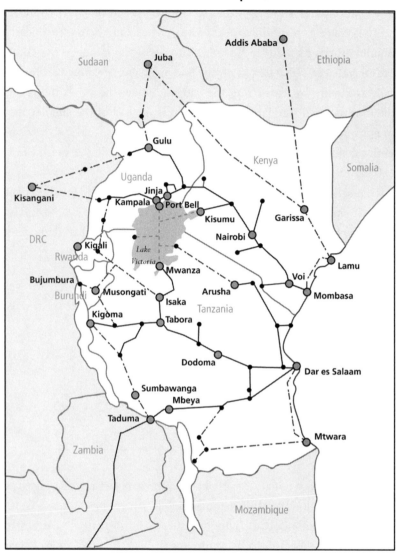

Current Railway Line
Proposed Railway Line
Ferry

Lake Victoria port of Mwanza. At Keza, the line will split with one line to Kigali (Rwanda) and the other to Gitega and Musongati (Burundi).

The current plan does not envisage the line being extended to Bujumbura, as its focus in Burundi is to serve the mines in the Gitega/Musongati areas. The design of this line involves upgrading the Tanzania railway system by converting the gauge (distance between the rails) to the international standard of 1.435 meters instead of the smaller meter gauge, building the line to handle heavier locomotives and freight wagons with a consequent increase in capacity, and increasing the speed limit to 120 kilometers per hour.

Deutsche Bahn Consulting expects that this line could handle as much as 16.28 million metric tons of freight on an annual basis by 2044. As the following table presents, the primary traffic that will be handled over the line is merchandise imports.[22]

Traffic Forecast—2044 (Central Rail Corridor)

(millions of tonnes)			
Traffic Type Optimistic	Realistic	Minimal	
Merchandise exports	1.87	1.85	1.87
Merchandise imports	10.79	9.13	10.79
Mineral exports	2.49	0.00	3.52
Mineral imports	0.08	0.00	0.10
Total	15.23	10.98	16.28

The traffic forecast also highlights the imbalance of merchandise trade that reflects a low level of manufacturing in the service area. With a 5.8:1 ratio of inbound to outbound merchandise traffic, many of the trains can be expected to be empty on their return to Dar es Salaam. What the forecast does not include is trade to and from the DRC, which could be significant. According to Mr. Narakwiye, all of the detailed planning has been completed. The next phases involve raising funds and construction. He expects that construction of the entire line will be complete in 2014.

While awaiting construction and completion of the new rail line,

Burundi's primary link for bulk and large volumes is Lake Tanganyika. Because Burundi is a landlocked country, it relies on the transport links through neighboring countries that have ocean access. The primary links include lake shipping to other ports on Lake Tanganyika and the rail line and road link between Dar es Salaam and the Tanzanian lake port at Kigoma. An essential element of this logistics dream is the revitalization of both lake services and the Port of Bujumbura.

The Port of Bujumbura was built in 1959, originally with an annual design capacity of 200,000 tons that was increased in 1989-92 to 500,000 tons per annum. Since 1992, the port has been operated by Société Concessionnaire de l'Exploitation du Port de Bujumbura (EPB), a public-private partnership company (public 43 percent, private 57 percent). Eighty percent of Burundi's external trade is routed through its only port at Bujumbura.[23]

Port of Bujumbura, Burundi, January 2010

The capacity-limited cranes depicted in the photo and the poor state of the roads immediately outside the port combine to limit the potential of the port as a major transfer and distribution hub in spite of its prime location on Lake Tanganyika. Only one crane has the capacity to lift a fully loaded 20-foot container (TEU) and it is not located alongside the main berths. Access to that berth and crane requires transit on an unpaved road outside of the port.

In 2005, the last year of published data, The Port of Bujumbura handled a total of 204,929 metric tons of goods. This reflected an 11.6 percent increase over the volume of the preceding year but was still only 41 percent of the port's throughput.[24]

Of even more importance is that, among the logistics and transport industry, the current lake service has a reputation for poor and sporadic service. Arnolac, a Bujumbura-based company, is the major operator,

Arnolac Fleet Information

Vessel Capacity (MT)	Notes	Vessel Capacity (MT)	Notes
200	Bulk	550	Bulk
250	Bulk	600	37 TEU
350	Bulk	850	Bulk
450	14 TEU	1,200	Bulk
500	Bulk	115,000 Liters	Bulk fuel
500	Bulk	415,000 Liters	Bulk fuel

with 70 percent of the vessels that operate on Lake Tanganyika. Its fleet is composed of 12 vessels equipped to handle fuel containers and break-bulk shipments. The capacities of the vessels range from 200 tonnes to 1,200 tonnes. Two of the vessels carry bulk petroleum.

Services are not operated on a scheduled basis; rather, the vessels sail according to demand. The physical state of the vessels, as the photo illustrates, varies considerably. Additionally, it is not out of the ordinary to see nearly half the fleet tied up along the berths at any time, with many of the vessels not being loaded or unloaded.

The closest port with direct links to an ocean port is at Kigoma. The state-owned Port of Kigoma is being leased by the Tanzania Ports Authority to MUAPI Ltd. (Muungano Wa Africa Port), a private Burundian Company, through 2013. The port's wharf is 200 meters long. On-quay rail (seven tracks) and a crane can handle loaded 20-foot ocean containers.

Lake Vessels at Port of Bujumbura, Burundi, January 2010

The Cargo Terminal has a 301-meter ship berthing facility, goods storage sheds with a capacity of 10,300 tonnes at a time and a container stacking yard with an area of 3,745 square meters, sufficient for up to

Kigoma Port, May 2010

380 containers. The passenger terminal can handle 150,000 passengers and 50,000 tonnes of parcels and luggage yearly. The shipyard contains a workshop and shipway for vessel maintenance and repair. Typically, 25 vessels call at the port every month.

In addition to services to Bujumbura, vessels link Kigoma with Kalunda-Uvira (DRC) and Mpulungu (Zambia). Road connections for Kigoma are poor. A gravel road links the town northeast to the national road network, and earth tracks link north to Burundi and southeast to Sumbuwanga.

Wharf at Kigoma Port, May 2010

Although Kigoma is the closest lake port to Burundi with a rail link to an Indian Ocean port, the poor state of the Tanzanian rail operations has forced bulk shipments of cement and sugar to be routed to Mpulungu (Zambia).

Instead of an eight-hour sailing time (Bujumbura-Kigoma), the vessels must traverse the entire length of Lake Tanganyika, 670 kilometers, which takes about 48 hours. As a result, while the freight rates between Bujumbura and Kigoma are about US$16/tonne, the rates to and from Mpulunga range between US$36/tonne for cement and US$41/tonne for sugar. This 2.4-times increase in the rates puts Burundian exporters at a disadvantage when compared to their competitors in countries with better transport alternatives. Likewise, Burundian importers and their customers must pay higher prices than those in other countries with better service to ocean freight services.

Among the many products handled by the lake vessels is coffee. Burundi is potentially one of the world's largest suppliers of coffee due to its climate and geography. In 2006, the country grew and shipped 31,000 tonnes of Arabica coffee.[25] Coffee is shipped by vessel from the port of Bujumbura, the capital city of Burundi, to the port of Kigoma in Tanzania, where it is loaded onto rail wagons and hauled to the Indian Ocean port at Dar es Salaam. Export destinations include Belgium, Germany, Holland, Japan, Australia and the United States.

The first Arabica coffee tree in Burundi was introduced by the Belgians in the early 1930s and has been grown in the country ever since. Coffee cultivation is an entirely small holder-based activity with more than 800,000 families directly involved in coffee farming on a total of 60,000 hectares with about 25 million coffee trees. Burundi coffee falls into the mild Arabica category, and is recognized as among the best grown in the Eastern Africa region because its quality is inherent to the hills and mountains where it is cultivated at altitudes ranging from 1,250 to 2,000 meters above sea level. The coffee is shipped in ocean containers to minimize loss. The combination of the infrequent lake service and the long transit time via rail from Kigoma to Dar es Salaam (up to 29 days) means that the Burundi shippers are at a commercial disadvantage to growers in other countries where the transport and logistics system is more efficient.

The infrequent service provided from Bujumbura to these other ports is stifling trade and forcing those in the other ports and countries to seek more consistently served routes. It is reported that the failure to keep to a schedule creates considerable stress on the other port communities and significantly disrupts the flow of trade. The reasons for this situation are unclear, but the short- and mid-term effects are very clear: Without a professionally managed lake service, the potential of establishing Bujumbura as a logistics and distribution hub for the region is being stifled.

Distribution Cluster

While Mr. Narakwiye is focusing on the transport and logistics system, his dream to create Bujumbura as a distribution center follows a proven concept of "cluster-based growth." Cluster developments allow "enterprises to overcome constraints in capital, skills, technology, and markets...that help their constituents grow, and compete by encouraging more effective knowledge and technology diffusion and product specialization, leveraging production value chains, and achieving collective efficiency."[26] Clusters develop and succeed when they can achieve improved productivity, which typically translates into higher revenues and profits, by upgrading systems and technology. The key elements that contribute to this accomplishment include:

- Establishing a supply-production-distribution supply chain,
- Acquiring and adapting knowledge and technology,
- Creating a local educated labor force,
- Cooperating among the cluster members to enjoy collective improvements in efficiency, and
- Securing support from local, nation and even international governments and agencies.[27]

Establishment of clusters requires aggressive efforts to attract business investment. As new companies are created and developed, the demand for improved transport services follows.

If such a cluster is to be created at Bujumbura, these factors must be part of the plan and, more importantly, be executed well. One of the advantages of establishing a logistics and distribution cluster at Bujumbura would be that the required investment would be low given the existence of the port, the lake service, and the existing U.N. distribution centers that soon will be shut down.

As the following table illustrates, a possible distribution cluster in Bujumbura meets the primary success factors.

Analysis of Possible Bujumbura Logistics/Distribution Cluster

Factor	Summary Analysis
Natural endowment	Adjacent to Lake Tanganyika, leverage the unused capacity of the existing lake port
Proximity to major local markets	Bujumbura, DRC, western Tanzania, Rwanda, and northwestern Zambia
Local entrepreneurs	Pent-up demand
Market push	Demand from DRC for better access to outside markets exists and growing, most of the traffic from the DRC is raw materials
Limited government intervention	Bujumbura Port already public-private enterprise

Conclusion

Bujumbura's location on Lake Tanganyika makes it a natural location for a logistics and distribution cluster. The port has more than 200,000 tonnes of excess annual capacity, an important factor if a cluster can be designed and managed to handle the expanding raw materials traffic from the DRC, which lends itself to handling bulk traffic flows.

By using Lake Tanganyika, a logistics and distribution cluster in Bujumbura is ideally suited to handle the flows of goods in and out of the DRC, which has indicated a strong interest in joining the EAC and is also recognized as one of the wealthiest countries in Africa based on its natural resources. Even though the country is subject to ongoing violence as competing groups fight for control of the valuable resources, trade is growing. Local entrepreneurs in Burundi and the DRC are continually emerging to create new businesses. We believe this cluster will evolve from the existing and growing traffic flows that are already carried by road between Bujumbura and Uvira (DRC), as well as the traffic that moves on the lake vessels. Until the new rail line is built, the existing service through the Port of Kigoma is an essential part of any plan. Burundi, the DRC and Zambia need to work with the Tanzanian authorities to ensure that the port and the critical rail link to Dar es Salaam are fully operational.

An important aspect of success is an open and transparent business environment. The creation of the public-private enterprise that manages and operates the Port of Bujumbura symbolizes the potential for creating the required environment. It will be necessary for the local and national authorities to reinforce and protect this environment if the cluster is to develop and grow to its full potential.

With a seamlessly integrated transport and logistics system, access to raw materials in the DRC and Zambia would be improved. This in turn would make it easier to increase the flow of those materials. If the transport and logistics system were sufficiently efficient and reasonably priced, additional refining and manufacturing locations would be created, thus increasing the number of jobs, income for the companies and the GDP of the countries. The increased production also would lead to increases in imported goods to meet the needs of the higher production levels and those of the workers.

The benefits also would accrue to Burundi and Tanzania. The higher flow of goods would increase the demand for more transport and logistics services. At the same time, the improved logistics systems should translate into lower costs for goods imported to the interior locations. The demand for the goods would increase, thus creating increased income and employment in Burundi.

Federal Democratic Republic of Ethiopia

Looking quickly at his watch after hearing the distant roar of an aircraft beginning its takeoff, Girma Wake, CEO of Ethiopian Airlines, confirmed that the Boeing B747-200 freighter was departing on time for the flight from Bole International Airport outside Addis Ababa, Ethiopia, to Liege Airport in Belgium. He knew from the morning briefing that it was loaded with the fruits of Ethiopia's agricultural based exports. Today, 99 tonnes of flowers and beans were headed to consumers in Europe. On its return, the airplane would be filled with a wide variety of manufactured goods paid for by the exports.

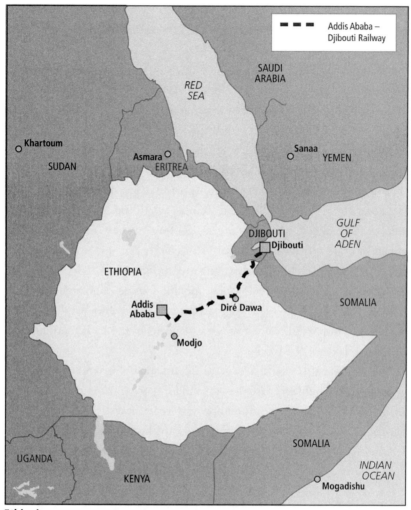

Ethiopia   Source: http://en.wikipedia.org/wiki/Ethiopia

As he turned back to his cup of coffee and the open report on his desk, he mused about how his landlocked country was developing a dynamic flower export business in addition to the well established coffee trade. The lush green grass and trees outside his office at the airline's headquarters underscore Ethiopia's natural ability to produce agricultural products. In his capacity as CEO, Mr. Wake was committed to developing a robust airline operation whose cargo services would support the needs of Ethiopia to generate export earnings to fund the economic and social developments.

Ethiopia is one of the oldest independent countries in the world. The Book of Aksum,[28] a Ge'ez chronicle compiled in the 15th century, states that the Ge'ez name, Ethiopia, is derived from "'Ityopp'is"—a son (unmentioned in the Bible) of Cush, son of Ham, who according to legend founded the city of Axum. It is also one of the oldest sites of human existence known to archeologists today. The capital, Addis Ababa, has become home to several international and pan-African organizations, including the African Union and the UNECA.

Officially known as the Federal Democratic Republic of Ethiopia, it is the second-most populous nation in Africa, with more than 79.2 million people, and is the 10th largest by area with 1.13 million km^2 (435,071 square miles). As the map shows, Ethiopia is landlocked. Eritrea and Djibouti block its access to the Red Sea. Somalia lies between it and the Indian Ocean. Kenya to the south and Sudan to the west form the other borders. The natural beauty of Ethiopia is varied and striking. It includes the Great Rift Valley, one of only two in the world that bisects the country from the southwest to the northeast. Deserts, mountains and major waterways have formed the land. Ethiopia is often referred to as the "water tower" of eastern Africa,[29] because of the fourteen rivers that rise in the country. In spite of the natural abundance of water there are few irrigation systems to support the burgeoning horticulture industry. The geomorphological structure of Ethiopia is reflected in the wide range of climates, including the hottest location on the African continent, soils and natural vegetation.

In 2007 and 2008, Ethiopia had Africa's fastest-growing non-oil dependent economy. Urban and rural poverty continue in spite of rapid economic growth in 2007 and 2008. During those two years, Ethiopia was Africa's fastest-growing non-oil dependent economy with rates of 8.4% and 8.0%, respectively.[30] Agriculture accounts for approximately 44 percent of the GDP, 80 percent of exports, and 44 percent of the labor force.[31] Agriculture supports other activities including processing, exporting and marketing. Like most agricultural activities in Africa, small scale operations dominate. Ethiopian agriculture is dominated by coffee, flowers, pulses (beans), khat, oilseeds, cereals, potatoes and vegetables.

As they dominate exports, agricultural products are the largest foreign exchange earner for Ethiopia. Not surprisingly, coffee is the single largest cash crop accounting for an estimated 60 percent of the national foreign exchange.[32] However, agriculture is plagued by periodic drought, soil degradation caused by overgrazing, deforestation, high population density, high levels of taxation and poor infrastructure, which makes it difficult and expensive to get goods to market. The potential exists for self-sufficiency in grains and for export development in livestock, grains, vegetables, and fruits.

Yet Ethiopian agriculture has remained underdeveloped. Most agricultural producers are subsistence farmers with small holdings averaging 1.2 hectares as of 2008.

And in spite of the potential bounty, as many as 4.6 million people need food assistance annually.

Coffee, which is thought to have been discovered in Yemen and the northeast region of Ethiopia, was first cultivated in the Arab world. There is credible evidence of coffee consumption as early as the mid-15th century in Sufi monasteries in Yemen.

A flowering *Coffea arabica* tree Source: en.wikipedia.org

As of 2007, Brazil, Vietnam and Colombia were the three largest producers of coffee, accounting for 29 percent, 12 percent and 9 percent,
respectively, of the 7.7 million tonnes in 2007. Ethiopia produced
325,800 tonnes or 4 percent of the world total, which made it the world's
fifth largest producer.

While Ethiopia's coffee production method is not much changed from
the 10th century, its coffee exports generated some US$350 million in
export earnings, which was the equivalent of 34 percent of the 2006
exports of the country.

In 2001, flower exports totaled US$660,000 or 0.15 percent of all
exports. By 2005, the exports had grown to an estimated $12.65 mil-
lion or 1.59 percent of all Ethiopian exports.[33] The industry's growth
was sparked in 2004 by aggressive moves by the government to attract
foreign investors to develop this new agricultural sector. Continued
government support, through the Ethiopian Horticulture Development
Agency, is expected to result in further growth of these exports. A
combination of ideal temperatures in Ethiopia's highlands, an average
monthly wage of US$20, the price of leased land of about US$13 per hectare, and significant government support aided the development of this
export business. In 2010, it was estimated that 80 active flower farms
were located within 30 to 200 km of Addis Ababa. The Ethiopian Horticulture Development Agency works with growers to establish minimum
operating specifications and codes of conduct. The Agency also provides
critical support and assistance in marketing this important segment of
Ethiopia's economy. A critical element of the Agency's efforts is to broad-
en the markets where Ethiopian flowers are sold. While traditionally
they have been sold at the major flower market in The Netherlands, new
markets are being developed in the Gulf States and Asia.

In addition to floriculture, the Ethiopian Horticulture Development
Agency supports the expansion of vegetable production for export, managing the investment of an estimated US$1 billion. This support includes
building capacity, investment, and marketing and promotional activities.
Some of the specific logistics programs include developing greenhouses at
about one-fourth the existing cost (US$10 per square meter), importing
critical systems on a duty free basis, eliminating taxes on profits for five

years, and extending the grace period for loan payments to six years. A key element is development of production hubs where farmers can bring their produce for cleaning, packaging and export preparation. While most of the products for Europe move by air, Ethiopia moves products destined to the Middle East by ocean services. This is particularly applicable for apples, berries and grapes, which have long enough shelf lives to endure the longer transit times. As one of the many landlocked nations in Africa, Ethiopia's links to international markets rely on roads through neighboring countries and air services primarily through the main international airport at Addis Ababa.

Transport Infrastructure

The Ethiopian government recognizes the importance of a good road network. By 2002, Ethiopia had 101,359 km of roads, both paved and gravel (federal and regional). Roads classified as "good" quality increased from 14 percent in 1995 to 31 percent in 2002, and to 89 percent in 2009. Significantly, the road density increased from 21 km per 1000 km^2 in 1995 to 889 km per 1000 km^2 in 2009. The average for Africa is only 50 km per 1000 km^2. Of equal importance is the plan to increase the proportion of the country area that is within 5 km from an all-weather road from 70 percent to 75 percent. Road links to adjoining countries including Djibouti, Somalia and Kenya require significant improvements. An ocean container will typically travel for 22 days from the time it is discharged from a vessel at the Port of Djibouti until it arrives in Addis Ababa. Only four of those days (18 percent) is taken up with movement, at an average speed of 19 km/h, while the rest of the time involves securing clearance to leave the Port, clearance at the Ethiopian border and other checks along the route.

Dr. Getachew Betru, Director of the Ethiopian Railway Corp (ERC), has been charged by the country's government to plan and develop a 5,000-km standard-gauge rail network by 2017. The ERC was created in November 2007 as a subsidiary of the Ministry of Transport and Communications.

The national network, which is to be electrified, is intended to support Ethiopia's agricultural sector, handling export grain and livestock as well as providing "high speed, high capacity, competitive and affordable" transport for passengers. Many overseas experts, including India's Overseas Investment Alliance (OIA)—which has been supplying electrical transmission and distribution systems under a 2006 agreement worth US$65M—have expressed an interest in developing the railway system. OIA signed an agreement in May 2009 with the government of Djibouti to undertake feasibility studies for a standard-gauge link into the region's main port.

As of September 2009, work was underway by firms from Italy and Spain to revitalize the 781-km meter-gauge Djibouti-Ethiopian Railway and increase its capacity to 10 trains daily. This is Ethiopia's sole rail link to a seaport. The work includes strengthening embankments, building new bridges, laying concrete sleepers, and replacing the remaining 20 kg/m rail with 40 kg/m on about a third of the route. Once completed, this critical meter-gauge line will once again become the primary link for Ethiopia to international markets. The upgrade's urgency has been in response to a string of derailments. Between Dire Dawa and Djibouti, trains have continued to carry fruit, vegetables, coffee and livestock for export and return with construction materials. At the end of July 2009, a Djibouti-bound freight train carrying 1,000 tonnes of export coffee and livestock derailed, killing 13 nomads who were apparently riding for free and injuring another 20 people, including the train crew.[34]

The East African Community railway plan includes a rail link between Addis Ababa and Lamu Island on the Kenyan coast. While this would provide Ethiopia with access to another seaport, the primary port for Ethiopia will always be at Djibouti.

The Port of Djibouti is located at the crossroads of one of the busiest shipping routes in the world, linking Europe, the Far East, Africa and the Arabian Gulf. The trading route between east and west stretches back some 3,500 years, since the time of maritime explorations of the Red Sea. As a strategic meeting point between two worlds, Africa and Asia, the Red Sea was a place of contact and passage used by the Egyptians, the Phoenicians, the Ptolemaists, the Romans, the Greeks, the Byzantine, the Arabs, and then by the Europeans in search of the spice trade route. Its apogee came with the opening of Suez Canal.

The port developed as an outlet of Ethiopia to the ocean. Construction on the port and the railway to Ethiopia began in 1897. The completion of the railway and the increased flow of traffic supported the expansion of freight flows at the port.

Between 1948 and 1957, construction of four deepwater quays and dredging of the port access channels was mirrored on land with the building of new warehouses and oil storage facilities as well as improved electricity and water supplies. A major line of business, bunkering passing ships, began in 1952. Bunkering traffic quadrupled in the decade after 1954, reaching a peak of 1.8 million tonnes in 1965. In 1985, the first modern container terminal opened. Since June 2000, the Port of Djibouti has been operated by DP World on a 20-year concession.[35] In 2008, the port handled a total of 356,462 containers and 6.6 million tonnes of traffic.[36] DP World noted that in 2009, the container terminal was operating at 85 percent of capacity in part because many containers remained in the port for extended periods of time.

Two dry (inland) ports have been developed in Ethiopia to handle seaborne trade. They are operated by the Dry Port Service Enterprise (DPSE), which was formed in 2007. As of March 2010, two dry ports, the initial one in Modjo, 76 km east of Addis Ababa, and a new one in Semera, were operational as part of the first phase of development. In June 2010, the DPSE announced a second phase expansion program valued at 220 million Br (US$16.2 million). "These two are the first phase of the construction," Ewnetu Taye, general manager of the enterprise, said. "We have planned to finalize the whole construction of both dry ports in three to four years (2013-2014)."

The expansion project of the dry ports in Modjo and Semera will include warehouses, container packaging equipment, cranes, parking lots, telecommunications lines, and buildings that will be used for offices by the Ethiopian Shipping Lines, Commercial Bank of Ethiopia (CBE), and Ethiopian Maritime Services Enterprise (EMSE). Total construction and operational start-up is estimated at 1.2 billion Br (US$88.9 million).

The Modjo port alone has saved 1.5 billion Br (US$111.1 million) in government expenditures by cutting the time it took to move cargo from Djibouti to Ethiopia from 30 days to 10. The port had handled 9,568

Addis Ababa Station in early evening
Source: en.wikipedia.org

containers by November 2009, 3,717 of which were empty containers, and 330 vehicles. As of 2010, only one exporter was using the Modjo Dry Port. The primary traffic served at the Semera Dry Port is vehicle imports. After going fully functional, the two dry ports will be able to store 70 percent of the country's imports.

Studies have been completed for additional dry ports in Moyale, Woy-ito, Hawassa (Awassa), Dire Dawa, Jimma and Mekele.[37]

Because of the limitations of surface transport links, Ethiopia relies on the services of Ethiopian Airlines and other carriers to move critically important agricultural exports and imports. Founded on December 29, 1945, Ethiopian Airlines' services began on April 8, 1946, with flights between Addis Ababa and Cairo. Service to Frankfurt in 1958 was followed by jet service to Nairobi in January 1963. By 1971, all of the airline's management and staff were Ethiopians. The airline serves locations on four continents with a combination of 42 passenger and all-cargo aircraft. It operates the largest fleet of all-cargo aircraft in Africa, including two each of B747-200F, DC-10F and B757F aircraft.

Ethiopian Airlines operates a cargo terminal at its hub at Bole International Airport that can handle all types of cargo, including perishable products. The airline is examining the potential to expand this capacity with another on-ramp terminal in response to the growing export traffic.

In July 2008, Ethiopian Airlines entered a strategic partnership with Lomé-based start-up ASKY Airlines, in which Ethiopian holds a 25 percent stake. Ethiopian Airlines is responsible for aircraft maintenance and operational management. The plan is to turn Lomé into Ethiopian Airline's regional hub for the West African market.

Ethiopian Airlines Boeing 767-300ER landing at London Heathrow

A critical element of the logistics landscape of any country is the financial sector. This sector facilitates trade through the issuance of letters of credit and collection of payments for services, duties and taxes, as well as general commercial banking needs. Ethiopia's financial system is underdeveloped and highly concentrated; a few banks control the sector. The banking sector is highly concentrated at an estimated 88 percent, versus 59 percent for Kenya, 67 percent for Tanzania, 63 percent for Uganda, and 81 percent for Sub-Saharan Africa as a whole. There is no stock exchange. Three state-owned banks dominate the small banking sector of just 11 banks, and there are no foreign banks in the country. The system remains isolated from the effects of globalization, while policymakers fear that liberalization will lead to loss of control over the economy. The government sets interest rates that are below the high inflation rate.[38]

Conclusion

Ethiopia is considering rebranding itself as "the water tower of Africa."[39] The Blue Nile rises in northwestern Ethiopia. Elsewhere, the mountains capture the warm humid air and rains fall on parts of the country. At the same time, other regions of the country suffer from prolonged water shortages.

Converting that precious natural resource and the rich soils into a critically important generator of export earnings is a long-standing policy of the country. The wide variety of agricultural products that can be produced in Ethiopia broadens the potential export markets. However, maximizing the benefits of this natural bounty is a complex task. While agriculture accounts for the majority of employment and nearly 80 percent of the country's exports, a significant portion of the population continues to rely on food assistance. The logistics and transport system in Ethiopia requires significant development on a variety of fronts. The internal and external road system requires further development. Similarly, the sole rail line to the closest seaport (Djibouti), which is finally undergoing much needed upgrades in 2010, will remain a bottleneck until it is converted to standard gauge.

From a financial perspective, the banking system is devoid of international banks and control of foreign currency is tight. The very high concentration level is a limiting factor on trade and economic development.

The bright spot in the logistics arena is aviation. Ethiopian Airlines is one of the continent's leading air carriers. The airline operates the largest all-cargo fleet and provides direct links to Ethiopia from North America, Europe, the Middle East and Asia as well as throughout Africa. But even though this is good news, air cargo services typically supplement higher capacity surface modes of road, rail and ocean services. There is a need to create a balanced multimodal transport system for this landlocked nation.

Republic of Ghana

The clouds had been building all afternoon. In the heat and humidity, they were a welcome sight, and thankfully acted as a shield to diffuse the heat of the sun. It was still three hours before the hordes of mosquitoes would rise from the shores of Lake Volta and bite unprotected living creatures all night long. As he looked south from the rise on his farm across the lake toward the hills of Kwahu Ridge that rose behind the village of Kotoso, Jon thought back to the weeks that had become months and now, a year, since he first decided to establish a farm in Ghana using modern techniques and technologies. There was not a breath of air, but hopefully the clouds would produce wind and rain that would not only keep the mosquitoes at bay but would also water the fields. However, too much rain could also turn the tracks into mud holes, making movement almost impossible.

Africa Atlantic Franchise Farms—Lake Volta

Here he stood, some four hours by vehicle and boat north of the Ghanaian capital of Accra, watching one of the young recent Florida State University graduates maneuver the tractor and plow over the newly cleared land to prepare it for planting. His plan, still being developed, was to convert the raw land that had never been farmed into a model enterprise that could radically change agriculture throughout Africa.

With the support of a local partner and the local paramount chief, Jon and his business partner, Kris, were planning to introduce larger scale farming to one of the richest agricultural areas in the world. He knew that the farm was a challenge enough. Already he was beginning to under-stand the value of logistics to get machinery, living accommodations and supplies to the site as well as to move the harvest to local and/or export markets. Incomplete paperwork had delayed clearing the shipment of equipment and supplies by nearly 60 days at the Tema port.   Without

Ghana

roads to the site, a barge had been purchased and a rudimentary landing constructed to move the two ocean containers from the end of the road some 100 kilometers from the Asambuco port. Rudimentary dirt tracks had been graded on the site.

The West African nation of the Republic of Ghana is surrounded by Côte d'Ivoire (Ivory Coast) to the west, Burkina Faso to the north, Togo to the east and the Gulf of Guinea to the south. After initial contact with the Portuguese, Ghana was established as a Crown Colony with the name "Gold Coast" in 1874. It was the first Sub-Saharan African country to gain independence, in 1957. Ghana was selected as the nation's name in reference to the Empire of Ghana, which had extended across much of West Africa before colonial times. Ghana is one of the world's largest producers of cocoa and has major gold reserves. Lake Volta, in the eastern part of the country, is the world's largest man-made lake.

Ghana has many natural resources, including an off-shore oil field that has initial estimated reserves of three billion barrels. Its economy is based on trade of natural resources, significant levels of international assistance and transfers from the Ghanaian disapora. Another source of revenues for the state is the Akosombo Dam, built in 1965, which generates hydro-electricity for Ghana and neighboring countries.

Transport

Transport in Ghana is accomplished by road, rail, air and water. Ghana's transportation and communications networks are centered in the southern regions, especially the areas in which gold, cocoa, and timber are produced. The northern and central areas are connected through a major road system; some areas, however, remain relatively isolated.

The deterioration of the country's transportation and communications networks has been blamed for impeding the distribution of economic inputs and food as well as the transport of crucial exports. Although the government allocated approximately US$2 billion in transport infra-structure investment between 1983 and 1992, transportation remains especially difficult in eastern regions, near the coast, and in the vast, underdeveloped northern regions, where vehicles are scarce.

Railways were first built in Ghana in 1903 by the British to move heavy equipment from the port at Takoradi to mines in the Tarkwa area in the Western Region. The railway system in Ghana was historically confined to the plains south of the mountains north of the city of Kumasi. Approximately 97 percent of the 947 kilometers of the narrow-gauge system was single-tracked. The rapid growth in tonnage carried by the railway system underscored its commercial importance. Between 1906 and 1926, annual traffic increased from 47,388 tons to 805,227 tons.[40]

Passenger traffic also grew rapidly during the same period, from nearly 700,000 to 1.5 million. After losing ground in the 1980s due to a lack of maintenance and investment, the Ghana Railways system carried 1.8 million tons of freight and 2.3 million passengers in 2003.

However, as of 2010, most of the railway does not operate. The fact that the track gauge in Ghana is different from the rail systems in Burkina Faso, Ivory Coast and Togo severely restricts the value of the two Ghanaian ports of Tema and Takoradi as major entry points for other countries in West Africa.

There have been numerous attempts to rehabilitate the rail system. In the early 1980s, investments were made in infrastructure, locomotives and rolling stock. In 2005, plans were unveiled to extend the railway system to improve economic development. In March 2007, a private-public partnership was proposed to rehabilitate the Eastern Railway from Accra to Ejisu and Kumasi, in addition to other routes. This was followed by another proposal in September 2007 to extend the Western Railway. In February 2008, the *Ghana General News* reported that the Ministry of Harbours and Railways and the Ghana Railway Corporation (GRC) expected to complete a new commuter line linking Accra and Tema by June 2008.

More recently, in September 2009, Mr. Hammah, Minister of Transport, announced plans to modernize the railway. The initial phase would concentrate on overhauling existing lines. With the exception of partial operations on the Western Line (from the port at Takoradi to Kumasi) and the suburban services at Accra, the other lines in the eastern and central areas are not operational. The plans also involved a modern signal and telecommunication system and widening of the track gauge from 1,067mm to 1,435mm, which would permit an increase in speed from 56 km/h to 160 km/h. The axle load would be increased from 16 tonnes on the Western Line and 14 tonnes on the Eastern and Central Lines to 25 tonnes. In the medium to long term, feasibility studies are to cover a new suburban rail service from Accra to Kasoa, Winneba and Madina, as well as to examine extending the railway to the north and connecting with the envisaged Ecowas line across West Africa. Other projects include construction of a "Tema-Akosombo multimodal freight service."[41]

In spite of all of these proposals, plans and studies, the railway system in Ghana is not able to support the demand for internal and international traffic that could significantly increase the economic and social wealth of the country. Because of the state of the railway, with limited services and a need for critical investment in the track, rolling stock and signal system, road transport has become the primary surface transport mode in Ghana and to the surrounding countries.

In 1997, Ghana was estimated to have a total of 39,409 kilometers of highways, of which 11,653 kilometers are paved (including 30 km of expressways). The Trans-West African Coastal Highway, part of the Trans-African Highway network, crosses Ghana and connects it to Abidjan (Côte d'Ivoire) and Lomé (Togo) as well as Benin and Nigeria. Eventually the highway will connect to another seven ECOWAS nations to the west. A paved highway also connects Ghana in the north to landlocked Burkina Faso, where it joins another highway in the Trans-African network, the Trans-Sahelian Highway. Most paved roads are only two lanes.

Marine transport is important to Ghana. The Volta, Ankobra, and Tano rivers provide 168 km of perennial navigation for launches and lighters, while Lake Volta provides 1,125 kilometers of arterial and feeder waterway. Ferries operate on Lake Volta at Yeji and Adwasco. The two seaports on the Atlantic Ocean are at Takoradi and Tema.

On July 4, 1958, the Ghanaian government established Ghana Airways to replace the former African Airways Corporation. By the mid-1990s, Ghana Airways operated international scheduled passenger and cargo service to numerous European, Middle Eastern, and African destinations, including London, Düsseldorf, Rome, Abidjan, Dakar, Lagos, Lomé, and Johannesburg, but it ceased operations and entered into liquidation in 2004. In 2005, Ghana International Airlines (GIA) began operations as the new national airline of Ghana but stopped services in early 2010.

Ghana has 12 airports, six with hard surfaced runways. The most important are Kotoka International Airport at Accra and airports at Sekondi-Takoradi, Kumasi, and Tamale that serve domestic air traffic.

Cocoa

One of the primary exports of Ghana is cocoa. An indigenous plant of Central and South America, cocoa was introduced to Ghana in 1878. It is a perennial tree crop of the humid tropics, grown under forest shade. A cocoa farm has an economic life of some 25-30 years. In Ghana it

Cocoa tree

is mostly grown by smallholder cocoa farmers. Ghana is the world's second largest producer of cocoa after Cote d'Ivoire and responsible for producing around 20 percent of the world's cocoa in 2005-06.[42] It is a very important source of income and foreign exchange earnings for Ghana. Cocoa accounts for US$1.2 million (33 percent) of Ghana's merchandise on exports, provides employment for around 6.3 million Ghanaians (30 percent of the population) and in 2006 contributed an estimated 8.5 percent of the nation's GDP.[43]

Cocoa is harvested twice per year. The main crop season begins in October and ends in February, while the light crop season is between May and August. Once fermented, the cocoa is carried to the villages for drying on raised bamboo or palm frond mats.

In Ghana, the entire cocoa production is controlled by a multi-layered organization known as the Ghana Cocoa Board (COCOBOD) and its subsidiaries. It has four primary objectives:

1. Maintain Ghana's position as the supplier of the finest and most consistent quality cocoa;
2. Pursue policies to maintain producer prices at profitable levels;
3. Support research to increase yields;

4. Fund disease control studies.

In 1993, the government of Ghana introduced a policy to liberalize the internal buying of cocoa. High quality cocoa beans are purchased from farmers by The Produce Buying Company (PBC), which then delivers the graded and sealed beans to specially designated Take Over Centers in the most efficient and profitable manner. The PBC's objectives are to:

- Satisfy cocoa farmers through quality service and other incentive packages;
- Build and maintain storage facilities for cocoa production;
- Recruit and retain a well-developed and motivated workforce;
- Encourage research institutions to develop technologically improved methods of cocoa production and their adoption by farmers to increase yield; and
- Conduct the company's business to the satisfaction of shareholders and other stakeholders.

The cocoa is purchased at a minimum producer price set by a Producer Price Review Committee (PPRC) from buying centers that are established in the cocoa production areas. On average, about 4,600 buying centers are in operation. After purchasing the cocoa, the Quality Control Division grades and seals it. The graded and sealed cocoa is transported using private cocoa haulers to designated take over points such as Tema port, Takoradi port and an inland port at Kaase, Kumasi. Control of the cocoa is the responsibility of the Cocoa Marketing Company until it is shipped overseas.

The Cocoa Processing Company Limited (CPC), based in Tema, has two processing lines. The Cocoa Factory processes raw cocoa beans into semi-finished products, such as cocoa liqueur, butter, natural/alkalized cake or powder, while the Confectionery Factory manufactures the Golden Tree chocolate bars, couverture, pebbles (chocolate coated peanuts), VITACO and ALLTIME drinking chocolate Powder, ChocoDelight (chocolate spread), ChocoBake and Royale natural cocoa powder. The CPC factories process only the choicest Ghana cocoa beans without any blending, probably the only factory in the world that can make such a claim. Ghana's cocoa has a high content of theobromine, which makes it the best cocoa for high quality chocolates. Unprocessed cocoa beans are stored, checked for quality, re-dried if necessary, sieved, and bagged into export sacks. Cocoa may be ready for export within seven days of arrival at the Cocoa Marketing Company (Ghana) Limited depot.

CMC is a wholly owned subsidiary of the Ghana Cocoa Board and has sole responsibility for the sale and export of Ghana cocoa beans. It also sells some of the cocoa products from the Cocoa Processing Companies in Ghana to overseas destinations. It is solely responsible for the sale of Ghana cocoa beans, cocoa liqueur, butter, cake and powder from the Cocoa Processing Company.

All sales by the Cocoa Marketing Company (Ghana) Limited are made to firms registered by the company as buyers on Cost, Insurance and Freight (CIF) terms without any commission. In special circumstances, however, the company can make sales on other terms such as Cost and Insurance (C & I) and Free On Board (FOB). The minimum quantity for a contract for cocoa beans to all the main ports of discharge is 50 tonnes while that for the cocoa products is 10 tonnes.

Sales are made for three-month shipment periods (for example, October/December, November/January, December/February) for cocoa beans and for a two-month shipment period (for example, February/March, March/April) for cocoa products. In both cases, the sales are made on the basis of major U.K. ports.

While cocoa exports are important to Ghana, a policy has been created to consume at least 40 percent of the crop locally. In addition, three foreign cocoa processing companies have now entered the market—Archer Daniels Midland (ADM), Cargill, and Barry Callebaut. The installed local processing capacity has increased from 100,000 tonnes in early 2000 to 450,000 tonnes in the middle of 2009. The following diagram describes the value and logistics chain for cocoa products.[44]

While total cocoa production figures are kept confidential, circumstantial data suggest that annual production expanded from more than 434,000 tonnes in 1999-2000 to 675,000 tonnes in 2007-2008. In all, 75 percent of Ghana's cocoa beans are exported to The Netherlands, Malaysia, United Kingdom, Japan, Estonia, United States, Belgium and Turkey. The Netherlands is by far the largest importer due in part to the major cocoa grinding installations of Cargill and ADM in Amsterdam.[45]

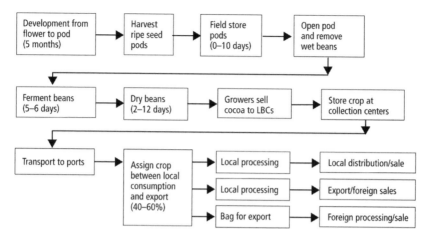

Source: C.H.W. Edwards, May 2010

Both companies dominate the cocoa grinding market. Western Europe is the major destination of the exports of cocoa powder, paste, butter and waste.

Conclusion

There is no disputing the importance of cocoa to Ghana as a source of employment and input to the nation's GDP. In order to realize even more economic and social benefits, investment in transport and logistics as well as production is essential. Ghana once operated a large and efficient railway network. That system created many social and economic benefits for the country. Now it barely exists, and Ghana is poorer for it. The proposed improvements are essential for the long-term growth of the nation. The benefits, both social and economic, arising from an efficient and effective railway operation will be wide ranging. Larger quantities of goods can be transported at lower costs. If the Ghanaian system is linked to those of adjacent countries, the ports of Tema and Takoradi can become major gateways to other West African nations, thereby generating additional jobs and income for Ghana.

Because Ghana is blessed with the Volta River and Lake Volta, inland water transport is another transport mode that needs to be developed. The primary route exists. The waterway needs to be prepared and maintained to handle commercial traffic. Snags, trees, and other barriers need to be removed. Channels need to be charted and marked. Vessels need to be obtained and crews trained. Unlike railways and roads, this transport mode can be created at lower costs and in a shorter time frame. The result will be to open up the interior of Ghana. The social and economic benefits of such developments will include higher incomes and improved lifestyles as goods, primarily agricultural products, can be more easily moved to Tema for export while imported goods can more cheaply taken inland.

The combination of an efficient rail system and inland waterway will provide a means to move more cocoa products more cheaply from the collection points to the processing facilities and port. The majority of the growers of cocoa in Ghana are small and thus inefficient. The overall concept being developed by Jon, Kris and their partners to create large farm-holdings and thereby derive economies of scale for both revenues and costs can potentially be applied to this important crop. Larger farms not only generate larger crops but also become traffic generators that attract transport and support logistics enterprises. As the volumes become concentrated, the efficiency of the transport and logistics system rises. As these efficiencies rise, rates can be cut, and profits, which ensure continued operation, can also increase. Additionally, as profits rise, tax revenues can increase which, if properly managed, can bring benefits to the entire nation.

The combination of improvements to the transport and logistics system and agricultural production can strengthen Ghana's position as the world's pre-eminent grower and exporter of cocoa beans and other agricultural products. By applying better systems for growing and producing agricultural products, Ghana can enter other export markets, develop other value added services and increase its gross domestic product and income.

By reducing production costs, through more efficient larger farms and lower transport costs by using rail and water services instead of relying on truck transport, all members of the cocoa supply chain have the potential to realize a combination of larger revenues and higher profits. This, in turn, will improve the economic wealth of individuals, companies and Ghana.

Republic of Kenya

The Kenyan Coast on the Indian Ocean is a mix of small villages, white sand beaches, waving palm trees, resort hotels, and a coral reef that protected the coast from the devastating Indonesian tsunami. This part of the eastern coast of Africa has been a gateway to the interior for many centuries. Arab traders and Chinese explorers have been visiting this coast for time immemorial. The port of Mombasa is one of the oldest ports along the Indian Ocean coast of Africa. Arab traders and Chinese and European explorers alike have employed the natural sheltered waters and easily protected environment of Mombasa Island as a base of operations. Fort Jesus that once protected the entrance to Mombasa has changed hands from the Portuguese, who built it, to the Arabs, who violently forced them out, to the English, who negotiated its takeover, to the Kenyans, who received it when their independence was granted in the 1960s. Nairobi, situated on the plains of Kenya, was developed by the English as the political headquarters for their colonies in east Africa. The land's rich soil was the foundation of one of the richest colonies in the British Empire.

Kenya issued a plan in 2006 entitled "Kenya—Vision 2030." The plan presented a new development blueprint with the goal of transforming Kenya into a newly industrialized middle-income country. The program is a comprehensive and integrated approach to address economic, social and political issues. The objective of the economic portion is to achieve an average annual GDP growth rate of 10 percent. The objectives of the social part of the plan are to create a clean and secure environment in which a just and cohesive society can thrive. Finally, the political element focuses on protection of individual rights and freedoms through the democratic non-political application of the rule of law.

As part of the overall program, the First Medium Term Plan (2008-2012) was issued to address specific challenges facing Kenya, including those that arose as a result of post-2007 election violence. A stable political environment and a growing economy are not important just for Kenyans, but for millions in the surrounding nations of the East African Community. Kenya is a major gateway to this part of Africa. Jomo

Kenyatta International Airport is one of the three largest air hubs on the continent. The Port at Mombasa is one of the major seaports of Africa and is an essential link to East African countries. Thus, Kenya plays a pivotal role in the economic and social well being of East Africa.

This chapter focuses on the opportunities and challenges of creating a company that exports the bounty of the Indian Ocean. While the export of flowers and other perishables dominates the air trade from Kenya, seafood exports are a relatively unknown segment of air trade that positions Kenya as an important node in the worldwide transport system. But developing a perishable export business is not easy, regardless of its location. The process of shipping live seafood caught off the coast of Africa to the tables of hotels and consumers in the Middle East and Asia demands a finely tuned system where delays are unacceptable and close attention to detail is critical. Regardless of how well the processing facility operates, the moment the packages leave for their journey, the shipper must rely on others to perform their duties at the highest levels. This does not always happen, for myriad reasons. If the system fails repeatedly, it can lead to the financial ruin of the shipper and the loss of revenue traffic for the transport companies.

In addition to examining how one Kenyan businessman is creating a business using the gifts of the Indian Ocean, the chapter considers the development of the country, on a broader scale, to establishing a stable political environment in which the economy can grow and all Kenyans can enjoy a better, safer and more prosperous life.

Seafood Exports

Sipping from a glass of mango juice, Hussein B., founder and managing director of Seithmar Marine Ltd., began to ponder two issues affecting his business. It had been a good day and it was turning out to be an above average week. His team had shipped 135 kilos of crab to Dubai and another 50 kilos were on the Akamba Express coach service to Nairobi that evening for distribution to local hotels. As the afternoon breeze began to pick up off the placid Indian Ocean and the breakers on the distant coral reef began to subside, Mr. B. knew that he had to deal with how to create and implement a marketing plan for his improved processing operation, and even more importantly, how to fight the ongoing issues of poor transport service that was causing loss of shipments.

The warm waters of the Indian Ocean and the seafront Mangrove Swamps are excellent habitat for a wide variety of seafood and shellfish. Hussein B. has built a business that exports crab and lobsters to the United Arab Emirates, China and Singapore. The operation extends from Lamu Island (Kenya) in the north to Mozambique in the south.

Live Indian Ocean lobster

Mr. B. has invested in a state-of-the-art processing facility for the live seafood at his primary location. A series of cleaning tanks use filtered seawater, designed to ensure that the entire shipped product is of the highest quality and meets the applicable (Hazard Analysis and Critical Control Points) standards. This investment and constant attention to the processing system is essential to assure that when the seafood leaves the

Live crab pot holding facility, Seithmar Marine

facility it is of the highest quality and has the best chance to survive the transport process. His packaging includes bottles of frozen water to keep the seafood at the proper temperature during the transit. If, however, the shipment is delayed, it can be destroyed, especially at locations with high temperatures.

Hussein B.'s operations span the east coast of Africa from northern Mozambique to northern Kenya. The logistics system comprises independent fishermen, company-owned boats to collect the catch, trucks to move the seafood to preparation stations and from the stations to airports, preparation and packaging facilities, and the services of airlines to move the shipments to the final destinations in the Middle East and Asia.

On the northern Kenyan coast, Siethmar Marine contracts with inde-

pendent fisherman to catch highly prized lobsters. Sailing wooden
dhows like those in use around
the Indian Ocean for thousands
of years, the fishermen catch the
lobsters and place them in floating
wooden crates some two to four
hours from Lamu Island for collection by Hussein's staff. The catch
is then loaded in trucks for the six-
hour drive to the primary preparation facility near Mombasa.
Each truckload weighs between
300 and 600 kilograms.

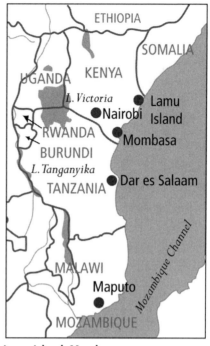

Lamu Island, Mombasa

Dar es Salaam is the site of another
processing location. Crabs caught
amongst the Mangrove Swamps
of Kilwa and Mtwara in southern
Tanzania are transported by truck
to the facility. There the crabs are placed in seawater tanks for two days
before being packaged for shipment. The shipments of live crabs go from
Dar es Salaam to Dubai and Singapore. To the south, at another operation in Mozambique, Indian Ocean lobsters and crabs are bought from
local fishermen, packaged and shipped via Johannesburg to Hong Kong
(lobsters) and Singapore (crabs).

Seithmar Marine sends at least two shipments of crab and one
shipment of lobster to Dubai, two shipments of crab to Singapore and
two shipments of crab and lobster to Hong Kong every week. From
the Mombasa facility, the shipments are delivered to Kenya Airways
at Mombasa International Airport approximately two hours before the
flight departure. As the shipments are destined for Dubai, Hong Kong
and Singapore, the flight from Mombasa is selected to reduce the transit
time before the next flight. The minimum time at Nairobi is four hours.
The shipments are prepared at the three processing facilities to maintain
a temperature between 20 and 22 Celsius. While chillers are available at

Mombasa and Nairobi, Hussein prefers that the shipments not be placed in them. Paperwork for the shipments is prepared by freight forwarders.

In spite of all the careful planning, preparation and packaging, shipments are lost. Transits at Nairobi International Airport can be prolonged. Shipments are left out in the hot African sun and spoil. Some shipments are routed to the wrong destination, and must be destroyed. Not only does Mr. B. lose valuable revenue, his customers have to go without the crabs and lobsters that they have planned to sell at their restaurants. Addressing these issues is an added task, not to mention an unprofitable one.

The accomplishments of Hussein B. and other entrepreneurs in Kenya are emblematic of the integration of Kenya into the world economy. The country and its business owners have taken advantage of the bounty of the soil and the sea, and have created an industry that collectively employs thousands of Kenyans. In early 2010, an estimated 5,000 Kenyans were employed in the Kenyan agricultural industry that ships an estimated 909,000 tons (2 million pounds) of fresh produce daily. The overwhelming majority (82 percent) of the foodstuffs and flowers are shipped to Europe, with the United Kingdom absorbing an estimated 33 percent of all products. The individual efforts, sometimes hampered by systems and infrastructure that are lacking or absent, reflect the vitality of Kenya and, it is hoped, are just the beginning of the economic and social growth of the country as it strives to meet the goals of Vision 2030.

The efforts of Hussein B. and other investors and entrepreneurs represent the individual efforts that are the building blocks of economic growth in Kenya. However, there is a need to create an environment in which their individual efforts and plans are not stifled or compromised.

First Medium Term Plan

In 2008, the Office of the Prime Minister of Kenya issued a detailed report, "First Medium Term Plan (2008-2012)," that outlined the progress of the Vision 2030 concept and identified specific actions. Among the many elements of the master plan for Kenya were several that specifically addressed economic and transport issues.

In 2007, Kenya registered a GDP growth rate of 7 percent. Prior to the worldwide recession it was hoped that the GDP growth rates between 2009 and 2010 would increase from 7.9 to 8.7 percent, and would reach 10 percent by 2012. Agriculture has always been a major economic sector. Government statistics show that it accounts for 24 percent of the country's GDP and for 75 percent of the industrial raw materials, and creates an estimated 60 percent of the nation's export earnings. About 8.3 million people, 21 percent of the nation's population, are employed either directly or indirectly in this economic sector. The business created by Hussein B. is embedded in those statistics, especially the export figure, as almost all of his business is directed toward exports. The government estimates that annual fish exports total some 4 billion Kenyan Shillings (approximately US$51.8 million).

To support the efforts of the 60,000 or so people active in the fisheries, including those on Lake Victoria, the government is to develop fishery related activities within the Exclusive Economic Zones on the Indian Ocean as well as on Lake Victoria. In addition, the government is planning to assist in marketing fish exports and to build three cold storage facilities, including one on Lamu Island and one at Malindi, close to the processing facility of Seithmar marine. Another component of the program is to establish a Food Security and Nutrition Policy. It is especially important, because when fully implemented, it will assure consumers in Kenya and elsewhere in the world that Kenyan food products are safe to eat.

These plans and actions are intended to improve the infrastructure that supports and assists this segment of the broader agricultural economic sector. Considering the significant contribution of the sector, a substantial amount of care and concern is required by the government to provide an environment in which independent businesspersons can create and grow their businesses. Some may argue that the role of a government is simply to provide an open, transparent and fair environment in which any business can be created and allowed to grow or fail without direct intervention. Others may argue that it is the role of the government to actively support businesses. Perhaps the answer lies somewhere in the middle, or perhaps the need for government active support changes over time.

On a broader scale, Kenya's plans to boost its economic, social and political environment to the next level is grounded in the rapid growth that has swept through Kenya in the last two decades of the 20th century. The reforms carried out in Kenya are exploiting the potential offered by geography and skilled labor through private sector-led development strategy. Continued structural reforms aimed at strengthening the country's external orientation and the role of the private sector should further advance Kenya's prospects. And Kenya boasts a number of characteristics and features that heighten its potential for strong long-term growth. For one, Kenya has developed a skilled, English-speaking labor force. Also, its natural beauty and coastal location provide unexploited potential, and Kenya has long been a major entry point into East Africa. Thus, it has the opportunity to leverage these characteristics not just for its own benefit but also to participate in the growth and development within the East African Community.

National Integrated Transport Policy

The Kenyan Ministry of Transport National Integrated Transport Policy of 2004 covers diverse issues, including transport infrastructure planning; development and management; legal, institutional and regulatory frameworks; safety and security; funding; gender mainstreaming; and use of Information and Communication Technologies, as well as environmental considerations. The aim of all this is to create a world-class integrated transport system responsive to the needs of people and industry.

A working paper, "A Report on Integrated National Transport Policy: Moving a Working Nation," was issued in May 2009 and identified a number of challenges that were inhibiting the transport sector from performing its role to support national and regional economies. The report identified nine challenges:

1. Poor Quality of Transport Services
2. Inappropriate Modal Split
3. Unexploited Regional Role of the Transport System
4. Transport System Not Fully Integrated

5. Urban Environmental Pollution

6. Lack of an Urban/rural Transport Policy

7. Institutional Deficiencies

8. Inadequate Human Resource Capacity

9. Lack of a Vision for the Transport Sector

In addressing the four primary modes of transport—roads, railways, maritime and aviation—the Kenyan government has begun to enact new laws, regulations and programs to improve infrastructure and services. The Kenyan Parliament enacted the Kenya Roads Act of 2007, which created three new agencies to be responsible for the development and maintenance of the road network. The agencies were the Kenya National Highways Authority, the Kenya Rural Roads Authority, and Kenya Urban Roads Authority, with the goal of managing and maintaining all road works on urban roads in cities and major municipalities.

The Kenya Railway Corporation (KRC) historically has been the primary transport link from the Port of Mombasa inland as far as Uganda. Its service level, performance and capacity have declined over the years due to a lack of investment in locomotive power and rolling stock. Even though the government assigned a concession of the KRC to the Rift Valley Railways (RVR) on November 1, 2006, significant challenges remain in the RVR's performance. A much delayed but long-hoped-for plan includes a widening of the track gauge to international standards as well as the purchase of new equipment, and the plan to introduce high-speed operations.

In contrast to the state of railway developments, the impact of a general modernization and computerization of Mombasa port facilities is reflected in the growth of tonnage and the construction of dedicated container handling equipment and facilities. While improvements have been made, further work is required so the port can meet the expanding needs of the Kenyan economy.

The expansion of facilities at Jomo Kenyatta International Airport, to include a new state-of-the-art terminal, is currently underway. Moi International Airport (Mombasa) and 40 airstrips have already been rehabilitated as part of the effort to improve air services. The Kenya Civil Aviation Authority has undertaken a program to upgrade equipment and internal structures to improve air safety.

A brief examination of the Port of Mombasa highlights the economic structure of both Kenya and other countries in east Africa. The Port of Mombasa, while not used by Hussein B. for his business, is a critical part of East Africa's transportation and logistics network. It is one of the four major ports on the east coast of Africa, and is the closest to the Middle East and India. It is larger than the port at Dar es Salaam. And historically, because of the colonization by England, it has a history as the primary gateway into much of east Africa.

The port is operated by the Kenya Ports Authority (KPA). The KPA's vision is to be recognized based on reputation and performance as one of the top 20 ports in the world. Its mission is to efficiently support seaborne trade. A set of five core values provide the basis for achieving this vision:

1. Conducting effective and reliable operations;
2. Responding to the needs of its customers;
3. Ensuring that operations are conducted on the basis of honesty, fairness and transparency;
4. Working with all partners in a collaborative manner to delivery services; and
5. Meeting corporate social obligation commitments.

In 2008, the latest reported year, the Port of Mombasa handled 445 vessel calls. An analysis of its import and export shipments illustrates that imports dominate trade of east Africa. In 2008, the port handled 13.8 million deadweight tons of import cargo. General cargo accounted for 39 percent of the imports, with dry bulk cargo at 21 percent and liquid bulk cargo at 40 percent. Exports totaled just 2.3 million deadweight tons. Of that, general cargo accounted for 83 percent of the exports. Soda ash was the single largest export at 24 percent of all exports.

The level of transit statistics reflects the importance of the port as an entry point into Africa. As the following table illustrates, traffic to and from Uganda dominates. As the statistics show, imports comprise almost 92 percent of the transit traffic. The largest exporter is Uganda, which reflects that country's relative economic size. Surprisingly, even though Tanzania has three ports, some Tanzanian import and export traffic is handled through this Kenyan port. The transit import traffic accounted for 32 percent of all import traffic at the port, while transit export traffic accounted for only 17.5 percent of all exports.

Port of Mombasa—Transit Traffic (2008)				
		Deadweight Tons (000)		
Country	% of Total	Exports	Imports	Total
Uganda	76.0	327.1	3,374.2	3,701.3
D.R. Congo	6.2	40.2	264.2	304.4
Rwanda	6.0	16.9	276.6	293.5
Tanzania	5.1	14.6	236.2	250.8
Sudan	4.6	3.2	220.1	223.3
Burundi	1.2	1.3	55.5	56.8
Somalia	0.9	N/M	43.2	43.2
Total	100%	403.7	4,470.6	4,873.3

Source: Kenya Ports Authority Annual Report 2008, Table 6

Vision 2030

In order to expand the Kenyan economy, several issues need to be addressed. While some of these are not specifically logistics issues, they affect transport and logistics operations and services. Vision 2030's goal to achieve a 10 percent long-run growth rate in the nation's GDP is ambitious. This is especially the case when one considers that Kenya's average annual GDP growth rate was around 3 percent from 1980 to 2005. From an international perspective, only 10 economies with populations greater than 1 million achieved an average per capita growth rate higher than 4 percent from 1980 to 2005, and only China was able to achieve an average growth rate of about 10 percent during this period. For the long-run high growth rates that Kenya aspires to achieve, it will be necessary to make progress along multiple fronts such as raising growth of total factory productivity, attracting foreign direct investment and foreign aid, and mobilizing domestic savings.

The plan for Kenya identifies five broad areas that must be improved to provide a foundation for achieving this ambitious goal. Those areas are the political institutions, the social fractionalization of Kenya, integrating Kenya into the global economy, the need for more investment, and addressing the cost of doing business in Kenya.

Institutions

Kenya's position is mixed. While international indicators suggest that Kenya does well, the 2008 political crisis highlighted the inherent weakness of institutions to ensure smooth political transition in a democratic context. Kenya ranks much lower on control of corruption, even compared with fast-growing Sub-Saharan African countries. Finally, income inequality is relatively high. Research shows that high inequality in incomes can be unfriendly to growth.

Social Fractionalization

After the 2008 elections, unexpected violence spread across the country, leaving some 1,500 dead and forcibly relocating hundreds of thousands. A major reason for the violence is the fact that Kenya, like all African countries, is an ethnic kaleidoscope of six major tribal groups. This fundamental situation means that many investors could think twice before developing a business in Kenya. The government acknowledges that this social fractionalization affects economic outcomes and hurts growth due to ethno-regional biases in policy, particularly the provision of public goods, and indicates a higher potential for conflict and derailing growth.

Integration into the Global Economy

While Kenya does not look much different from sustained growth countries at the beginning of their growth acceleration, in terms of level and structure of exports, Kenya's export growth has lagged behind those of other countries.

Need for More Investment

High risk and low returns limit investment in Kenya. The average return on investment is low mainly because business costs other than the cost of labor and capital are high. This includes the high cost and unreliable supply of infrastructure services, particularly transportation and energy, as well as opportunity costs due to logistics bottlenecks, such as delays of shipments and trading costs at the border. Risks due to corruption and the security situation remain serious deterrents to investment. Second, access to finance is limited and costs are high for certain categories of borrowers, such as rural and small entrepreneurs. Investment by smaller businesses can be constrained because of poor and costly access to finance in part because of the high cost of collateral requirements. Informal businesses also have greater problem in accessing credit. Access to credit declines as one moves from urban to rural areas and is the thinnest in arid areas.

An important source of investment—flow of foreign aid—is also low, at around 3 percent of GDP. A variety of improvements in governance and investment climate are required to stimulate these flows. Example of the improvements include ensuring that transaction costs of aid are low and that the aid goes to projects with priorities for growth and poverty reduction. There is a danger that too much aid going into the services sectors would likely impede efforts to maintain a competitive real exchange rate. The caveat about the revenue effort is important because a low level of aid appears to have motivated fiscal reforms in Kenya in the 1990s. The tax burden (including fees and levies) is perceived to be high. Experience elsewhere suggests that negative perceptions about the tax burden could be rooted in unreliable and costly public services.

To support capital accumulation, there is considerable scope for greater use of foreign savings, in the form of foreign direct investment and remittances. Kenya's private savings rate is relatively low and is expected to improve slowly. A rapid increase in private savings rate would require an initial slowdown in the growth of personal consumption. Therefore, foreign savings in the form of foreign direct investment (FDI) could help relax the domestic savings constraint, especially in the beginning of the period of growth acceleration. FDI would bring with it newer technology and products, and help improve productivity, as happened in the horticulture and garments sectors. Indeed, Kenya is likely to rely considerably for its productivity growth on technological change embodied in new investment. Lastly, FDI is likely to be a source of access to other markets, particularly in niche products, as has happened elsewhere in East Asia. FDI would increase as the public infrastructure, crime, and security situations improve.

Cost of Doing Business

The high costs of doing business have reduced Kenya's global competitiveness in tradable goods and services. The extent of loss of competitiveness is highlighted in the following table, which compares Kenya with other countries. To these must be added opportunity costs of delays due to logistics bottlenecks. Largely because of these costs, Kenya is rated low on various cross-country indexes of global competitiveness.

Costs of crime, security, bribes, and lost production are several times higher in Kenya than in other countries Cost as % of sales

Factor	Kenya	Tanzania	Uganda	India	China	S. Africa
Production lost to power outages	7.1	10.7	10.2	7.8	2.0	0.9
Production lost due to crime	3.9	1.1	1.0	0.6	0.3	0.6
Bribes	3.6	3.4	3.7	2.1	1.9	0.3
Payment for security	2.9	2.3	1.4	1.3	0.8	0.9
Product lost in transit	2.6	1.6	1.2	0.8	1.2	0.8
Total Costs	20.1	19.1	17.5	12.2	6.2	3.5

Source: ICA 2007

To accelerate growth, rapid improvement in total factor productivity (TFP) will be critical. Reducing business costs and improving integration with the global economy through trade and investment would provide sources for enhancing total factor productivity. A target contribution of about 2 percent to overall growth by TFP growth could provide a reasonable challenge. In comparison, TFP growth contributed 1.8 percent per annum to the per capita growth rate during 2003-06.

Conclusion

The creation of a business that exports the bounty of the Indian Ocean by a Kenyan businessman exemplifies the entrepreneurial spirit in east Africa. With a base in Kenya, Hussein B. obtains crabs and lobsters from Mozambique to the Somali border in Kenya. He uses independent fishermen to catch the seafood, and through a network of boats, trucks and processing facilities, prepares shipments for export to the Middle East, China and Singapore. His company relies on critical air services from Mombasa and Nairobi in Kenya, Dar es Salaam in Tanzania and Johannesburg in South Africa.

As Mr. B. builds his business, Kenya has created and is implementing a comprehensive program that will raise the growth rate of the nation to one of the highest in the world. Vision 2030 is addressing a broad array of issues, many of which affect or enhance transport and logistics infrastructure and services in Kenya. Historically, Kenya has been a primary entry point into Africa. As illustrated by the statistics of the Port of Mombasa, Kenya is a transit point for East Africa. As Kenya improves its transport and logistics network, the benefits will expand beyond its borders. Not only will this strengthen the economies of the surrounding countries, but their economic expansion will generate higher trade flows that will create business, revenues and tax income for Kenyans.

Building an infrastructure requires a long-term perspective. While small businesspersons learn how to optimize their available resources, many are unable to create comprehensive networks. They have to rely on those that are created by the government or by other service providers. Ensuring the political environment that supports and enhances the development of this essential component of modern day economies is an essential role of every government. Kenya has embarked on its journey to establish and protect such an environment. Small businessmen like Hussein B. and his customers around the world are among the many beneficiaries.

Republic of Rwanda

The Republic of Rwanda is known as the land of a thousand hills. During the period of genocide, those hills ran red with blood and echoed the screams of victims. But that is in the past. The process of reconciliation has spread throughout the country. The many benefits of this process are readily identifiable. One of the most visible results is the monthly clean-up that occurs on the last Saturday of each month. Everyone, from the President to the common citizen, stops his or her work to clean up the land. The result is a country whose natural beauty is not covered by trash. Not only is it visibly pleasing to the visitor, it is emblematic of a country that is working hard to recover from its past, to wash away the old and renew itself for a bright future.

Another key feature of Rwanda is the dominant position of women in business and politics. Women account for nearly 60 percent of all of the legislators and ministers. This pattern reflects the matriarchal organization that is typical of African families. With its search for the best way to build and manage a country, the government of Rwanda has sought the input of technocrats from the Southeast Asian nation of Singapore. A major impact of that support and guidance that has been fully embraced by President Kagame and his ministers is the drive to eliminate corruption. The people of Rwanda recognize that the short-term benefits that come from the levy of extra charges, turning one's back to the damaging effects of an overloaded truck, or the repeated flouting of safety rules and regulations are damaging their future.

The government is committed to stopping corruption and creating an environment that promotes economic and social well being and development, using billboards like the one at left, which states: "Corruption is the enemy of development."

Like its neighbor to the south, Burundi, Rwanda is a landlocked nation. But Rwanda, through its aggressive attack on the damaging effects of corruption and its commitment to creating a transport and economic environment based on public-private cooperation, is seeking to develop itself into a critical link in the logistics environment in east Africa. This chapter examines the negative impact of corruption in transportation and its deleterious effect on economic growth and development.

Looking out over the lush green hills of her native home of Kigali, Madame Therese considered what she had heard on the phone call. As the regular afternoon shower cleared the air and moved westward, the distant thunder returned her focus to the notes of the call. A critical

Choice Boutique Hotel, Kigali

shipment for the new boutique hotel she was developing was still delayed at the port in Dar es Salaam.

The ship carrying the containers of furniture and supplies had just docked. It had been in Oyster Bay anchorage for 21 days—three times longer than it had taken to sail to the port. She now wondered how long it would take for the shipment to be off-loaded, inspected, and cleared for forwarding to the hotel. She wondered what "special charges" would be added to the process. She also had to consider the knock-on effects in delaying yet again the planned opening of the hotel.

A businesswoman with other successful enterprises, Madame Therese had faced these challenges many times during her career. While she could almost understand the logistics and transport delays, given the simple fact that Kigali was at the end-of-the-road systems from the port cities of Mombasa in Kenya and Dar es Salaam in Tanzania, it was the extra, unofficial charges and fees that had to be paid. When, she wondered, would this situation be addressed and remedied? When would shippers, consignees, logistics and transport operators band together to fight the pervasive practice known as "Chai Kidogo" that delayed or diverted shipments or added unnecessary costs to the shipments? Madame Therese could take solace in that the government of Rwanda, led by the President Kagame, had announced a concerted effort to fight corruption and had published a report that named specific sources of added costs, including those in other countries. Maybe, just maybe, this would be the beginning of the end of these extra payments and delays.

Essentially all of Rwanda's imports and exports are handled by the major Indian Ocean ports of Mombasa and Dar es Salaam. This means that the trucks bringing goods to Rwanda or taking exports from the country must pass through one or two other countries between points in Rwanda and the seaports. A 1997 UNCTAD study noted that Rwandan importers and exporters bear some of the highest costs for transport and insurance payments in the world. That same study noted that more than 48 percent of the Rwandan total export value was comprised of transport and insurance payments, compared to an average of 14.1 percent for all landlocked countries combined and 17.2 percent for least developed countries. For Rwanda to effectively compete with her neighbors in the global market, she will have to significantly lower these exorbitantly high transport costs. Short of that, the competitive advantage will be minimal.

Cost of Corruption

Madame Therese was thankful that this critical shipment was not coming from the Port of Mombasa. The Northern Corridor, which begins at the Port of Mombasa and traverses both Kenya and Uganda, accounts for about three-fourths of the imports and exports of Rwanda. It is also known for the many delays and extra charges paid by the drivers. According to a study prepared by the Private Sector Federation-Rwanda, these corruption payments can typically add almost US$1,200 to the cost of a shipment.[46] In contrast, the experience along the shorter Central Corridor between Dar es Salaam and Rwanda result in negligible payments of US$7.50 per shipment.[47]

As the report states, the "extra" payments and other costs that increase transport costs between Rwanda and the Indian Ocean ports come in different forms. The following tables identify the types of payments and the amounts.

The information in these tables, based on a small sample of trips, highlights the source of these added costs to imports and exports. In terms of frequency and amount, the weighbridges along the Northern Corridor are the primary reason for increased operating costs. Based on reported figures, these alone can increase a round trip between Kigali and Mombasa by US$1,995.02. The added cost for exports of US$864 is the equivalent of 26 percent of the calculated standard costs for exports, according to the World Bank's "Doing Business 2010" report. The weigh-bridge cost for an import shipment is equivalent to a 23-percent increase of the calculated standard costs for exports, according to the report. Rwanda already faces some of the highest legitimate costs for

Cost of Corruption—Along the Northern Corridor—Exports

	Total number of occurrences	Number of occurrences where bribery occurred	Total bribes in USD Uganda	Total bribes in USD Kenya	Total amount paid in USD	% Share of total value of bribes
Border	4	1	$ 0.00	$ 40.11	$ 40.11	5%
Police Roadblock	22	17	$ 1.84	$ 10.03	$ 11.87	1%
Weighbridge	10	10	$ 196.20	$ 616.05	$ 812.25	94%
TOTAL	**36**	**28**	**$ 198.04**	**$ 626.08**	**$ 864.23**	**100%**

Cost of Corruption—Along the Northern Corridor—Imports

	Total number of occurrences	Number of occurrences where bribery occurred	Total bribes in USD Uganda	Total bribes in USD Kenya	Total amount paid in USD	% Share of total value of bribes
Weighbridge	10	10	$ 275.90	$ 906.87	$ 1,182.77	100%

Cost of Corruption—Along the Central Corridor—Imports

	Total number of occurrences	Number of occurrences where bribery occurred	Total bribes in USD Rwanda	Total bribes in USD Tanzania	Total amount paid in USD
Border	2	0	$ 0	$ 0	$ 0
Police Roadblock	21	9	$ 0	$ 7.50	$ 7.50
Weighbridge	5	0	$ 0	$ 0	$ 0
TOTAL	**28**	**4**	**$ 0**	**$ 7.50**	**$ 7.50**

(Source: Private Sector Federation-Rwanda, "Assessment of Non Tariff barriers (NTB's) Along the Northern & Central Corridors—EAC," 2008, Tables 6, 7 and 11)

imports and exports in the world; by adding approximately 25 percent, it is not surprising that the government of Rwanda has initiated an aggressive campaign to fight corruption. Unfortunately, in the case of imports and exports, the problem does lie within its borders. The added costs attributable to Uganda are 32 percent for export shipments and 23 percent for imports. The extra costs on the Northern Corridor occur primarily in Kenya.

While the Rwandan government is actively seeking to end corruption,

Rwandan importers and exporters must cope with a combination of other situations that put them and the economy of Rwanda on a less-than-equal footing with other countries in the EAC, especially Kenya and Tanzania as well as other less developed countries elsewhere in the world. The hurdles that Rwandan companies face on both corridors include:

- Extensive sections of poor quality roads and numerous diversions around construction sites;
- Repeated weighing of trucks, whether sealed or not, especially along the Northern Corridor;
- Non-Tariff Barriers (NTBs), such as customs delays, road blocks, and bond guarantees;
- A lack of harmonization and cooperation between Rwanda and the countries;
- Different information and communications technology that hinder customs clearance between the countries; and
- Other delays that effectively double the transit time between Rwanda and the two seaports.

Improvements to the roads are a function of available funds. Many of the projects have been underway since the late 1990s. Until all of the individual projects are completed, delays will continue for road haulage on the Northern and Central Corridor roads.

Ten of the weighbridges are in Kenya. They were installed at the recommendation of donors, including the World Bank, to control the weight of trucks using the highway between the Port of Mombasa and the Kenya-Uganda border. Unfortunately, the role of the weighbridges has morphed into a source of non-tariff charges instead of ensuring that trucks are not overweight and damage the road surface. A system has evolved to speed up the payments at the weighbridges. It is possible for a driver to pre-negotiate payments for subsequent weighbridges through middlemen. In this way, the delays at subsequent weighbridges are reduced.

In addition to these extra payments, road haulage companies must deal with other costs. Border crossings are a major source of delays. In some cases, money is exchanged to get paperwork signed and stamped quickly. In other instances, the sheer volume of vehicles creates delays.

The study noted that only 43 percent of total transit time from Kigali to Mombasa was spent driving.[48]

Combined, these issues increase costs that in turn reduce the competitiveness of the Rwandan economy. Higher cost imports that become inputs into export-generating enterprises raise the cost of goods sold, and thus increase the prices of the exported goods. This can be very damaging if the Rwandan exports are in direct competition with those from a country that does not have costs that are as high. The higher cost for imported goods for domestic consumption also can reduce the wealth of the country. The payment of the higher costs is translated into an additional flow of money out of Rwanda, for which there is no reciprocal increase in the country's GDP. Essentially, the additional costs to pay for the movement of imports to Rwanda is an economic tax on those goods.

The impact of higher transport costs, additional insurance premiums for the inland transport and the Chai Kidogo payments affects the cost of doing business for companies in Rwanda. In the case of the new hotel in Kigali, these costs were passed on to guests. The added costs for a shipment of furniture or cutlery can be amortized over room-nights or meals served. But the fact remains that this added cost increases the charges borne by guests. A tourist who has the flexibility to select one location over another might ignore Rwanda, in spite of its many attributes, simply because the average cost is higher than that for a venue in another country.

As the following table illustrates, the cost of furniture purchased for a new hotel rapidly escalates from the time it leaves the manufacturer's plant. Once landed at an east African port, the tariff and non-tariff costs increase the price of the shipment by almost 25 percent. By the time the shipment is delivered to the hotel, the final cost of the furniture has more than doubled.

In contrast, a similar shipment destined to a hotel in Tanzania would cost US$16,475 or 18.8 percent less than the same shipment for a hotel in Kigali (see the following table).

While the two hotels are not necessarily in direct competition, this example does illustrate the economic penalty that business people in

Estimated Cost Impact to Move Imported Goods to Kigali

Cost	Amount Per Container (US$)	% of Total
Ocean Transport Costs (e)	2,500	12.3%
Inland Transport + Insurance (1)	3,595	17.7%
"Chai Kidogo" payments (2)	1,183	5.8%
Total Inland Transfer Costs to Kigali	**4,778**	**23.6%**
Rwanda Import Duty (3)	3,000	14.8%
Value of Contents	10,000	49.3%
Total Delivered Cost	**20,278**	**100%**

(e) The ocean transport costs have been estimated based on a TEU.

Sources:

(1) World Bank, Doing Business 2010, pg. 148

(2) Private Sector Federation-Rwanda, "Assessment of Non Tariff barriers (NTB's) Along the Northern & Central Corridors—EAC', 2008, pg 22

(3) Rwanda Revenue Authority, Customs Tariff, Chapter 94

Estimated Cost Impact to Move Imported Goods to Dar es Salaam

Cost	Amount Per Container (US$)	% of Total
Ocean Transport Costs (e)	2,500	15.2%
Inland Transport + Insurance (1)	1,475	9.0%
"Chai Kidogo" payments (2)	0	0%
Total Inland Transfer Costs	**1,475**	**9.0%**
Tanzania Import Duty (3)	2,500	15.2%
Value of Contents	10,000	60.7%
Total Delivered Cost	**16,475**	**100%**

(e) The ocean transport costs have been estimated based on a TEU.

Sources:

(1) World Bank, Doing Business 2010, pg. 148

(2) Private Sector Federation-Rwanda, "Assessment of Non Tariff barriers (NTB's) Along the Northern & Central Corridors-EAC', 2008, pg 22

(3) EAC Customs Union, Common External Tariff

Rwanda must face. It could be argued that the cost of a hotel room in Kigali would be 18.8 percent higher than one in Dar es Salaam if all other costs were the same. If that were the case, tourists might decide against going to Rwanda for their vacation.

As Madame Therese considered these additional costs, she also was

concerned about the actual trip that the truck carrying her precious shipment would take. The most direct route from the port at Dar es Salaam
and Kigali was via the so-called Central Route. Unlike the highways she
had driven on in France and the United States, this route was a collection
of roads that led across Tanzania and then through Rwanda to Kigali.
All were paved, but most were only two lanes wide. She knew that the
truck would average less than 40 kph, so the trip would take at least 41
hours of driving plus other time for en-route delays, including crossing
the border at Rusmo into Rwanda. If she was lucky, the shipment would
arrive within the next four to five days after the shipment was off-loaded
and loaded on the truck and the truck was released to leave the Port of
Dar es Salaam.

East African Community Central Corridor

Sector	Length (Km.)	Sector	Length (Km.)
Tanzania (Sub-Total)	**1,399**	Nzega-Isaka	170
Dar es Salaam-Mlandizi	55	Isaka-Lusahunga	245
Mlandizi-Morogoro	140	Lusahunga-Rusumo	57
Morogoro-Dodoma	265	**Rwanda (Sub-Total)**	**150**
Dodoma-Manyoni	127	Rusumo-Kayonza	87
Manyoni-Singida	118	Kayonza-Kigali	63
Singida-Shelui	110	**Total Length**	**1,549**
Shelui-Nzega	112		

Source: Cape Consult, "Scoping Study on Identification of the Missing Links and Bottlenecks
Affecting the Performance of the East African Community Central Corridor," November 2008, 10

The frustration of the road haulage from the port to Kigali was
enough, but added to that were the problems of getting the shipment off
the ship, onto the truck and the truck off the port. The Port of Dar es
Salaam is the primary seaport for Tanzania as well as Burundi, Rwanda
and Uganda of the East African Community. Non-EAC countries that
use this port include the DRC, Malawi and Zambia. As a result, traffic at
the port exceeds its capacity.

A series of operational issues create additional delays, including:

- Lack of a computer system;
- Duty payments are made after the manifest is submitted;

- No interface between the Tanzania Revenue Authority and banks, which delays issuance of payment receipts;
- Only manual screening of shipments and documents;
- Preparation and release of the delivery orders is a long process;
- Severe congestion due to delayed transit containers that must stay in the port; and
- Insufficient equipment to handle the increasing volumes.

The combination of these factors only worsen the productivity of the port, which creates further delays and adds to loss of productivity at this critical East African seaport. This means that all importers and exporters must allow additional days when planning their shipments. At the same time, the road haulage operators are forced to incorporate added costs to their operations to reflect the extending waiting times. These added costs are passed on to the shippers, which further add to the overall cost, especially for those in interior countries like Rwanda.

The country's geographic situation—it is between 1,500 and 1,700 kilometers to the nearest seaport and only about 5 percent of the road length of the Northern and Central Corridors are in Rwanda—lends itself to numerous opportunities for Chai Kidogo to be levied outside of Rwanda. Also, there is little harmonization and standardization among the countries. All of this means that Rwanda has limited opportunities for economic growth and development. From a logistics cost and operating perspective, many impediments and challenges must be overcome to develop and maintain business links with Rwanda. Depending on the price elasticity of demand for the particular goods, Rwandan exports are at an immediate disadvantage in comparison with similar products from neighboring countries like Tanzania, Uganda and Kenya. At the same time, imported goods to Rwanda are more costly than for its neighbors. But as the Wheel of Commerce demonstrates, commerce is affected by a wide range of factors and inputs. A major factor that affects transport and logistics services, and operations and the businesses that they service, is public policy and practices.

This is particularly important in the case of Rwanda. Government policies in Rwanda are dedicated to strengthening and broadening the economic and social growth of the country.

Rwanda Vision

A document entitled "Rwanda Vision," issued by President Kagame, is the primary vehicle for improving Rwanda. As the foreword states, "the Vision 2020 is a reflection of our aspiration and determination as Rwandans, to construct a united, democratic and inclusive Rwandan identity, after so many years of authoritarian and exclusivist dispensation."[49] The plan contains six key elements—good governance, an efficient State, skilled human capital, vibrant private sector, world-class physical infrastructure, and modern agriculture and livestock—all geared toward national, regional and global markets. Importantly, the plan notes, "this Vision is not only for government. Vision 2020 is a shared purpose for all Rwandans."

The plan identifies seven challenges that must be overcome for the development of Rwanda, including:

- Diminishing agricultural productivity and arable land distribution. As the population has increased, there is less than one hectare for every nine Rwandans. With more than 90 percent of the population in agriculture, alternate sources of jobs have to be created.
- The reliance on high-cost transport for both imports and exports is a hindrance to industrial and other forms of development.
- The reliance on coffee and tea production is not sufficient to support the entire economy. The few mineral deposits in Rwanda need to be explored and quantified in order to broaden the narrow economic base.
- Governance, including the management of public resources, remains insufficient due to lack of sound institutions and competent personnel. Past governments relied on costly and, in some cases, indifferent foreign technical assistance instead of building local capacity.

The severe shortage of professional personnel constitutes an obstacle to the development of all sectors. Illiteracy is rampant among both the urban and the rural population, with 48 percent of Rwandans unable to read and write. The prevalence of major diseases, such as malaria and

HIV/AIDS, as well as malnutrition, reduces the population's productivity.

Rwanda's public debt, which stands at about US$1.5 billion, is larger than the current national GDP of US$1.3 billion (2000 data). It is increasing at a rate higher than the country's capacity to generate wealth to service the debt. A return to a sustainable level of debt, where existing debt can be serviced comfortably without jeopardizing the country's growth prospects, is envisaged for 2015. However, continued debt relief and grant financing by donors will still be needed—at least in the medium term—and a significant rise in export earnings is vital to avoid returning to the current situation.

The 1994 Genocide devastated the Rwandan economy as well as its population. GDP was halved in a single year, 80 percent of the population was plunged into poverty and vast tracts of land and livestock were destroyed. The impact of more than 1 million deaths in the 100 days of genocide set back economic development of Rwanda. Among the dead were many of the nation's best educated and trained. Infrastructure was also destroyed. The result was devastation of Rwanda's social, economic, transport and political fabric. Recovery from the long-term impacts of this horror required successful reconciliation throughout the entire population of Rwanda and a return to political stability and security.

The following table illustrates the multi-dimensional plan for Rwanda. The six pillars of the plan are supported by three "cross-cutting" areas

Pillars of the Vision 2020	Cross-cutting areas of Vision 2020
1. Good governance and a capable state	1. Gender equality
2. Human resource development and a knowledge-based economy	2. Protection of environment and sustainable natural resource management
3. A private sector-led economy	
4. Infrastructure development	
5. Productive and Market-Oriented Agriculture	3. Science and technology, including ICT
6. Regional and International Economic integration	

Source: Republic of Rwanda, Rwanda Vision 2020, Table 2

that are viewed as means to accomplish the objectives of the plan. These three "cross-cutting" areas reflect the fundamental structure of Rwanda.

Rwanda is committed to improving the lot of 53 percent of its population—women. To eradicate discrimination, Rwanda is committed to updating its laws and introducing an environment where positive discrimination for women must be practiced. By 2010, 58 percent of the government ministries and legislative members were women. This fact demonstrates that Rwanda is not just stating a plan, but enacting the plan to achieve its stated goals.

Rwanda is a beautiful country under tremendous pressures caused by a strong population growth and limited arable land. The country's natural resources have been harmed through a combination of massive deforestation, the depletion of bio-diversity, erosion and landslides, pollution of waterways and the degradation of fragile ecosystems, such as swamps and wetlands. The government is committed to protecting its natural resources. The monthly clean-up program is an example of this commitment.

The plan notes that in Rwanda, the rate of adoption and integration of science and technology in socio-economic life is very low, and that there is a shortage of technically qualified professionals. In order to facilitate achievement of the Rwanda Vision 2020, the nation is committed to teaching science and technology at secondary and university levels. New computers and their support systems are being put in place as part of this goal.

The combination of these efforts is directed toward the achievement of six focused programs that support each other, and will grow and improve the economic structure of Rwanda. Three of the "pillars" that are of particular interest to those in the transportation and logistics industry are:

- Infrastructure development,
- Regional and international economic integration, and
- A private sector-led economy.

Infrastructure Development
The plan for infrastructure development encompasses better land use

management, urban development, and improvements to the transport, energy, water and waste management systems in the country.

The transport plan contains three primary elements. Rwanda Vision 2020 notes that "it is imperative to develop alternative, lower costs of transport to the sea, notably through a regional rail extension to Isaka (Tanzania) and an extension to the Ugandan Railway system."[50] These two links provide Rwanda not only with two rail routes to the two major seaports, but also with a means to avoid the delays and costs associated with road haulage.

Another route that combines rail and water system is a link to the Banguela Railway. The Banguela Railway runs from Angola's Atlantic Ocean port across that country, and also has direct links to the DRC and Zambia. Creating a link to this railway would establish Rwanda as an eastern entry point to this part of Africa and would create an alternate transport route for Rwandan importers and exporters to world markets.

Given its location, air transport is potentially an important mode for the nation. The country is proceeding with the development of a new international airport located close to the Rwanda-Burundi border. The concept of this new airport, which will be built and operated by a public-private arrangement, is intended to serve as a regional hub for the great lakes region.[51] There is also a need to extend and improve the Rwandan road network to improve access for rural inhabitants.

Improving regional and international trade links is important to Rwanda for many reasons. Employment in export-driven companies typically commands higher wage rates. Access to other markets not only opens up new opportunities for companies to sell their goods, but also provide sources of new technology and investment. Rwanda recognizes that pursuing a policy to open and liberalize its trade regime with minimal trade barriers and also to encourage foreign direct investment is extremely important to the nation's social and economic development.

In order to achieve this goal, the government is committed to facilitating the creation and existence of competitive enterprises, exports and entrepreneurship. Specifically, Rwanda plans to develop and promote economic zones for ICT based production that will also be available to sharpen the competitiveness of Rwandan firms.[52]

The plan is not dedicated to fighting its situation as being landlocked. Instead, it wants to exploit Rwanda's comparative strategic potential as a trade and commercial entrépot. One strategy is for Rwanda to take advantage of growing regional cooperation in the Great Lakes/Eastern African Region. The objective of this part of the plan is for the nation to consolidate its niche in the services and communication sectors.

Expansion of a viable private sector is key to Rwanda's economic and social development. The private sector will be part of the economic engine of the country as well as the foundation for emergence of a vibrant middle class of entrepreneurs, which will help develop and embed the principles of democracy. Although foreign direct investment will be encouraged, a locally-based business class remains a crucial component of development.

Unlike many other developing countries, the role of private enterprise as a full partner in the economic development process is recognized by Rwanda as an essential aspect of the country's economic and social development. The Rwanda Vision 2020 plan specifically states "the Government of Rwanda will not be involved in providing services and products that can be delivered more efficiently by the private sector. It is, therefore, committed towards a comprehensive privatization policy that will help reduce costs and prices and widen consumer choice. The State will only act as a catalyst, ensuring that infrastructure, human resources and legal frameworks are geared towards stimulating economic activity and private investment."[53] This fresh approach highlights the innovative efforts of Rwanda to escape the past horrors and mismanagement that have limited the economic and social development of the country.

As noted by the World Bank in its "Doing Business 2010" study, Rwanda is fulfilling many of these objectives. Between 2008 and 2010, Rwanda's ranking among 183 surveyed nations jumped from 143 to 67.[54] During that period the government passed a total of seven major reforms focusing on easing restrictions on starting a business, employing workers, registering property, getting credit, protecting investors, trading across borders, and closing a business. These actions demonstrate the government of Rwanda's ability to implement the Rwanda Vision 2020

Rwanda Score Card			
Indicator	2000	2008	% Diff.
Population (000)	7,960	9,720	22.1%
PPP GNI (USD)	580	1,010	74.1%
Gross Domestic Product (USD Billions)	1.73	4.46	157.8%
Annual GDP Growth Rate (%)	8.1	11.2	37.0%
Per Capita GDP (USD)	220	459	108.6%
Exports and Imports (USD Billions)	0.61	1.61	163.9%
Merchandise trade as % of GDP	15.2%	30.5%	100.6%

Source: World Bank World Development Indicators 2000 and 2009.

The table presents a few selected indicators that suggest that the Rwanda Vision 2020 is in fact taking hold and contributing to the long hoped-for social and economic improvement of Rwanda.

During this eight-year period, the GDP of Rwanda has grown by nearly 160 percent. This is extremely important at the per capita level. While the per capita GDP has not grown as rapidly because of the increase in the population of Rwanda, in 2008 it was US$1.26 per day instead of the 2000 level of US$0.60 per day. On a comparative basis, the per capita gross national income purchasing power (PPP GNI) level of Rwandans increased from the equivalent of US$1.59 per day to US$2.77 per day. The PPP GNI is a more accurate indicator of the income of the average citizen as it reflects the real cost of living in the local community as expressed in terms of U.S. dollars.

Conclusion

Rwanda's national focus on addressing corruption represents a recognition that the short-term benefits of these added payments are not in the long-term benefit of the population and nation. While Rwanda cannot directly change the situation outside its borders, such as the extra costs incurred by truckers moving shipments from the nearest seaports, it does have the ability to influence changes through the East African Community. The benefits of reducing corruption are well known and documented by the World Bank, Transparency International and others. And although conceptually it might sound easy to eliminate this corrosive state of affairs, the simple fact is that the situation is ingrained and eliminating these extra payments will require decisive leadership and constant monitoring.

In spite of being a landlocked country, Rwanda has set out on a course that involves innovative public and private partnerships to aggressively develop its economy and the social well being of its citizens. Using the model of Singapore, a small city-state in Southeast Asia, Rwanda is on track to become a shining light in East Africa. The focus on improving the transport and logistics infrastructure will facilitate economic development. By providing and maintaining a transparent environment, businesses will be attracted to Rwanda. Those investments will contribute to rising incomes with myriad benefits that will spread throughout the country.

United Republic of Tanzania

The largest country in the East African Community is also one of the richest in terms of natural resources. Coal, lime, gas and other products are found throughout Tanzania. With the Indian Ocean to the east and the great lakes of the Great Rift Valley to the west, Tanzania is a natural transport and logistics center for this part of Africa. Unlike many other countries in Africa, Tanzania is not subject to the historical impediments of tribal history.

During the socialist period, the relocation of people broke down traditional tribal groupings. Observers note that the people consider themselves Tanzanian first and foremost, with only a cursory acknowledgement of their heritage. That is of tremendous importance and stability as the country seeks to elevate its economic status. The development of gas fields from the border with Mozambique to Kenya in the north is a foundation that can, if properly used, fund critical transportation developments throughout the nation. Those developments are not beneficial just for Tanzanians, but also for people in countries that border the United Republic of Tanzania.

This chapter examines the role of the recent gas finds, with particular focus on Mnazi Bay in the Mtwara administrative region. We also look at the transportation plans for the Mtwara Development Corridor, and highlight the interplay between development and expansion of transport systems and economic development.

A Dirt Road near Mtwara

Even though his shoulder still hurt from being slammed against the window post of the 4x4, a result of the rough ride, John Dragonetti's face lit up as he looked out the window at the production station at the head of the pipeline on Mnazi Bay in Tanzania. The rough dirt road that had been cut through forest

White car on dirt road to Mnazi Bay

and across the coastal plain from the paved road south of Mtwara was a rudimentary affair. The seismic team had made the road to get its machines to the bay where it proved the gas field. The economic impact of the gas field was expected to become a major foundation stone for this southeast corner of Tanzania along the Mozambique border.

The unimproved dirt road marked the first time that villages in this part of the Mtwara administrative region had more than rough tracks linking them to each other, to the regional headquarters in Mtwara and to the rest of the region. In a recently completed report, The World Bank noted "only one-third of rural inhabitants [in Africa] live within 2 kilometers of an all-season road" and "African rural communities have by far the lowest accessibility to an all-season road in the developing world."[55]

The importance of the road cannot be understated. Already, it has become the primary transport link between the previously isolated villages, remote farms and regional center in Mtwara. A few cars and small delivery trucks bounce over the unimproved road and avoid the local residents using overloaded pushbikes carrying charcoal, the common fuel for heat and cooking. School children can now use the road rather than pass through the forest and across fields between their houses and the schools. Women carrying large pails of water from bore holes to

Village near Mnazi Bay, Mtwara District, Tanzania

their homes and gardens can take advantage of the road, as well.

Fortunately, in contrast with other rural areas in Africa, the presence of the gas field supported the need for the road. In many parts of Africa, the population density and economic benefits do not outweigh the construction and maintenance costs of most rural roads. This road, built with private funds, had overcome at least part of the cost equation. The opening of the road and the expected utility demands of expanding gas field operations likely mean that power and powered well pumps will come to the previously isolated villages scattered along the road.

Based on the seismic teams' findings, a number of wells had been drilled both on and offshore. The gas was unique and of high quality. It was "dry," which meant that it did not require a lot of processing, unlike gas in other fields, which needs processing before it can be used. In the initial stage, gas that was being drawn from only one well was transmitted by pipeline to an electrical generating plant near the town of Mtwara. In spite of not operating at full capacity, the new power plant was producing electricity at higher levels than the coal-fired plant that it would soon completely replace.

John had more than three decades in the oil and gas industry, includ-

Mnazi Bay gas processing plant

ing experience in the Middle East and East Africa. He had now come out of retirement to help an old friend develop a plan for this unique gas field following the failure of the initial developer. Standing in the production station, he began to quiz the site manager about such things as gas pressures, monitoring systems and the level of condensate. Additional questions concerned the other capped wells he had seen on his way to the facility and the potential for additional wells both on and offshore.

With most questions satisfactorily answered and still nursing his bruised shoulder, he turned to the value of the road and the other social improvements, such as schools, hospitals and employment for the villagers that would follow development of the gas field.

Interior of Mnazi Bay gas-fed new Mtwara electrical power plant

Gas from the first well was transferred by a local pipeline to a new power plant located just outside the town of Mtwara. The plant was expected to replace an older facility. The new plant was already producing a more consistent flow of electricity for the benefit of local residents, commercial and industrial users, and would soon be transmitting gas to a second province, Lindi. All of these developments would increase the economic opportunities for the residents and companies in the region. Their lives were already changing. He hoped that the change would benefit all, and would not disrupt but improve their lives. If the project moved forward, John expected that he, too, could become a resident, and benefit from the transport and logistics and related economic improvements.

Mtwara Special Development Initiative

The Mtwara administrative region of the United Republic of Tanzania stretches approximately 235 kilometers westward from the Indian Ocean along the Tanzanian-Mozambique border. The region's population as of the 2002 census was 1.36 million, about 2.7 percent of the nation's population. Mtwara is served by a number of national and regional roads that connect it to other administrative regions in Tanzania and to Mozambique. A regional airport handles scheduled service to Dar es Salaam, and a small port is served by small (up to 1,500 TEU capacity) feeder container vessels. The local economy is dominated by agriculture, livestock and fishing.

The importance of the Mtwara administrative region of Tanzania within a broader context has been recognized by others inside and outside of East Africa for many years. In 1992, the Mtwara corridor was identified by the South African Transport and Communications Commission (SATCC) for its strategic importance.[56] The SATCC had previously created the Spatial Development Initiative program. These projects were identified as being "trans-territorial and trans-national" and the report noted "transport links become nodes, which will create a networked grid, hopefully paid for by the renewal of mineral prosperity, but allowing systematic regional development that can knit together different countries."[57] The statement reinforces the importance of transportation

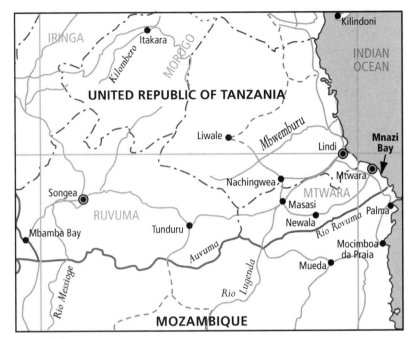

Mnazi Bay

to economic development. It has recognized for many years that "the growth of roads, railways, canals and the like is inextricably woven with the whole process of economic growth and regional development."[58] With its location along the border of Tanzania and Mozambique, combined with the eastern shore on the Indian Ocean, the Mtwara administrative region is a potential gateway to southern Tanzania that requires improvements to its transport infrastructure to realize its full potential.

On December 15, 2004, the Heads of State of Malawi, Mozambique, Tanzania and Zambia signed a multi-lateral accord establishing the Mtwara Development Corridor Regional Spatial Development Initiative Program (Mtwara SDI). The objectives of the Mtwara SDI are to: 1) promote investment along the corridor, 2) establish an information system to support the investment, and 3) define an integrated strategy to enhance the enabling environment for investment.[59]

The South African government, through its Department of Trade and Industry, committed about US$1.25 million in technical support to accelerate the regional development within the corridor. The

Mtwara Development Corridor covers an area of 160,785 km², which is equivalent to 41 percent of Tanzania. As of 2002, 23 percent of the Tanzanian population (8.433 million people) lived in the region with an average per capita income of Tsh 252,000, which was only slightly (1.9 percent) below the then national average of Tsh 257,000.[60]

Poor roads, rail lines and other transport services can depress productivity by as much as 40 percent.[61] This lesson is not lost in the Mtwara Development Corridor's plan. The importance of transportation as an enabler for economic development is reflected in the plan that incorporates six transport sub-systems within either wholly or in part in Tanzania.[62] These are:

- A coastal road system between Dar es Salaam (Tanzania) to Pemba (Mozambique);
- The port at Mtwara and an associated potential Special Economic Zone development;
- An inland transport system incorporating road and rail links from Port of Mtwara to the Mbamba Bay on Lake Malawi;
- A series of bridges and ferry services across the Ruvuma River between Tanzania and Mozambique;
- The lake system that links Mbamba Bay (Tanzania) with Nkhata Bay (Malawi) and Metungula (Mozambique); and
- Air transport services and related airports (such as Mtwara) or airfields linking all parts of the development corridor with major regional airports such as Dar es Salaam.

Because of its location on the southern boundary of Tanzania, most of these transport projects are in or touch the Mtwara administrative region of Tanzania. The planned improvements can increase accessibility and attractiveness for new projects that in turn will generate employment and raise the average per capita income of the residents of the region. The existing transport network of the Mtwara region is composed primarily of a network of roads. Limited water transport along the Indian Ocean coast is focused at the small port of Mtwara. The lone airfield in the region is also at Mtwara.

The transport investment plan incorporated in the Mtwara Development Corridor plan envisages an expansion of the existing transport links as well as the addition of rail to the modal mix.

The coastal road system between Dar es Salaam and Pemba is a critical artery that not only links the two countries, but also provides access to communities along the Indian Ocean coast of these two countries. While the roads tend to be well maintained and paved, they are usually only two lanes and critical sections remain that are not paved or require maintenance to ensure a free flowing movement of passenger and freight traffic.

The Port of Mtwara is a critical transport node. However, it does not have the capacity or infrastructure to handle expected increased traffic flows. Currently, access to the port is a combination of poorly paved and sand roadways. With the exception of the ramp areas alongside the piers, the internal roadways in the port are a combination of dirt and sand. These roads can become all but impassable during the rainy season, as there is no observable system to draw water off the road surface. There are no paved areas for the heavily laden trucks waiting to enter the port. The access road leading to the port passes in front of a major distribution center that becomes so clogged during the peak cashew nut harvest season that vehicles going to and from the port are forced off the road to get past the waiting trucks.

The need to revitalize the rail system between the Port of Mtwara and Mbamba Bay is critical. This is especially important to handle the expected coal volumes from the mines that are located near Lake Nyaska.

As the volume of trade increases in east Africa, improvements to the bridges and other crossings across the Ruvuma River between Tanzania and Mozambique will be become ever more crucial. This is particularly important, as these crossings are integral parts of the coast road system between Dar es Salaam and Pemba.

The value of the lake transport system on Lake Malawi is significant. Such services can handle large volumes of freight and passengers and can provide critical connections between Tanzania, Zambia and Mozambique.

Air service within the development corridor and to points outside, including Dar es Salaam and Maputo (Mozambique), is essential to move managers, sales people and other critical staff to and from regional centers.

The identification of these critical links reinforces the importance of transport systems to economic development. According to the report, non-transportation investment projects have the potential to generate more than 50.9 million tonnes of goods each year. Moving those products to market requires an efficient and effective transportation network. The expected volumes can easily swamp the capacity of the existing links. The largest volume of traffic—coal—cannot be efficiently moved by truck. Around the world, coal is moved by rail. If Tanzania is to realize the full potential of the world demand for coal, a rail line from the mines to the Port of Mtwara and a dedicated coal-loading facility at the port is not only desirable, it is mandatory.

The competing demands on the transportation network need to be logically and realistically analyzed. As pointed out by many reviewers of transport networks, "the primary purpose of a network…is to service transportation demand."[63] As the authors further point out, "the principal characteristic of a transport network is to merge different flows so that they move over a common link."[64] In other words, instead of building separate links between discrete pairs of origins and destinations, the effectiveness and efficiency of a transport network can be maximized by combining dissimilar flows that fully use the transport network and increase the efficiency, and that reduce the cost of the transport link. In the case of some traffic flows, like coal, other bulk goods and gas, unique transport links such as railways and pipelines are best able to satisfy the transport needs from the perspective of cost efficiency.

Mnazi Bay Development

The new dirt road to Mnazi Bay is emblematic of the lowest form of road links. Even though it is incapable of carrying large volumes of traffic, its importance cannot be understated. Not only does it provide a fundamental link within that part of the Mtwara administrative region, it also provides a visible and vital artery for commerce. Using the geographical riverine model, the dirt road to Mnazi Bay is the brook or stream that in turn feeds into a river. Without this lowest class of

Mnazi Bay road

waterway, water from the hills has no way of being pulled by gravity to the largest body of water. So too, without the dirt road, commerce within, into and out of the region has no way of moving without great difficulty.

The dirt road represents the importance of access to all population and agricultural centers regardless of their size and location. The people of this part of the Mtwara administrative region are luckier than many who live in rural areas elsewhere in Africa. The combination of low population densities; insufficient financial resources of local, regional and national governments, and insufficient volumes are barriers to building and maintaining rural roads in most of Africa. As noted by the World Bank, building a rural road more than two kilometers to a rural area is difficult to justify economically.

But, the development of the gas field in Mnazi Bay has changed the economics to benefit the people who live near it. Built by private money, this rural road has not stretched the resources of the local administration. In time, especially as the gas field is further developed, the road will likely be improved to all-weather standards. These improvements probably will involve stabilizing the dirt sub-base, covering the surface with gravel and installing a water management system to carry away water that would otherwise wash away portions of the road. In time, the road may even be paved.

Mtwara

On a broader scale, the various projects in the Mtwara region are expected to generate a wide variety of products, including cashew nuts (both raw and processed), forest products such as jatropha and black wattle, seafood such as tuna and prawns, parts and scrap metal from ship breaking, glass, titanium pigment, supplies, machinery and parts for the Mnazi Bay gas field, cement, coal, iron ore, and sponge iron. These investments will change the economic landscape of the region. The different products also will require a variety of transport services. The following table identifies the primary products that originate and/ or move through the Mtwara region. Most of the products, with the exception of coal and some of the lime volumes, are expected to move by truck to the Port of Mtwara, for export.

The products have been ranked by volume from largest to smallest.[65]

Based on an average load of 15 tonnes per truck, the estimated traffic volume from these projects will generate more than 91,300 annual loaded truck movements, or more than 182,600 total movements. These do not include such factors as local movement of goods within the region or traffic that is passing through the region between Tanzania and Mozambique. With the exception of the coal shipments and an estimated 50 percent of the lime and seafood moves, all of the traffic will move by truck. Those movements will place significant pressure on the region's road system.

Mtwara Port

The key transport element within the Mtwara administrative region is the Mtwara Port. The port is one of three major ports managed by Tanzania Ports Authority; the others are Dar es Salaam and Tanga. The deep-water port at Mtwara was built between 1948 and 1954. Development of the deep-water port was accompanied by railway construction from Mtwara and Nachingwea. When the groundnut scheme failed, the railway line fell into disuse and is now defunct. The port, however, continues to function but is underutilized. Mtwara Port can handle 400,000 tonnes of imports and exports annually. It is mainly designed to handle conventional cargo by both break-bulk and container vessels. It is esti-

Transport Demand—Mtwara

Product	Origin	Transport Mode(s)	Port	Traffic (000,T./ year)	Est. Annual Truck Movements
Coal	Mchuchuma, nr. Lake Nyasa	Rail	Port of Mtwara	15,000	N/A
Black wattle charcoal	Mtwara, Lindi & Ruvuma regions	Truck	Port of Mtwara	675.0	45,000
Bio diesel/ organic fertilizer	Mtwara, Lindi & Ruvuma regions	Truck	Port of Mtwara	250.0	16,667
Charcoal from coal	Iringa District	Truck	Within Tanzania	100.0	6,667
Sesame	Lindi Region	Truck	Port of Mtwara	80.0	5,333
Lime—agricultural and cement	Songea District	Truck,	Within Tanzania rail	76.0	2,533
Woodchips	Mtwara, Lindi & Ruvuma regions	Truck	Port of Mtwara	50.0	3,334
Processed hardwood	Mtwara Region	Truck	Port of Mtwara	39.0	2,600
Rare earth minerals	Nkasi District, Rukwa Region	Truck	Dar es Salaam or Mtwara	33.0	2,200
Coffee	Mbinga District Ruvuma Region	Truck	Port of Mtwara	30.0	2,000
Raw timber and semi-processed timber	Mtwara, Lindi & Ruvuma regions	Truck	Port of Mtwara	30.0	2,000
Tuna	Mtwara	Truck	Port of Mtwara	24.0	1,600
Aquaculture	Ruvuma Region	Truck	Port of Mtwara	13.6	907
Cashew Nut (processed)	Mtwara Region	Truck	Port of Mtwara	7.0	467
Seafood—shark, prawns, crayfish, octopus, crab,	Lindi and Mtwara regions	Boat & Truck	Port of Mtwara	2.4	80
Total				16,410	91,388

Notes: 1. Assume 15 MT per truck. 2. Assume 50 percent of lime and seafood moves by truck.

mated that the port of Mtwara can handle up to 750,000 MT with the same number of berths if additional equipment is put in place for handling containerized traffic.

The following table summarizes the essential characteristics of the Mtwara Port.

Foodstuffs dominate imports at the port. They include maize flour, rice, beans, sugar, wheat/wheat flour, beer, cement and other general

Mtwara Port Characteristics

Feature	
General	The deep-water quay is dredged to -9.8 meters chart datum. There are no tidal restrictions for vessels entering and leaving the harbor, but there is an enforcement length restriction of 175 meters due to the shape of the channel, particularly the MSEMO SPIT area.
	A sheltered anchorage exists in the inner bay (basin). The basin can accommodate six vessels of 175 meters. The number of vessels can be increased if numerous shoal patches are removed.
	Access to the port can be affected by the ocean swells in the narrow bight that connects the bay to the Indian Ocean.
Quay Wall	The port has a quay wall of 385 meters, which can accommodate two ships and one coastal vessel at a time. The draught is 9.85 meters and with the introduction of new and more reliable solar powered navigational aids, the port will be accessible to ships around the clock.
Equipment	Cargo handling equipment include three mobile cranes of 25 tonnes, 15 tonnes and 4 tonnes; four tractors, 18 trailers, eight forklifts and one front loader of 7.5 tonnes, which can be upgraded to 15 tonnes. Marine crafts available at the port are one pilot boat and one mooring boat. The port does not have specialized equipment for handling container traffic because the volume at present does not justify such investment.
Storage	Transit sheds are available, with a total storage capacity of about 15,000 tonnes.
Current Traffic Performance	The average annual cargo throughput at Mtwara port for the past five years is 100,000 tonnes, which is only 25 percent of its capacity of 400,000 tonnes.

Source: Tanzania Ports Authority web site

cargo. Principal export commodities are raw cashew nuts, cassava roots, simsim and sisal. The present under-utilization of the port is essentially due to poor access to the low economic performing hinterland. The Mtwara Port Master Plan envisages expansion of the quay wall westward by 400 meters and eastward by another 400 meters, which will double the number of berths to five. A total area reserved for expansion is 200 acres. Besides this area, another 60 acres are reserved for port-related development activities. This is an ideal location for EPZ and distribution activities. However, depending on the demand for land for development and commercial activities, the bulk of the 260 acres can be dedicated for this purpose with little effect on port operations.

The immediate hinterland of the Mtwara Port is composed of the Tanzania regions of Mtwara, Lindi and Ruvuma. These are agriculturally rich areas famous for cashew nuts, coffee, tobacco and simsim farming, and also coal and other mineral deposits. Beyond these regions, and provided that a good inland transport network is put in place, the port should be able to cater to neighboring countries of Malawi, Mozambique and Zambia. In spite of its limited facilities the port has the potential as a trans-shipment facility. Its location at the southern end of the Tanzanian coast suggests a role in handling shipments to/from Indian Ocean islands including Comoros, Madagascar, Mauritius, Reunion and the Seychelles. Additionally, the Mtwara Port can serve the seaborne trade of Malawi, especially if the road and rail links to Lake Malawi are built as part of the Mtwara Development Corridor plan.

Currently, four ports handle Malawi trade. They are Nacala, Beira, Durban and Dar es Salaam. The following table compares the distances and estimated transit time from Lilongwe to the five ports from each of the ports as well as Mtwara.

Port	Transport Mode(s)	Distance (Kms.)	Estimated Transit Time (Days)
Tanzania			
Dar es Salaam	Road/Rail	1,640	3
Mtwara	Road—Water—Road	1,183	4
Mozambique			
Beira	Road/Rail	1,554	4
Nacala	Rail	1,007	3
South Africa			
Durban	Road/Rail	3,020	8

Source: Tanzania Ports Authority

With the exception of Durban, which is the largest Indian Ocean port in Africa, the distance from Lilongwe to the other ports ranges between 1,007 and 1,640 kilometers. Based on expected travel times, the transit times are three or four days. According to this analysis, Mtwara Port can become a port for the landlocked country of Malawi. The value of the Mtwara Port will be accentuated with the other improvements to transport links in the corridor.

On April 16, 2008, a Memorandum of Understanding was signed by the Tanzania Ports Authority and Gulf Resources Ltd. to jointly determine the potential of a public-private partnership for the development, modernization and expansion of the Mtwara Sea Port, including regulating the associated Export Processing Zones and Free Port facility. Although the original date of completion for the study was mid October 2008, developments at the Port are not visible some two years later.

The expansion of the Mnazi Bay gas field in the next couple of years will not only result in higher volumes of gas for use locally and for transmission to points north such as Dar es Salaam, but also holds the potential for new industries. One possible use of the gas is to make fertilizer. A local source of fertilizer will reduce costs for the local agricultural community and will provide yet another source of export income. This, in turn, will generate additional traffic for the port to handle, further pressuring the staff and facilities.

The two-lane, narrow, poorly maintained roads will have to be improved to take on this volume of traffic. With its growing importance as a transport hub, much attention needs to be focused on access to the Port of Mtwara. Dirt roads have to be paved, narrow two-lane roads have to be widened, and a rail line to the port for coal and lime exports has to be planned and built. The rail line and road links must be separated for safety and capacity reasons. With the likelihood of a coal-handling terminal, the Port of Mtwara will have to be significantly expanded on the land as well as on the water. Additional berths, a purpose-built coal handling facility, and truck and container staging areas will be needed to handle the expected volumes.

Although the traffic volumes that will require expanded facilities and capacity at the Mtwara Port are not yet present, the age-old challenge of when to build which facilities for what volume of traffic must be met head on. The coal mines will not be able to expand if the rail link and coal-loading facility at the port is not ready. The cashew processing plant will not be able to operate at its full potential if road access to and handling facilities at the port are limited.

Conclusion

Solutions exist that do not revolve exclusively around seeking financial support from donors from around the world. Establishing an open, transparent and welcoming political and legal environment that supports public-private partnerships is the optimal approach to take. The long-term focus of governments is best employed to build and maintain long-lasting infrastructure components where rates of return are measured not exclusively in terms of short-term financial gain, but in terms of in-creased employment, rising per capita income and rising tax revenues.

This approach can be meshed with the faster, more flexible, more aggressive focus of private investors whose horizons are much shorter, but who have the ability and the skills to bring new projects on line and through their efforts, create businesses that employ the newest technology, create jobs, and generate incomes. The plan for the Mtwara Development Corridor recognizes this mix in terms of the traffic producing ventures—the mines, the plantations and the farms. But it is in the transport and logistics arena where the public-private partnership can also be applied for the benefit of many.

The comprehensive program for the Mtwara Development Corridor encompasses both industrial, agricultural, extractive and transport investments. As the program notes, the importance of transportation services cannot be ignored. In order to realize the full potential of this concept, a series of public-private partnerships appear to be the best alternative. Of particular interest is how to maximize the economic value of the Mnazi Bay gas field and to ensure that the Mtwara Port is expanded to meet the growing needs of the Mtwara administrative region, southern Tanzania and the surrounding countries.

The simple dirt road to Mnazi Bay, built with private funds, is but a small link in the entire network. It is important for two reasons. The first is that it demonstrates the potential of public-private partnerships. The road was built with private funds, when there would have been no justification based on a traditional public cost-benefits analysis. Secondly, now that it is built, the potential exists for the local government to take over the maintenance and upgrade efforts, especially when tax revenues grow from the increasing gas output from the Mnazi Bay gas field. In the end, it will be the local inhabitants who should see the greatest benefits of this development.

[1] World Bank Group, *Africa's Infrastructure: A Time for Transformation,* (World Bank, December 2009), 1

[2] Ibid. 3

[3] Ibid. 5

[4] Ibid. 7

[5] Ibid. 222

[6] Ibid. 229

[7] Ibid. 232

[8] Ibid. 235

[9] Ibid. 236

[10] Ibid. 249

[11] Ibid. 249

[12] Ibid. 259

[13] Ibid. 262

[14] Ibid. 268

[15] East African Community Secretariat, Protocol On The Establishment of the East African Customs Union, March 2, 2004

[16] Ibid. 1-2

[17] East African Community Customs Union, www.eac.int/customs/

[18] East African Community, Common External Tariff, 2007 Version

[19] East African Community, EAC Trade Guide, www.customs.eac.int/index.php?option=com_content&view=article&id=101&Itemid=103

[20] World Bank, *Africa's Infrastructure—A Time for Transformation,* Figure 10.4, 218

[21] Mongabay.com, www.Global.Mongabay.com

[22] Deutsche Bahn Consulting, "Etude de Faisabilité du Projet Ferroviaire Isaka-Kigali/Keza-Gitega-Musongati," 2009, Table 14-24, 158

[23] Port of Bujumbura

[24] Société Concessionnaire de l'Exploitation du Port de Bujumbura (EPB), www.pmaesa.org/media/docs/burundi.pdf

[25] Coffee Board of Burundi, 2007

[26] Douglas Zhihua Zeng, ed., *Knowledge, Technology, and Cluster-Based Growth in Africa,* (World Bank, February 2008), 1

[27] Ibid. 3

[28] http://en.wikipedia.org/wiki/Ethiopia

[29] "Tap that water—Dams in Africa," *The Economist,* May 8, 2010, pg. 49

[30] *World Development Indicators,* The World Bank, 2009, Table 1.1 and *The Little Data Book on Africa,* The World Bank, 2009, Pg. 36

[31] *World Development Indicators,* The World Bank, 2009, Tables 3.2, 4.2. and 4.4

[32] www.treecrops.org/country/ethiopia_coffee.htm, Sustainable Tree Crops Program

[33] Embassy of Ethiopia, Washington, DC, www.ethiopianembassy.org/pdf/Flower%20 Combo.pdf

[34] Railway Gazette, "Grand designs from Ethiopian Railway Corp.," www. railwaygazette.com (September 11, 2009)

[35] DP World, Port of Djibouti—Port History, www.dpworld-djiboutiport.com

[36] DP World, Port of Djibouti—Statistics, www.dpworld-djiboutiport.com

[37] Wudineh Zenebe, "Dry Ports to Receive 220 Million Br Expansion," http:// allAfrica.com (April 6, 2010)

[38] Bekezela Ncube, "Ethiopia," http://fic.wharton.upenn.edu/fic/africa/Ethiopia%20 Final.pdf (2007)

[39] "Tap that Water—Dams in Africa," *The Economist,* May 8, 2010, 49

[40] "Ghana Railway," www.Ghana-Net.com

[41] "Ghana to Upgrade Railways," *Railways Africa,* www.railwaysafrica.com (September 8, 2009)

[42] International Cocoa Organization, 2006

[43] International Monetary Fund, 2007

[44] Ghana Cocoa Board

[45] "Towards a Sustainable Cocoa Chain," Oxfam International Research Report, January 2008

[46] Private Sector Federation—Rwanda, "Assessment of Non Tariff Barriers (NTB's) Along the Northern & Central Corridors—EAC," 2008

[47] Ibid. 21, 22, 28

[48] Ibid. 5

[49] Republic of Rwanda, Rwanda Vision 2020

[50] Ibid. 16

[51] Ibid. 16

[52] Ibid. 18

[53] Ibid. 15

[54] World Bank Group, *Doing Business 2010: Reforming through Difficult Times,* (World Bank, 2009), 4

[55] World Bank Group, *Africa's Infrastructure: A Time for Transformation,* 211, 212

[56] National Development Corporation of Tanzania, "Draft Strategic Perspective of the Mtwara Development Corridor Process in Tanzania," August 14, 2006, 11

[57] Ibid. 11

[58] Peter Haggett, *Locational Analysis in Human Geography,* (London: Edward Arnold, 1969), 79

[59] Ibid. 3

[60] Ibid. 5

[61] World Bank Group, *Africa's Infrastructure: A Time for Transformation,* 2

[62] Ibid. 13

[63] Peter Haggett, Richard J. Chorley, *Network Analysis in Geography,* (London: Edward Arnold, 1969) 109

[64] Ibid. 111

[65] Ibid. Appendix One

CHAPTER 10

OTHER COUNTRIES

In the Canadian Arctic, logistics are not an afterthought. The climate, the geography, the distances and the desire to protect the land must be incorporated into the logistical plan to support the exploration, development and operation of one of the richest areas in the world. Moving vast quantities of fresh water from Patagonia in Chile to regions around the world requires innovative thinking. Filling bottles or even bulk containers is not sufficient to meet the demand. India, long known for crippling bureaucracy, is becoming a symbol of innovative projects being completed in very short periods of time. Employing a true democratic approach, these projects are built on consensual agreement. Singapore and the United Arab Emirates symbolize the power of wedding vision and action to the development of state-of-the-art transport and logistics services. Those facilities and services in turn have contributed to the economic and social development in their respective nations.

Canada

Flying in the comfort of a modern jet north to Yellowknife, capital of the Northwest Territories, it is difficult to understand the challenges faced by those who live in the Canadian Arctic on a daily basis or the privations faced by those who first explored this land. The Canadian Arctic has attracted explorers for hundreds of years. Alfred Lord Tennyson once wrote "There is nothing worth living for but to have one's name inscribed on the Arctic chart."

It is a harsh land that was scoured by countless volcanoes when the earth's crust was first being formed. Numerous ice caps have rubbed the surface clean of most soil and left a landscape pockmarked with innumerable lakes, rivers and streams. The climate can be violent and sublime on the same day—a blizzard might be swept away and replaced by a cloudless clear blue sky, and temperatures can dip to -25, -40 and even -60°C.

But the Canadian Arctic is one of the richest territories in the world. Those ice sheets that scraped the land laid bare rich deposits of minerals. Oil and gas deposits have made Canada the second largest holder of petrochemicals in the world.

Supporting the exploration, extraction, processing and delivery of this natural wealth to the rest of Canada and the world is the role of the hardy transport and logistics professionals who work in an environment that sends many others streaming out of the north toward warmer climes. This chapter examines the challenges and unique solutions that have been created to provide transport and logistics services in one of the most challenging parts of the world. We look at ice roads—roads built for a short season on frozen lakes. We also describe the essential role of aviation from its earliest beginnings in the 1920s.

Watching the Boeing B737 make a slow turn on the snow-covered ramp outside his office, Gary Reid, president of Braden Burry Expediting Ltd. (BBE), looked at his watch and noted the flight was late. After a brief conversation with his Operations Manager Rod Noseworthy, his suspicions were confirmed. Bad weather at the destination caused the delay. This time it was ice fog, but it could have easily been a whiteout, such are the vagaries of Arctic flying. Safety was, of course, of paramount concern. Moving the teams to the mine and hauling in much needed supplies for those working at the isolated site was also important, but would wait until it was safe to fly. In an environment like the Canadian Arctic, where the temperatures can plunge and a blizzard can last for days, no one takes unnecessary chances.

Providing logistics services in the Canadian Arctic involves dealing with a wide variety of challenges. First is the sheer size of the area. Also, the weather can easily overcome humans and machines. The geography of the territory requires a unique combination of transport modes. Finally, the First Nation peoples and the Inuit demand that their ancestral lands be protected from pollution and disruption and their people be employed in any ventures. The land is sacred, and the land and waterways have spiritual meanings for the Inuit and First Nations people. (The name of

a large portion of the Canadian north—Nunavut—means "Our Land.")
The combination of these issues leads to unique transportation and logistics solutions.

Since 1925, Canada has claimed the northern reaches of the North
American continent from 60°N latitude to the North Pole and between
60°W and 141°W longitude. This part of Canada, which includes the
Northwest and Yukon Territories and Nunavut, covers more than 1.51
million square miles (3.91 million square kilometers), an area larger than
India and equal to half the continental United States. Among its many
features is the Northwest Passage, an all-water route between Europe
and Asia that claimed many lives during its discovery and until recently
has been open for only a very short sailing period each year.

The largest part of the Canadian Arctic is composed of permanent
ice and tundra north of the tree line. It is studded by thousands of lakes,
rivers and streams surrounded by smoothed hills, permafrost and tundra.
Massive ice sheets that covered the region during the various ice ages
created this landscape.

Canadian Artic

The region's climate varies significantly. In the southern parts, the average temperature ranges from -18°C (-0°F) in the winter to 25°C (77°F) in the summer. Daylight hours in the summer average about 15 hours, while winter daylight averages about 8.5 hours. However, in the northern parts, it is very cold. The average temperatures range from 15°C (59°F) in the summer to -35°C (-31°F) in winter. At these temperatures, steel axles can snap like a piece of wood and vehicle brakes and steering systems seize up. Winter daylight hours are about 5.5 hours, but in the summer the daylight hours average 18.5 hours.

The entire region is sparsely populated. According to the Canadian Census of 2006, 101,310 people lived in this vast area larger than the all of Western Europe. About 51 percent of the population of the three territories is native—a combination of Inuit, First Nations and Métis. The First Nations are the primary indigenous peoples of Canada. The Inuit live throughout most of the Canadian Arctic and sub-Arctic. Métis are mixed race people.

The three territories, Yukon, Northwest and Nunavut, each have a greater proportion of Aboriginal inhabitants than any of Canada's provinces. The First Nations and Inuit peoples are guardians of their spiritual home of water and land. With the increased wealth from the minerals found on their land and the unique political structure they hold in Canada, they have created major corporations that serve the needs of the explorers and developers of the northern wealth. An example of these native-owned corporations is NorTerra, Inc. This company, whose motto is "Proudly Contributing to the Economy and People of Canada's North," includes five operating companies. Those companies are:

- Northern Transportation Company Limited, which specializes in marine transport in Canada's Arctic and Alaska;
- Canadian North, an airline that operates almost exclusively in Canada's Arctic;
- Weldco-Beales Manufacturing, which makes specialty fittings for construction, mining and oil equipment;
- Braden-Burry Expediting, the largest logistics company in northern Canada; and
- Northern Industrial Sales, serving the needs of logging, mining,

oil and gas industries in the British Columbia and northern Canada.

Through their involvement in the exploration and development of the natural resources of Canada's Arctic, companies like NorTerra actively protect this special environment for the generations that will follow. The severe erosion of the land during the ice ages, with ice caps miles thick, as well as the repetitive rhythm of ice and water, has worn down the old volcanoes, scraping the soil off the bedrock and exposing many ore deposits.

Typical Canadian shield: pines, lakes, bogs, and rock Source: en.wikipedia.org

The region known as the Shield is one of the world's richest areas for minerals. Mining, originally for gold, began in the late 1890s. Additional deposits of copper, gold, nickel, silver and uranium have been mined since the 1930s. Over the past 20 years, numerous diamond mines have opened. In recent years, additional gold, iron ore and uranium deposits have been discovered and new mines started. The potential is even larger given that only about 3 percent of the surface area has been systematically geologically explored.[1] As an example, new geological discoveries confirm that precious gems also are present in sufficient quantities and quality to support commercially viable operations.

After decades of prospecting, diamond mines are being developed all over the Canadian Arctic. One, Ekati, was opened as Canada's first diamond mine in 1998 by the Australian company BHP Billiton.[2] In 2003, the Diavik mine, owned by

Aerial view of the Diavik Diamond Mine, Lac de Gras, Northwest Territories

Source: en.wikipedia.org

Rio Tinto, began production some 40 kilometers south.[3]

Logistics: Not an Afterthought

A multimodal approach to logistics has been the common theme in the Canadian Arctic. During the Klondike Gold Rush in the Yukon in the late 1890s, men and materials were moved by steamship, by foot over treacherous mountain passes and on rafts down rivers to remote sites in the center of what became the Yukon Territory of Canada. Before the introduction of mechanized equipment, dog sleds were the preferred way to cover long distances during the winter. From the late 1920s, aviation became a more important transport alternative, initially when the rivers and lakes were free of ice, and then providing access to the remote territory in the winter as technology and knowledge grew.

In the 21st century in northern Canada, moving people and supplies to remote locations is a multimodal combination of transport dictated by the seasons. When the ice melts, the waterways, especially the major rivers like the Mackenzie River that begins its 1,738-kilometer (1,080-mile) run to the Arctic Ocean at Great Slave Lake, become the bulk load highways in the Northwest Territories. Tug and barge units leave ports from Vancouver, Montreal and Churchill to haul supplies to northern locations. During the short summer season, tugs and barges carry the large quantities of supplies to staging areas or directly to the mine sites and remote communities if they are accessible. Paths for the tugs and barges from southern Canada include a route around Alaska from Vancouver and another from Montreal down the St. Lawrence River north along the Labrador Coast, through Hudson Bay and on the Northwest Passage. Both of these routes terminate on the Arctic Ocean coast in the Northwest Territories. The typical load on each barge is around 12,000 tonnes of machinery, parts, fuel, and other non-perishable supplies. Shorter routes from Churchill, Manitoba, also are used to move supplies to isolated communities in the Canadian Arctic.

For two months during the late winter, winter/ice roads to selected locations become the means to move bulk fuel, large equipment and other bulk supplies.

The only year-round alternative is airlift. It is very expensive when compared with the other modes, and the capacities of the aircraft are smaller than barges or trucks. But if there is a paved, gravel or ice runway, the air carriers that serve the northern reaches of Canada provide critical access to these locations. With more than 30 years of experience in the Arctic, Gary knew that until all-weather roads were built, access to the remote communities, mines, and oil and gas fields would be a combination of ice roads in a two-month period in winter, tugs and barges during the short two-month summer and year-round airlift from major logistics centers like Yellowknife.

The jet was loaded and starting its engines. Soon it would taxi out for take-off. The ice fog must have started to dissipate at the destination. Even though its capacity could not match that of trucks, air service remained the vital link in supporting exploration and operation of mines and oil and gas fields for most of the year in the Canadian Arctic. Balancing the challenges of arctic weather, the distances, the remoteness and the need to protect and preserve the natural environment made the lives of the many men and women working in arctic logistics always challenging and interesting.

From the beginning of the exploration process until the mine or the field is exhausted, moving personnel to and from the sites, transporting supplies and removing the trash from the sites, and then transferring the products out, involves a complex and highly choreographed logistics process in which many parties play a role. It has been estimated that logistics associated with a complete project can account for between 50 and 80 percent of an entire project's cost. Logistics in the Canadian Arctic is not an afterthought; it is foremost on everyone's mind. Whether it is the 10 pounds (4.5 kilograms) of food allowed for every person each day, the thousands of liters of fuel for the power generators, or transporting gold bars or diamonds from the mines, the role of logistics experts of Braden Burry Expeditors and other companies is a critical cog in the development of the natural wealth of the Canadian Arctic.

BBE is a member of the NorTerra Inc. group of companies. NorTerra is owned by the Inuvialuit Development Corporation, on behalf of the Inuvialuit of the Western Arctic, and the Nunasi Corporation, on behalf of the Inuit of Nunavut. The ownership by native Canadians—the

Inuvialuit and the Inuit—reinforces the commitment of the company to the logistics needs of northern Canada and underscores the company's commitment to protect the fragile environment, which is the spiritual foundation for the Inuit and First Nations people. Protecting the environment is an accepted part of the logistics services, in addition to the applicable government rules and regulations.

Winter Road

Access to the mines and remote settlements in the winter has always been a challenge. Dog sleds were replaced by "Cat trains" or by bulldozers pulling ski-equipped skids piled high with supplies. The "Cat trains" used unimproved trails to get to the various sites. In the late 1950s, a former Royal Canadian Mounted Policeman named John Denison pioneered the concept of an ice road. He proved that by plowing snow off the frozen lakes and building portages across islands and between the lakes, a temporary road could be constructed that would allow much larger quantities of supplies to be moved from Yellowknife to remote mine sites as much as 520 kilometers away. The first road linked silver mine on Great Bear Lake to Yellowknife.

The Tibbitt-Contwoyto Winter Road (TCWR) varies in length depending on the mining operations in Canada's Arctic. At its maximum the road has been as long as 600 kilometers (373 miles) with some 64

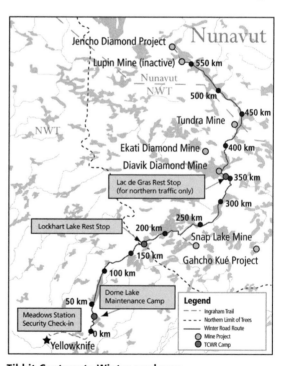

Tibbit-Contwoyto Winter road map

land portages accounting for 15 percent of the road's length connect the rest of the road which is on the frozen surface of lakes. Since 1998, the road has been built and maintained by Nuna Logistics. In recent years, the road has only extended to the Diavik Mine (360 kilometers), with spurs to serve the Ekati Mine and another new diamond mine owned by DeBeers.[4] The map shows the full extent of the TCWR.

The road follows part of the original road that was cleared to the now closed Tundra Mine in 1960-1961 by John Denison. The original road followed a route from Discovery Mine up the Yellowknife River to the Tundra Mine crossing a number of lakes including Gordon and Mackay.[5] This route was used until 1968 when the mine closed. The road was reopened in 1979 to aid an equipment haul to the new Lupin Mine at Contwoyto Lake in Nunavut. However, the owners of the Lupin Mine decided not to continue using the road at this time and relied instead on Lockheed Hercules aircraft to haul in machinery during construction of the mine.

First Air Lockheed Hercules all-cargo aircraft at Cambridge Bay Airport, Nunavut Photo credit: First Air, www.firstair.ca/About_First_Air/fleet.html#L382G

In 1983, the ice road to Lupin Mine reopened as a much cheaper alternative to yearly freight haul using aircraft. Another gold mine, the Salmita Mine (operated between 1983 and 1987) also benefited from this ice road. Until 1998, the road was licensed and operated by Echo Bay Mines Limited, owners of the Lupin Mine. Since 1999, the road has been licensed and operated by the Tibbitt-to-Contwoyto Winter Road Joint Venture, a partnership between Echo Bay Mines Ltd., BHP Billiton, and Diavik Diamond Mines Inc. (Rio Tinto Group). The road is engineered by EBA Engineering Ltd. Currently, Nuna Logistics (primary road) and RTL Enterprises Ltd. (secondary roads) are responsible for the annual construction, maintenance, dispatching, and camp catering for the winter road.

The road is constructed during January with plows, graders, water trucks, bulldozers, snow blowers, and specialized low ground pressure equipment. The road is built extra wide on the ice—50 meters (164 feet)—but narrower on land portages ranging between 12 meters (39 feet) and 15 meters (49 feet) wide so windblown snow does not block it, and so it also provides for extra spacing when trucks meet and pass each other. As the trucks move along the ice, their weight depresses it, which in turn builds a wave under the ice in the unfrozen water. If the waves meet they can push the ice upward and create cracks that weaken the ice.

During construction, the first vehicle on the route is a Swedish Army reconnaissance vehicle designed to float if it falls through the ice. It tows sonar that profiles the thickness of the ice. Behind it, the snow is cleared off the road so that the ice underneath freezes faster and thicker. Once initially built, the road is checked by drilling holes into the ice. If the ice needs to be thickened, water trucks are called in to add water to that specific area. The road is operational only during February and March, an average of 67 days per year. The ice has been proven by engineers to support light vehicle loads at 70 centimeters (30 inches) thick and increasing to full highway truckloads as the ice thickens, often exceeding 100 cm (40 in).

Vehicle speed is closely monitored. Fully loaded trucks travel on the ice at 25 km/h (16 mph) with some areas reduced to just 10 km/h (6 mph). Empty trucks have a maximum speed limit of 60 km/h (37 mph) on the ice.

Three road camps serve drivers hauling loads. They are at Dome Lake Maintenance Camp, Lockhart Lake and Lac de Gras. Dome Lake is for maintenance crews and emergency use for drivers; Lockhart Lake provides drivers with food, showers, and a place to do laundry; and Lac de Gras is for road crews, emergency use and for facilities for drivers traveling north of the Ekati Diamond Mine. At an average speed of 25 kph, the Ekati Mine can be reached from Yellowknife in about 16 driving hours over a two-day period, allowing for mandatory rest stops.

Trucks operate in convoys for safety reasons. Up to four trucks are dispatched from Yellowknife every 20 minutes. Heavy and wide loads are dispatched from Yellowknife between midnight and 6 a.m. to avoid daily commuter traffic. Diesel fuel is the dominant commodity trucked north on the road because it is more difficult to move the required volumes by air. The other most typical supplies carried north include cement, tires, prill (ammonium nitrate for explosives), construction materials and machinery and parts.

The year 2007 saw record usage of the ice road, with 10,922 loads north totaling 331,000 tonnes or 364,865 short tons). That record number does not include the 818 back hauls south, totaling 15,000 tonnes (16,535 short tons). The road was open for 73 days from January 27 to April 9 and closed for only 91.5 hours (70 hours due to storms and 21.5 hours due to minor incidents). More than 700 drivers were registered during 2007, with nine accidents and one minor injury (a bruised shoulder). The table below illustrates the significant tonnage

Tibbitt-to-Contwoyto Winter Road
Operating Statistics

Year	Open Date	Northbound Close Date	Number of Northbound Truck Loads	Estimated Weight (tons)
2000	January 29	April 3	3,703	111,090
2001	February 1	April 13	7,981	239,430
2002	January 26	April 16	7,735	232,050
2003	February 1	April 2	5,243	157,292
2004	January 28	March 31	5,091	152,730
2005	January 26	April 5	7,607	228,210
2006	February 4	March 26	6,841	205,230
2007	January 27	April 9	10,922	327,660
2008	January 29	April 7	7,387	221,620
2009	February 1	March 25	5,377	161,310

Source: Tibbitt to Contwoyto Winter Road Joint Venture, "2008 Winter Road Updates," http://jvtcwinterroad.ca

Note: Northbound weight estimated at average of 30 tons per truck load.

carried on the winter road in a very short period of time.

Many other winter ice roads are carved through the Canadian Arctic. The Tuktoyaktuk Winter Road traverses the frozen channels of the Mackenzie River delta and the frozen Arctic Ocean that connects the Northwest Territory communities of Inuvik and Tuktoyaktuk. It is the 194-km (121-mi) extension of the Dempster Highway that connects the Klondike Highway in the Yukon over a 736-km (457-mi) distance to Inuvik. This winter road is used to serve the gas hydrate fields and exploration facilities. It also provides access to ice-locked barges used on the Mackenzie River and in the Arctic Ocean, and is used to move supplies to the hamlet of Aklavik.

Another ice road in the Province of Ontario links the railhead of Moosonee with the Victor Diamond Mine. This road includes stretches along the shore of James Bay to Attawapiskat and then due west into the far northern part of Ontario. The primary traffic is fuel for the generators at the mine. A local logistics company in Moosonee rents 27 tanker trucks for a one-month period. The trucks and fuel are moved by rail to Moosonee. In 2008, a total of 32.8 million liters (8.66 million U.S. gallons) of fuel was transported this way to the mine.[6]

Gary chuckled to himself about the TV show ("Ice Road Truckers") that had highlighted the 570-kilometer Tibbit—Contwoyto ice road—the world's longest ice road. While that unique transport link had received a lot of press—and yes, it was important—it lasted for just 45-60 days each year. The extended exposure to the sun and warming daytime temperatures meant that the ice road's life would soon come to an end. Some 700 trucks, most of them carrying diesel fuel for the power generators at the remote mines, still had to make their deliveries via the ice road. Even though it was much colder further north, a melting road was of great concern to the logisticians, truckers and mine operators. Would they get the precious fuel into the site before the road melted? It was a recurring worry this time every year. The distant roar of the jet taking off from Yellowknife reinforced his belief that aviation would remain the primary means of moving people and supplies into remote communities, mines and oil and gas fields throughout the Canadian Arctic.

Arctic Aviation

Unlike trucks, which have to rely on ice roads during the winter and the tugs and barges that must wait until the Arctic Ocean, Hudson Bay, the Mackenzie River and other waterways are free of ice, the air services continue to move people and supplies to remote locations on a year-round basis.

Because of the payload and range limitations of the aircraft between World War I and World War II, aircraft initially were used for exploration purposes—transporting prospecting crews into remote sites and collecting them at the end of the season. As early as 1928, the use of flights to support exploration of the Canadian Arctic was impressive even by today's standards.[7] Using float planes or those equipped with skis, the original aviation pioneers ventured into uncharted territory where communication and logistical support was either non-existent or far and few between. As an example, in August 1928, pilot C.H. "Punch" Dickens flew over 4,000 square miles of mainly unmapped land in a 12-day period. That flight, funded by a combination of several prospecting companies, was conducted to determine the conditions that prospecting parties could expect in the Northwest Territories. In January 1929, a flight of more than 1,600 miles (2,575 kilometers) to pick up a party of stranded prospectors proved that winter flying was possible.[8]

Given the thousands of lakes and rivers in the Canadian Arctic, aircraft were equipped with floats to carry prospectors and their equipment into remote sites. Float-equipped airplanes and helicopters are used during the summer months to provide access to remote sites where the mineral bounty of the Canadian Arctic is still being discovered.

The rich Arctic aviation history of Canada is reflected in the many scheduled and charter carriers that serve this vast part of the world. Native-owned air carriers and specialized carriers using older aircraft, including DC-3, DC-6, Lockheed Electra and even C-46 airplanes, provide critical air service for this region.

While Buffalo Airways focuses almost exclusively on all-cargo flights, other air carriers provide both cargo and passenger services. Even in 2010 and for the foreseeable future, flight operations to remote sites involve landing on gravel and/or ice runways.

Facilities at remote sites are basic and limited. A forklift equipped with a slave pallet is used to load and off-load freight. There are no warm passenger terminals and jet bridges to the waiting aircraft. Passengers brave winds and snow as they move from waiting vehicles and the aircraft.

One of the airlines almost exclusively dedicated to serving the Canadian Arctic is Kanata, Ontario-based Bradley Air Services Limited, operating as First Air. It serves communities in Nunavut, Nunavik, Northwest Territories as well the Provinces of Alberta, Manitoba, Ontario, Quebec, and one in the Yukon Territory. Its main base is Ottawa Macdonald-Cartier International Airport, with hubs at Iqaluit Airport and Yellowknife Airport. The airline is wholly owned by the Inuit people of Quebec through the Makivik Corporation, which purchased the company in 1990.

The airline's fleet is composed of a wide variety of aircraft selected to serve the many types of stations and traffic handled by the company.

As the fleet table shows, all but the B767 of the First Air fleet have been adapted to operate on and off gravel and ice runways in addition to traditional paved runways. This reflects one of the unique aspects of flying in the Canadian Arctic. Additionally, most of the planes are configured

First Air Fleet

Type	Number	Comments
Aerospatiale ATR-42	9	Max 42 seats, combi aircraft, ice/gravel runway capable
Hawker Siddley HS 748	2	Max 40 seats, combi aircraft, ice/gravel runway capable
Boeing B727	2	One 200C series, max 174 seats, combi aircraft, ice runway capable and one 200F series cargo aircraft only, ice runway capable
Boeing B737	6	Four 200C series, max 115 seats, combi aircraft, ice/gravel runway capable, two 200 series, max 99 seats, all passenger aircraft
Boeing B767	1	767-223 Super Freighter, cargo aircraft only, max payload: 98 700 lbs.
Lockheed Hercules	2	Cargo aircraft only, ice/gravel runway capable, max payload of 40,000 lbs. First Air operates the only 2 civilian Hercules in Canada

Source: First Air website, as of January 2010.

Note: "Combi" means that the aircraft can carry both freight and cargo on the main deck.

to carry both cargo and passengers. The two Hercules freighters are the heavy lifters of the Canadian Arctic. They are in continuous operation year-round, moving large pieces of mining machinery, fuel and other supplies. Specially built slave pallets fit inside the Hercules for faster off-loading and loading. These aircraft also carry ocean containers filled with special equipment. While significantly more expensive than the road or water alternatives, the cost of the airlift option is acceptable because of its year-round capability and accessibility to locations where there are no all-weather or winter roads, or water access.

Conclusion

In spite of the vast distances, the challenging topography, the harsh climate and the concerns of the aboriginal people, the development of mines and oil and gas fields continues in the Canadian Arctic. The lessons learned by the logistics experts in meeting and overcoming the natural challenges of this world region are applicable around the world. Snow is not unlike sand, in that very hot temperatures can cause just as many operational problems as very cold temperatures, and protecting the natural environment is universal.

Ice roads are used for 1-2 months each year, while water transport operates for another 1-2 months. Throughout the year air services provide the vital lifelines to remote mines and oil and gas fields. In spite of facing some of the worst weather in the world, Canadian logistics firms, airlines, trucking companies and vessel operators provide safe and reliable services to a growing array of companies that are attracted to Canada's Arctic and the natural wealth that lies beneath the surface of some of the oldest parts of the earth's crust.

There is little doubt that as more of the Canadian Arctic is subjected to highly detailed geological surveys, additional rich mineral deposits of all kinds will be discovered. With the process of exploration, permitting and construction taking years and, in some cases, decades, the need for specialized logistics experts and firms in the Canadian Arctic is not likely to decline. Each new location brings with it a new operational challenge. Canadian Arctic logistics experts thrive on adapting existing equipment and services. Moving hundreds of thousands of tons of equipment and supplies, along with thousands of prospectors, engineers, managers and operating employees (not to mention their luggage) is an ongoing, never-ending activity in one of the coldest parts of the world.

Chile

About 20 kilometers south of Balmaceda Airport, the paved road ends. The next nearly 500 kilometers to Caleta Tortel in the Southern Patagonia region of Chile is on a twisting gravel road, in many places only one lane wide, that penetrates one of the wildest and least inhabited parts of the world. In fact, the last 124 kilometers (77 miles) between Cochrane and Caleta Tortel is officially known as a penetration path (the lowest category of routes in Chile). The drive is overshadowed by towering, snow-capped peaks, winding alongside crystal clear lakes that mirror those same mountains, across bridges that traverse rushing streams and rivers, and past steep pastures and forests. Only a few settlements exist.

The road passes through an untouched part of the Republic of Chile. Here, nature is truly in control and mankind has made only slight inroads. The road, which is still under development with widening and straightening of curves, is evidence of man's limited ability to penetrate one of the most remote regions of the world. But that remoteness is critical to the unique business that is taking shape in the Southern Patagonia Ice Fields.

The road journey passes through the XI Aysén Region of General Carlos Ibáñez del Campo. It is one of Chile's 15 first order administrative divisions. Although it is the third largest in area, the region is Chile's most sparsely populated, with 105,000 people in an area of some 108,494 square kilometers. The capital of the region is Coyhaique, located some 45 kilometers northwest of Balmaceda Airport. Balmaceda Airport was sited by Chile to reinforce its claim on territory adjacent to Argentina. The airport is located within meters of the national border. Aircraft landing at the airport on internal Chilean flights pass through Argentinean airspace.

The landscape of this part of Chile has been molded by glaciers that have formed numerous lakes, channels and fjords. Two ice fields, the

Northern Patagonian Ice Field, just south of Coyhaique, and the Southern Patagonian Ice Field from Tortel south are the world's largest after those in Antarctica and Greenland. Until the construction of Route 7 (the Carretera Austral, or Southern Highway) in the 1980s, the only overland routes from north to south through the

Carretera Austral, Northern Patagonia

region were extremely primitive tracks. The narrow gravel road is a vast improvement for those living in or traveling into this remote part of Chile. It once took upwards of two weeks for pack animals and riverboats to make the journey from Cochrane to Caleta Tortel; that same trip can now be covered in about three hours.

Chile, located on the southwestern coast of South America, sports a diverse array of geographical regions. The northern reaches of the country contain the world's driest desert, while the southern end is fewer than 1,000 kilometers from Antarctica. This long, narrow country stretches 4,300 kilometers from its northern border with Peru to the tip of the continent, and averages only 175 kilometers (109 miles) west to east. It is bordered by the Pacific Ocean to the west and the Andes Mountains to the east. The country, which became independent of Spain in 1818, is recognized for its many natural resources including copper (one of the largest deposits in the world), iron ore, seafood, wood products, and various fruits, vegetables and wine. Now, a family is developing a new natural resource that could radically change how we think about that resource and how it is moved from sources of supply to locations of demand.

At the road's end, a small community of 510 souls, Caleta Tortel, is the gateway into the Southern Patagonia region of Chile. A noteworthy peculiarity of southern Chile is the large number of glaciers formed on the western and southern slopes of the Andes and other high elevations. These glaciers discharge directly into these deeply cut estuaries. This phenomenon is not found elsewhere in the same latitudes.

Jorge Montt Glacier

The Jorge Montt Glacier, the primary source of water for Waters of Patagonia, is a tidewater glacier situated on the northern edge of the southern Patagonia Ice Field. The glacier drains an area of about 510 km² (197 sq mi). But like many other areas around the world, it, too, is subject to rising air temperatures. Between 1975 and 2000, the glacier's ice thinned at an average rate of 3.3 m (10.8 ft) per year over the entire glacier, and as much as 18 m (59.1 ft) per year at the lowest elevations. The end of the glacier, which meets the tidewater, has experienced a major retreat of 8.5 km (5.28 mi) in those 25 years as a result of rapid thinning. The glacier calves off icebergs into the Baker Channel. While it

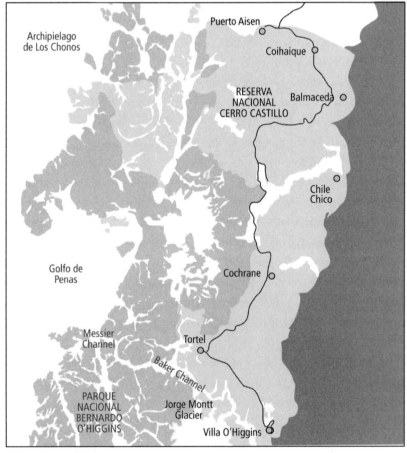

Chile: Montt Glacier

remains a major source of fresh water, even this source could eventually disappear.

The experience of the Jorge Montt Glacier is not unique in Southern Patagonia. A joint study by the U.S. National Air and Space Administration and Chile's Centro de Estudios Cientificos (Center of Scientific Studies) concluded that the Southern Patagonian ice fields were thinning at an accelerating pace, faster than other areas on the planet. They found that the runoff from these melting ice fields was contributing to an ongoing rise in global sea level.

Conventional topographic data from the 1970s and 1990s were compared with data from NASA's February 2000 Shuttle Radar Topography Mission to measure changes in the volumes of the 63 largest glaciers in the region over time. The researchers concluded the thinning rate of the Patagonia Ice fields more than doubled during the period from 1995 through 2000 versus the period from 1975 to 2000. The 1975-2000 rate of loss in ice mass equaled about 9 percent of the total annual global sea level rise from mountain glaciers of 0.45 millimeters (0.02 inches) per year. (Note: The total global sea level rise from all known sources is about 1.8 millimeters, or 0.07 inches, per year.)

The researchers attribute the increased thinning to climate change, and the unique dynamic response of the region's glaciers also to climate change. It must be noted that precipitation in the region has continued to increase as the climate has warmed. Thus while the melting continues, precipitation continues to fall, refreshing both the glacier and water supply. The Jorge Montt Glacier is adjacent to the Parque Nacional Bernado O'Higgins. The national park is the fourth largest in the world and provides a natural barrier to development that ensures the clarity and freshness of the melt water.

The Jorge Montt Glacier empties into the Baker Channel. This natural estuary provides a direct link from the glacier to the Pacific Ocean. Baker Channel, also known as Calen Inlet, empties into the southeast corner of the Gulf of Penas through Tarn Bay. The Baker Channel is fed by the Baker River, which drains the land north of Caleta Tortel and is one of the largest in Chile, as well as the rivers and streams including those coming off the glaciers. The channel is a very deep estuary, with depths of more than 150 meters. Its narrowest point is approximately one nautical mile. The Baker Channel empties into the Gulf of Penas near where the 500-kilometer (338-mile) Messier Channel also enters the same gulf. The Messier Channel provides a shortcut for ships on an inland waterway link from the Straits of Magellan to the Pacific Ocean.

In the early morning hours, before the sun's light washed away the brilliance of the Milky Way and Southern Cross, Ian Szydlowski looked out from the wheelhouse of the M/V Huemule as it began its short voyage to the source of fresh water. A low, narrow fog bank made the towering mountains appear to float over the water. Their dark shapes loomed above the small vessel as it sailed through still, turquoise waters. The waters, actually fingers of the Pacific Ocean some 50 nautical miles to the west, were filled with fresh water, at least for the top 16 meters, from the melting glaciers.

Three hours after raising the anchor at Tortel, the engines of the M/V Huemule were throttled back as the vessel approached the face of the Jorge Montt Glacier. The Huemule is Ian's office and home as he and his brother establish one of the world's most interesting, fascinating and most important businesses—water.

M/V Huemule at Jorge Montt Glacier

Water

Water and air are essential for mankind's survival. Access to clean, non-polluted water is becoming increasingly difficult. Uncontrolled use of pesticides, a disregard for protecting water sources, draining underground aquifers without thought as to how long it takes to replenish them, and an expanding world population that is overwhelming traditional

Jorge Montt Glacier

water sources combine to imperil people the world over. An estimated 97 percent of all water on the earth is salt water found in the oceans. An estimated 60 percent of the remaining fresh water is locked in a frozen state in glaciers and ice fields.

The largest sources of frozen water are Antarctica, Greenland and Chile. That leaves a mere 1.2 percent of the world's water that is freely available for the needs of humans and animals. With a world population that exceeds 6.5 billion and is predicted to rise by almost 50 percent in the next 40 years, the demand for water continues to grow. But the supply of readily available, safe, fresh and potable water is not expanding.[9]

According to a United Nations' study, "World Water Development Report," an estimated 43,659 cubic kilometers of renewable water was on hand in the world as of 2000 (the last available year of data). As the following table illustrates, with the exception of the Middle East, the study estimated that 9 percent of the fresh water was withdrawn from the hydrologic cycle. Unless other sources of fresh water can be found, the withdrawal rates will have to increase. In the case of sub-Saharan Africa, access to potable, safe water has to be increased, and quickly.[10]

Lack of adequate water supplies can have far reaching impacts on the social, economic and political fabric. The burgeoning population increases in Arizona have meant that the critical water supplies for the agricultural regions of southern California in the United States have been reduced to the extent that this once major supplier of foodstuffs for all

2000 Water Resources

Region	Renewable Resource (km³)	Total (km³)	Withdrawal Percent of Renewable Resource	Per Person (m³)
North America	6,253	525	8.4	1,664
Asia	13,297	2,404	18.1	644
Europe	6,603	418	6.4	574
Latin America & Caribbean	13,570	265	2.0	507
Africa	3,936	217	5.6	265
World	**43,659**	**3,829**	**8.8**	**626**

Source: UN World Water Development Report, 2007

of the U.S. is literally drying up. The continuing droughts in countries like Kenya are creating an unstable and untenable economic and political environment. Farmers in northern Kenya who once had cattle herds measured in the hundreds have seen those numbers decline to the low teens. Not only has less water created an economic crisis, another issue is that the few remaining water sources are polluted. Insufficient clean water is recognized as the primary factor that leads to disease and death. Without access to more water, the inhabitants face a grim future. As the chart shows, there is a lot of water, but as in the case of almost every commodity, it is not always located where it is needed.

While the rise of the world's population is placing stress on the world's water supplies, agriculture consumes the majority of the water. Domestic, municipal and industrial users account for an estimated 25 percent of the world's water demand; the remaining use is related to agriculture. Different types of agriculture require different volumes of water per kilogram of food. As an example, a vegetarian-based diet which is common in Asia and Africa requires an estimated 2,000 liters a day, while a meat-based diet common in the Americas and Europe requires almost 5,000 liters per day. In contrast, individuals in developing nations consume between 100 and 250 liters of water each day.

In 2008, Goldman Sachs noted that global water consumption was doubling every 20 years, a rate of growth unsustainable for the long term. JPMorgan Chase has estimated that five food and beverage companies—Anheuser-Busch, Coca-Cola, Danone, Nestlé, and Unilever—consume an estimated 575 billion liters of water annually. The manufacturing of semiconductors is another heavy user of water. A single 200-mm chip requires 13 cubic meters of water. As a result, even though agriculture is the dominant user of water, industrial use is also increasing. It is a particular problem in areas with limited water supplies. And in spite of the impact of loss of water resources, only an estimated 17 percent of companies have a plan to respond to such a crisis. The combination of higher population needs for water and the increased use of water for manufacturing is placing more stress on the world's water supplies.[11]

The remaining water is not all potable—that is to say, suitable for human or animal consumption. Without access to clean water, the long-term future of human existence on the earth is limited. Those who live in deserts know the true value of water. For many millions who do not have this understanding, the reality of less available fresh water is starting to become a part of daily life. Farm families in northern Kenya must live on as little as 2.5 gallons a day. In contrast, Americans consume nearly 50 times that amount, most of which is wasted, becomes polluted and leads to a reduction in long-term supply. Many experts expect the lack of adequate supplies of potable water to be the basis for future conflicts. Individuals and countries will battle over access to this essential but diminishing resource. Evidence is emerging that desalination, once thought to be the answer for supply, is a source of pollution and in some cases is leading to the destruction of major bodies of water because draining is turning the bodies into toxic deserts.[12]

Tony Allan, a professor at London's Kings College, and Koichiro Matsurua, head of UNESCO, both believe that water will become a tradable commodity as demand increases but supplies do not. Water will be priced according to its true value, a situation that is not common today. Finally, more water conservation and consumption reduction programs, such as the one implemented by Coca-Cola toward a goal of reducing water consumption by 20 percent by 2012, will be implemented in the near future.

The impact of a lack of safe, clean, unpolluted water is staggering. Rotary International has adopted the provision of safe water as one of its projects and has assembled a set of startling statistics to illustrate the extent of the problem. In the October 2008 issue of "The Rotarian," the organization noted that:

- 1.1 billion people don't have access to safe water, and this number is expected to almost double by 2025;
- 4,000 children die each day of preventable water-borne diseases;
- In developing countries an estimated 90 percent of sewage and 70 percent of industrial waste is untreated before being dumped into surface water; and
- Per capita daily water consumption ranges from 380 liters in the United States to 200 liters in Europe to only 10-20 liters in

Sub-Saharan Africa.

In China, all aquifers and rivers are now believed to be polluted. That means that about 24 percent of the world's population has no access to clean water. The massive desalination plants in the Middle East are turning salt water into toxic mixes of heavy metals and salts that, when pumped into the Arabian Gulf, are slowly turning that body of water into a desert. Water programs and related economic development programs based on what is now believed to have been the wettest period ever in the southwestern region of the United States are no longer valid. Cities including Las Vegas, Los Angeles, San Diego, Phoenix and Albuquerque are faced with diminishing supplies of water. Albuquerque, which until the 1970s believed it was sitting on top of an aquifer as large as Lake Superior, the world's largest fresh-water lake, implemented a comprehensive regime of measures to limit water consumption. Those measures have proven that effective education and programs can reduce water use and husband this critical resource.

Many other cities around the world have not embraced the fact that potable, clean, unpolluted water is no longer freely available. Prices continue to be set at non-renewable levels, controls on usage are not being enforced, and poor infrastructure remains unrepaired, causing water loss. Also, officials and citizens generally lack the education needed to address this critical situation that could endanger our world as we know it, and not in centuries, but in years.

Waters of Patagonia

Recognizing this, the Szydlowski brothers have acquired the rights to collect and bottle the natural melt flow from a series of glaciers in Southern Patagonia. The volume of melt water is so large in this part of Chile that the surface waters of the Pacific Ocean some 50 miles offshore have no traces of salt; they are fresh and potable. The company has acquired tens of thousands of hectares that it will protect from development in order to ensure the supply of fresh water. The only neighbor is Chile's largest national park, Parque Nacional O'Higgins. As Ian points out, their actions are, in effect, translating the intrinsic value of the land into an economically viable activity without disturbing the land.

By late August 2010, the first bottles of glacier water are expected to emerge from a bottling plant that has been constructed adjacent to the small river that carries the melt water from one arm of the glacier. The plant was designed and equipped with the assistance of Zenith International, a Bath, England-based consultancy specializing in the international food and drinks industries. The small plant will have a production capacity of 1,000 bottles per hour.

In keeping with the company's policy of preserving and protecting the natural environment, the plant has been designed to have a small carbon footprint, which is especially critical as it is located in the midst of a natural environment where any imbalance could disrupt the critical water supply. In fact, the watchwords of Waters of Patagonia are "Integritas, Consonantia, and Claritas," which mean "wholeness, harmony, and radiance," respectively.

While their plans are to bottle this very high quality water, the real objective of Waters of Patagonia is to collect and transport fresh water in bulk quantities to areas around the world where access to safe water is either in limited supply or soon will not be available.

As in every business, the success of a venture can be reduced to a few key factors. In this case, the challenge is almost exclusively a logistics issue. The supply of water exists and the demand for safe water also exists. The challenge is create an effective and efficient transport and logistics system that conveys the safe water from origin to destination. As the company's creators believe, the essential mechanisms of a successful operation that will transform the water business includes creation of movable pipelines that facilitate worldwide distribution, a dependable supply and water quality.

The need for safe water around the world is undisputed. A supply of safe water in Chile has been confirmed. The remaining challenge and opportunity is how to move the water from its source to where it is needed in a safe and efficient manner. As the founders of Waters of Patagonia point out, the most critical water issues that the world is currently facing is making the redistribution of water an urgent necessity and incorporating realistic costs into the pricing of this valuable commodity.

The company has identified four primary logistics options. The following table summarizes the critical characteristics of each option.

Waters of Patagonia—Logistics Options

Option	Description	Unit/Quantity	Packaging	Transporter
1	Bottle	Bottle 0.5L	Palletized and containerized	Landing Craft + Container Vessel
2	Bulk container	TEU 22 MT	Ocean container	
3	Tanker vessel	59,000— 320,000 m³	Bulk	Tanker
4	High capacity bladder	300,000,000 m³	Bulk	Tug

Option 1 is suitable for relatively small quantities of high-priced product. The company has registered the name "Crevasse" for its high-end bottled water. It will be bottled at a plant it has built on the Crevasse River. The initial production capacity will be 1,000 bottles, or 500 liters, an hour.

Because the bottling plant is located on a shallow river with a mean low tide depth of about 5 meters (16 feet), the company has to employ a specially designed logistics system to move the bottles from the plant to the major seaport at Punta Arenas. This system is based on a geared landing craft that transports containers between the seaport and the bottling plant. A geared landing craft is the optimal vessel because its shallow draft is needed to access the location of the bottling plant, and it has a crane with adequate capacity to move products on and off the vessel at the plant. The basic operating plan for Option 1 is portrayed in the following table. It is a simple plan that negates the need for complex and expensive

Typical non-geared landing craft

handling equipment at the bottling plant while providing use of an efficient form of transport. Using this conceptual plan with 16,000 filled bottles per TEU (20-foot ocean container), a total of 96,000 bottles (48,000 liters) of Crevasse Water can be shipped every nine days. This option dispenses with the need to move loaded containers on and off the craft.

Option 2 will use a similar operating plan to move water in bulk from the bottling site to any destination. Instead of using tankers, this operating scenario is based on bladder-equipped ocean containers. These containers are already used to export Chilean bulk wine.

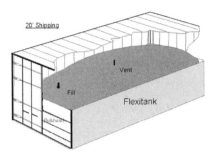

Each container can carry approximately 22 tons of water. Under option 1, the maximum weight of water per TEU is only eight tons.

Bulk shipping container (TEU)

Flexitank, Inc. www.flexitank.com/Intermodal. asp

The first two logistics options can be accomplished with a simple geared landing craft that is similar to the preceding photo except that it will be equipped with a crane to facilitate the movement of equipment on and off the vessel at the bottling plant and/or Punta Arenas.

As volumes increase, the company has two options. The first is to terminate the vessel at a closer port in southern Chile, Puerto Natales. Puerto Natales can be reached in 24 hours. Trucks then can be loaded and used to move the filled bottles to the larger port of Punta Arenas in approximately five hours. The second alternative would be to carry 12 containers either to Punta Arenas or Puerto Natales. This option would require a more sophisticated loading system at the bottling location.

The first likely destination of bulk water shipments will be in northern Chile, at Antofagasta and the surrounding mines. The water there has become so polluted that arsenic levels in the city's drinking water are well above acceptable levels. Many of the contaminants leach out of the mines some 1,500 meters above the city and find their way not just to the water supply of the region but also into the Pacific Ocean. That market is approximately 3,000 kilometers north of the glacier. Another potential market for water is in Europe, where a major supermarket chain that sells 1,000 liters of water each day would purchase the water in bulk and then bottle and sell it under its own private label. Both of these markets

Logistics Plan—Bottled Water

Step	Activity	Location	Elapsed Time (hours)	Notes
1	Bottle 96,000 bottles	Bottling Plant	106.0	1,000 bottles per hour + 10 percent allowance for set-up, etc.
2	Move boxes of filled bottles to packing area at wharf	Bottling Plant	1.0	Bottling plant generates 1 pallet per hour—transfer done while next pallet is being built. Time allowance for last pallet after bottling is completed for week.
3	Palletize boxes and shrink wrap	Packing Area	1.0	Can wrap two pallets an hour. Time allowance for last two pallets after bottling and transfer.
4	Stuff containers in landing craft	Landing Craft	6.0	6 TEU using portable un-powered conveyor system
5	Sail to Punta Arenas	En-route	48.0	
6	Off-load loaded containers	Punta Arenas	1.0	Use dock crane for transfer
7	Load containers with empty bottles and dunnage, and prepare vessel for return trip		7.0	
8	Sail to bottling location	En-route	48.0	
9	De-stuff containers	Landing Craft	2.0	
	Estimated Total Time		**220.0**	

Note: Steps 2 and 3 occur during bottling operations (Step 1).

would require the use of tankers, as the volumes will overwhelm the limited capacity of the landing craft based alternative.

Using tankers, the third logistics option, is not an innovative transport method for water. Over the decades the island territory of Bermuda has relied on water tankers from the United States from time to time when the rains failed to come and refill the cisterns that collect rainwater from the white-roofed buildings. However, while those movements are carried out on an ad hoc basis, the plan of the Chilean company is create continuous movements of water from Southern Patagonia to other places around Chile and the world.

The use of tankers, especially on routes to the Middle East, is particularly intriguing from a variety of perspectives. First, tankers carrying petroleum products return empty. This means that the loaded portion of the voyage must be priced to cover the cost of the empty backhaul where the next shipment will be collected. Second, to maintain stability on the return, empty voyage tankers must take on ballast water. That water, which is not necessarily fresh water, often contains native species that can disrupt the natural environment when discharged as the next load of petroleum product is loaded. Establishing a roundtrip operation, water in one direction and petroleum products in the other, would have a significant impact on the cost of transport for both products and could contribute to protecting natural environments.

The question then arises as how to efficiently use the vessel for two

An enclosed bladder

Source: http://royalliner.com/bladder.htm

purposes. Because water and crude oil don't mix and the presence of one liquid in the other spoils it, any technical solution must ensure that crude oil/petroleum products and the fresh water are kept separate and that remnants of one load do not contaminate the next load of a different product. One potential answer is the use of a flexible liner or bladder that fits inside the tanks of the ship. Such products are readily available. Adapting this solution to the tanker might involve minor modifications to the vessel, to ease the insertion and removal of the bladder, but those changes should not be problematic.

The likely operating plan would involve discharging the load of crude oil. After a standard inspection of each tank, the hatchway to each tank would be opened. The bladders would be inserted into each tank, and the vessel would then sail to the water loading location to fill the bladder-lined tanks with fresh water. Upon arrival at the destination, the water would be discharged from the tank, and the liners/bladders would be removed and inspected while the ship's tanks are also inspected and made ready to receive the next shipment of crude oil/petroleum product.

This logistics chain would significantly reduce the number of nautical miles traversed by an empty ship. It also would preclude the use of ballast water, and substantially reduce the transport costs for the crude oil and water shipments. In a perfect world, where the crude oil destination was adjacent to the water source, this operation could almost halve the transport cost of both liquids. But while such a situation is unlikely to occur all the time, the cost of transportation, even after allowing for the depreciation costs for the liners and the costs to install and remove the liners, would be significantly reduced.

The ultimate logistics option, number 4, is based on technology developed by a Canadian engineer. That technology is based on the construction of portable aquifers. These enormous bladders, with potential capacities of 300 million liters, would be filled in southern Chile and towed to where the water was required. Rather than floating horizontally on the surface of the ocean, the aquifers would sit in the water in a vertical orientation. This vertical alignment would serve a number of purposes. First, the water in the container would naturally begin to cycle from top to bottom and return. This action would reduce the amount of water subject to the heating action of the sun. It also would allow the water to remain "fresh" during periods of storage at the destination locations. Ian and his brother believe that the water in these portable aquifers could be either drawn out based on normal consumption rates to recharge

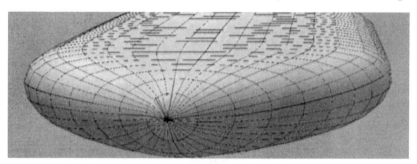

Artist's rendition of the high capacity bladder
Source: Waters of Patagonia (with permission)

the local water systems, or pumped out quickly into natural aquifers to replenish them.

The movement of fresh water from the ice fields of Southern Patagonia in Chile heralds the emergence of a new international business. Other sources of fresh water, including New Zealand, Greenland and Iceland, are potential sources of a rapidly dwindling resource upon which mankind and animals depend. Unlike the two sources in the Northern Hemisphere, Chile and New Zealand sources have significantly lower exposures to airborne dust and other contaminants. Unlike the northern sources, Chile and New Zealand are located closer to a known natural ozone hole that is contributing to rising temperatures in the southern hemisphere and are further from the larger areas of demand for safe fresh water.

The permits allow Waters of Patagonia to siphon off just some of the melt water. This reduces the impact of their operations on the natural environment. However, that relatively small percentage can easily translate into the difference between no water and access to a supply that is sufficient to meet the needs of many parts of the world. In this case it is simply a matter of transport and logistics solutions.

Conclusion

Water is essential to life on earth. Access to water is limited or non-existent in many regions of the world. If life is to continue, available fresh water must be available where it is needed. Moving vast quantities of fresh water from a source to an area of demand is a transportation and logistics challenge, especially when the quantities exceed the typical volumes associated with bottled water. An estimated 97 percent of all water on the earth is salt water found in the oceans. An estimated 60 percent of the fresh water is locked in a frozen state in glaciers and ice fields. Only 1.2 percent of the world's water is freely available for the needs of humans and animals. With a world population that exceeds 6.5 billion and is predicted to rise by almost 50 percent in the next 40 years, the demand for water continues to grow. But the supply of readily available, safe, fresh potable water is not expanding. Faced with this dilemma, a Chilean company has secured rights to capture melt water from one ice field. The quantity of water is sufficient to satisfy the thirst of hundreds of thousands, if not millions, where access to potable water is limited or all but non-existent.

From its base in the Patagonian region of Chile, Waters of Patagonia is developing a program that will provide high-quality fresh water, captured from a melting glacier, and ship it around the world. Capturing the water is relatively simple. Bottling the water is likewise a straightforward process. But moving very large bulk shipments of fresh water over long distances is a challenge that has only been accomplished for petroleum products. While some might look at the company as a supplier of water, in reality it is a logistics company.

The company has designed a family of transport and logistics solutions to move different quantities and categories of its fresh water. They range from 0.5-litre bottles, small bulk shipments in specially equipped 20-foot ocean containers and adaptation of crude oil tankers, up to a massive towed bag that can accommodate 30,000 cubic meters of fresh water. Bottles are the first step as the water is introduced to the market place as an up-scale product around the world. Filling and shipping ocean containers, similar to the current methods of moving bulk wine, are the second step. Adapting tankers to carry water in one direction and other products on a return voyage heralds the third step in the logistics evolution of the company. Eventually the huge towed bags will be able to transport very large quantities of water, enough to satisfy the needs of thousands of consumers at competitive cost levels.

India

As Mr. R. Srivastava reviewed the file concerning the Off-Shore Container Terminal at Mumbai Port, he could almost hear the impassioned statement of Mrs. Rani Jadhav, then the Chair of the Mumbai Port Trust, when she and her colleagues presented their plan to his predecessor. They had summed up their presentation with the simple statement that they would not let the port die. It had always been the primary port of entry to India, and still had a role to serve, but needed the help of the central government. In a demonstration of India's can-do attitude, the proposed Off-Shore Container Terminal was completed five years after

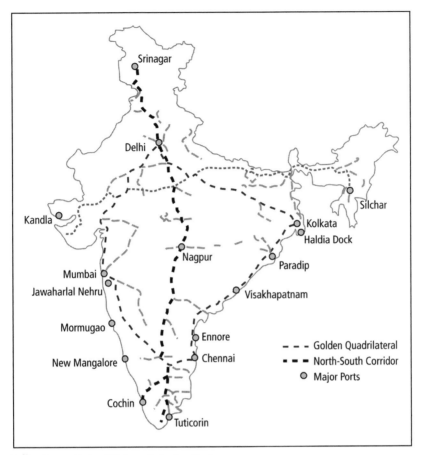

India   Source: National Highway Authority of India

receiving approval.

Looking across the piles of files on his desk, Mr. Srivastava thought about how each project reflected India's concerted effort to rapidly improve its infrastructure to accommodate the expansion of the nation's economy and the rising consumer demands of its population.

Outside, the waves of heat danced on every surface. Summer had arrived in northern India and the heat would continue to build until the monsoon season and then autumn. Barely a breath of air ruffled the palm fronds. People and animals sought the shade to gain some respite from the scorching sun.

On Parliament Street, like many others in Delhi, Mumbai, Chennai and across the sub-continent nation, the onslaught of traffic funneling into two lanes from four and the constant honking of horns served as a reminder that India's economic fortunes were on the rise. Barely brushed by the downturn of the 2008 recession, India's economic growth is changing the economic and social landscape of the world's largest democracy in striking ways. Estimates of the Indian middle class, approximately 400 million, is larger than the entire population of the world's largest consuming nation, the United States. Spending their new-found wealth in corner shops and brand new malls, they demand more and better quality products. While most consumer goods are made domestically, the growing waves of imports crossing port quays and passing through air cargo terminals serve as a constant reminder that India has shed its insular, protected economic stance and is benefiting from those changes.

In 1991, as India came close to financial default, the political leadership and legislature embarked on a massive overhaul of policy and procedures in the public and private sectors. The policy changes included extensive economic liberalization. The socialist-led policies of protecting domestic suppliers and tight control of financial flows and imports were swept away. The large domestic economy provided a foundation for the economic and social revolutions to take hold. As a result, the Indian economy has recorded growth rates prior to the recession of 8-10 percent per annum. This, in turn, has placed higher demands on the transport and logistics sector. With a return to the past growth rates and an elasticity of 1.25, the transport sector is expected to expand at rates of 10-12 percent annually in the medium and long-term range.

Transport Infrastructure—Ports

The transport and logistics story of India is about its ports and rail-ways. They jointly handle the majority of goods and passengers that traverse the nation. More than 200 ports, strung along 7,500 kilometers of coastline, serve all manner of vessels from very large crude carriers to small fishing boats. Those ports link India to the rest of the world. Across the nation, the world's second largest railway system operates about 11,000 trains a day, carrying an estimated 20 million passengers and 2 million tonnes of freight.[13] These two transport modes are critical to the continued economic growth and prosperity of India. The trade is facilitated by an innovative customs system that reduces paperwork and speeds both imports and exports through the ports of entry.

The vast majority of international trade passes through 12 major ports in India. They are located on both the east and west coasts of the country. As the following table illustrates, the growth of the Indian economy has stressed the capacity of these ports. Based on the 2008-09 traffic, the ports as a group only had 6.8 percent excess capacity. In four instances, ports at Chennai, Mormugao, Mumbai and Visakhapatnam handled traffic in excess of their published annual capacities.

Among the files on Mr. Srivastava's desk were 276 projects for these 12 ports. The National Maritime Development Program included port

Port	Annual Capacity	2008-09 Traffic	2008-09 Surplus/ Deficit	Additional Planned Capacity	Total Planned Capacity	2011-12 Traffic Estimate	2011-12 Percent of Total Capacity
Major Indian Ports							
(Millions of Tonnes)							
Chennai	55.75	57.49	**(1.74)**	23.50	79.25	57.50	73%
Cochin	28.37	15.23	13.14	35.40	63.77	38.17	60%
Ennore	16.00	11.50	4.50	51.20	67.20	47.00	70%
Haldia Dock Complex	46.70	41.79	4.91	21.20	67.90	44.50	66%
Jawaharlal Nehru	57.96	57.29	0.67	43.90	101.86	66.04	65%
Kandla	77.24	77.22	0.02	58.80	136.04	86.72	64%
Kolkata	15.76	12.43	3.33	18.85	34.61	13.43	39%
Mormugao	33.01	41.68	**(8.67)**	37.46	70.47	44.55	63%
Mumbai	43.70	51.88	**(8.18)**	48.16	91.86	71.05	77%
New Mangalore	44.20	36.69	7.51	22.50	66.70	48.81	73%
Paradip	71.00	46.41	24.59	55.00	126.00	76.40	61%
Tuticorn	22.81	22.01	0.80	43.43	66.24	31.72	48%
Visakhapatnam	62.23	63.91	**(1.68)**	52.40	114.63	82.20	72%
Total	**574.73**	**535.53**	**39.20**	**511.80**	**1,086.53**	**708.09**	**65%**

Source; Ministry of Shipping, Government of India, "Investment Opportunities in the Port Sector, New Delhi, 2010

projects totaling Rs. 55,804 crore (US$12.8 billion), of which an esti-
mated 62 percent were expected from private investors. As the table
shows, those projects will result in a near doubling of the major ports'
capacity. But even with those projects, the Ministry of Shipping expects
that by 2011-12, the major ports will already be loaded to an average of
65 percent of annual capacity. In fact, five ports—Chennai, Ennore,
Mumbai, New Mangalore and Visakhapatnam—will be handling traffic
at or above 70 percent of their capacity.

The oldest port in India, Mumbai, which in 2008-09 operated at 119
percent of capacity, had pushed for the Off-Shore Container Terminal
to add 9.6 million tonnes of annual capacity to allow the port to handle
container ships with capacities of 6,000 TEU. Like so many of the port
projects, this one was issued under a Build-Operate-Transfer program
for operation by M/s. Indira Container Terminal Pvt. Ltd. Begun in
March 2007, the addition is planned to be operational in 2011.[14]

Additional projects aimed at improving the capacity and throughput
of the Mumbai port include deepening the draft alongside certain berths,
adding a chemical berth, and making various improvements to the road
and rail links to the port. The total cost of the projects, all planned
for completion by 2012, is Rs. 3,532.76 crores (US$812.5 million). The
source of the project funding includes 61.5 percent from Mumbai Port
Trust sources, 33.6 percent from private investment and the remaining
4.9 percent from the state government.

At the nearby Jawaharlal Nehru Port, which as India's largest container
port handled an estimated 60 percent of the country's ocean container
traffic, also is aggressively expanding its capacity to 10 million TEUs by
the 2014-15 period.

Transport Infrastructure—Railways

From its limited and scattered beginnings in 1853, Indian Railways
has grown into the largest rail system in Asia and the second largest
in the world under single management. Route miles stood at 14,484
kilometers (9,000 miles) in 1880, and now reach 63,327 kilometers
(39,350 miles), linking 6,853 stations throughout the nation. The railway
operates an estimated 4,000 freight carrying trains daily. In the 1970s,

authorities decided to electrify a significant proportion of network. As of March 2008, 18,274 km or 13 percent of the railway's route miles was electrified.[15] The annual freight tonnage hauled annually is approaching 110 metric tonnes. Freight haulage generates about 70 percent of all its revenues and the majority of its profits. Those profits are then used to cross-subsidize the loss-making passenger services.

The majority of the track network is broad gauge (1,676 mm, or 5 ft 6 in). It is the most widely used gauge in India (86.8 percent of entire track length of all the gauges and 80.7 percent of entire route-kilometers of all the gauges) as of March 31, 2008. Indian Railways is converting all tracks to the broad gauge to increase operational capacity and efficiency. Other improvements related to freight carriage include increasing the maximum payload of freight wagons by 26 percent to 68 metric tonnes, reducing the turn-around time of freight cars by two days to five days by operating the goods sheds (freight stations) 24 hours a day and seven days a week, and spreading electrification to feeder routes, thus eliminating the need to switch from electric to diesel locomotives. The combination of these efforts increased the number of daily loaded trains by 45 percent to 800.

To accommodate the growth in demand, Indian Railways is pursuing a four-pronged plan.[16] Key elements of the plan to remove all capacity bottlenecks on critical sections include:

1. Improving the golden Quadrilateral to run more long-distance mail/express and freight trains at a higher speed of 100 kmph.
2. Strengthening the rail connectivity to ports and development of multimodal corridors to the hinterland.
3. Constructing four mega bridges—two over River Ganga, one over River Brahmaputra, and one over River Kosi.
4. Accelerating completion of those and other important projects.

The second element illustrates the recognition of the value of the rail system to moving freight to and from the ports. All of the major Indian ports are linked to the national railway system, although Kandla is served by a narrow (meter gauge) line. The importance of container traffic is reflected by the past growth and predictions on the Western Corridor. This region handles traffic to and from the Jawaharlal Nehru

India, Golden Quadrilateral

Source: National Highway Authority of India

and Mumbai ports in Maharashtra and ports of Pipavav, Mundra and Kandla in Gujarat destined for Internal Container Depots (ICD) located in northern India. Containers are expected to account for 80 percent of all traffic by 2021-22, as the annual TEU volume increases from 0.69 million TEUs in 2005-06 to an expected 6.2 million TEUs. By 2022, Indian Railways expects that the Western Corridor alone will handle 16.6 million tonnes of goods, annually, not including containers. This growth, as well as the movement of other commodities, will require as many as 109 trains each way per day. That is the equivalent of a train in either direction every 13 minutes.

Private companies have emerged to handle freight traffic. One of the major companies is the Container Corporation of India Limited

(ConCor), based in New Delhi. Formed in 1988, the company has a network of more than 59 terminals, offering scheduled and on-demand rapid rail and road services between the hinterland and ports, and between major metropolitan areas.[17] The company provides inland transport by rail for containers with its own fleet of container wagons and domestic containers, as well as management of ports and air cargo complexes. It also has established a cold-chain system. ConCor has developed multimodal logistics support for India's International and Domestic containerization and trade, including door-to-door services. Mr. Y. Vardhan, director of International Marketing and Operations of ConCor, noted that his company was adding 26 rakes (45 wagons each) each year to the existing fleet of 250 rakes in order to keep up with the growing demand for his company's services. ConCor bases its forecasts on a ratio of 2.5:1. If the economy grows at 8 percent annually, then the Container Corporation of India expects that the flow of containers in India will grow by 20 percent.

Among the many plans to improve freight carrying capacity is the Dedicated Freight Corridor (DFC) project. This project, which stretches from Kolkata in the east via New Delhi to Mumbai on the central west coast, represents one of the largest railway freight-focused projects anywhere in the world.

On October 30, 2006, the Dedicated Freight Corridor Corporation of India Limited (DFCCIL) was created to plan, develop, secure funding for, construct, operate and maintain the Dedicated Freight Corridor. The DFC's 2,762 km (1,716 miles) is divided into two corridors. The Eastern Corridor stretches from Ludhiana to Sone Nagar and the Western Corridor traverses Jawaharlal Nehru Port near Mumbai to Tughlakabad/Dadri along with the two corridors linked at Khurja. Upgrading transportation technology, increasing productivity and reducing unit transportation costs are the focus areas for the project.[18] The DFC has been developed to address the extreme loadings of 115-150 percent on trunk routes (Howrah-Delhi) and (Mumbai-Delhi) as well as the expected increased demands on the rail lines in the "Golden Quadrilateral" that link the centers of Chennai, Delhi, Howrah and Mumbai, which carry about 55 percent of the entire system's freight traffic.

The mission of DFCCIL is to:

- Construct, maintain and operate the dedicated freight corridors as a profitable commercial entity;
- Provide a modern, quicker and safer freight transportation system;
- Maximize the railways' share of freight transport business by leveraging quality and pricing of rail freight transport services;
- Leverage reduced emission of green house gases by encouraging a modal shift from road to rail; and
- Institutionalize an organizational environment that breeds sincerity, speed and success.

The specific objectives of the project include:

- Reduce unit cost of freight transport through increased operating speeds and higher productivity;
- Provide customized logistic services;
- Segregate freight trains from passenger trains;
- Create additional rail infrastructure to meet expected demand;
- Introduce high-end information technology focused on rail freight transport; and
- Introduce fixed operating timetables and guaranteed transit times for rail freight services.

The DFC will introduce a number of design features to Indian Railways to accomplish the objectives of the project. As the following table illustrates, the DFC will be able to handle more traffic per route mile than is typical on the existing broad gauge system. The critical characteristics include:

Dedicated Freight Corridor Design Characteristics

Characteristic	Existing System	DFC
Containers per wagon	Single stack (2 TEU)	Double stack (4 TEU)
Train length	700 m	1,500 m
Train load	4,000 MT	15,000 MT

With the addition of state-of-the-art signaling and beefed up roadbed, the DFCs will be able to operate longer and heavier trains at higher speeds than elsewhere in the Indian Railways system. The plan is to have both corridors fully operational by 2017. The alignment of the new line in the Western Corridor is generally parallel to existing trackage.

Excise & Customs

In addition to the physical improvements at the ports and on the railway, India has implemented an innovative system to provide an efficient and transparent mechanism for collection of indirect taxes and enforcement of cross border controls with a view to encourage voluntary compliance. The strategy for achieving its mission includes:

- Benchmarking of operations and adopting best practices;
- Enhancing the use of information technology;
- Streamlining Customs, Central Excise and Service Tax procedures by employing modern techniques like risk management;
- Inspections and accredited clients facilitation;
- Evolving cooperative initiatives with other government and private agencies and building partnerships with trade, industry and other stakeholders;
- Measuring conformance to service delivery standards; and
- Developing professionalism through capacity building.[19]

The system has sped up the clearance of inbound and outbound traffic. As of early 2010, 60 percent of all import shipments were cleared solely on the basis of submitted entries. As described by Y.G. Parande, Special Secretary, Central Board of Excise & Customs, the effort began in 1997 as an internal project with significant input and comments from the many stakeholders involved in the movement of goods in and out of India. Development of the system involved addressing a series of challenges, including:

- Identification of all of the impacts of a new system;
- Bringing together all stakeholders including shippers, consignees, manufacturers, customs house brokers, port authorities, banks, clearing agents, warehouse and terminal operators and transport companies;
- Increasing the productivity of customs inspectors without any

redundancies;

- Finding and attracting new people into the Customs department to develop the system; and
- Teaching Customs Inspectors how to provide services in a transparent environment that simplifies procedures, reduces discretion of the Inspector and reduces the potential for corruption.

The system is composed of two elements. The Indian Customs & Excise Gateway (ICE) provides a means for customs entries to be entered through a single portal. Information is automatically relayed among those stakeholders that require access or knowledge. As an example, when a shipment is ready for release, a notice is sent to the consignee and the bank to release the payment for the duties and taxes. Upon receipt of the payment, the terminal operator and clearing agent are advised that the shipment is released and ready for collection.

Another element of the system is the Risk Management System. This sub-system builds a database to identify shipments that require special attention by Customs Inspectors. The sub-system studies past entries and identifies exceptions.

In keeping with the basic premise that India is the largest democracy, ICE meets every two weeks with all stakeholders to review the system and discuss the next steps in the system's development. The meetings openly address all aspects of the operation and services of Excise and Customs, including evidence of corruption. The group's objective is to implement an export focused sub-system.

Conclusion

The world's largest democracy, so associated with suffocating bureaucracy, is quietly but effectively implementing a series of programs that are in turn facilitating the economic growth and social development that has positioned India as one of the world's economic engines.

Developments at ports, on the railway and within Excise and Customs reflect not just the extensive array of projects, but also the speed at which these projects are being planned and completed. Building the Off-Shore Container Terminal at Mumbai Port in less than five years; conceiving, building and expanding a completely new port (Jawaharlal Nehru Port) to rank within the world's top 25 in two decades; creating a completely new freight-only railway across the sub-continent in 11 years (planned); and introducing a state-of-the-art computerized shipment clearing system in five years are all examples of the commitment within India to build the necessary transport and logistics infrastructure to support the commercial activity of the nation.

These and other programs are designed to handle traffic volumes that India could never have imagined in the early 1990s. Through the implementation of policies that loosened the shackles on the natural inventiveness and entrepreneurial spirit of Indians, the nation is benefiting. Domestic companies once thought to need protection behind high tariffs and trade restrictions have embraced the new market openness and are now trawling the world, acquiring companies on other continents. While restrictions continue, such as those concerning establishing stores, international trade and investment in India is exploding.

This growth has overwhelmed many of the nation's transport and logistics infrastructures. The nation's premier airport, Mumbai International, has to contend with the fact that some 30 percent of its property is occupied by illegal dwellings that cannot be removed. Mumbai Port, long the primary access point for trade in Western India, handled more traffic than its official capacity in 2008-09 and in spite of planned improvements is expected to have just a 23-percent excess capacity as soon as 2011-12. Indian Railways, one of the world's largest rail lines, has embarked on a multi-pronged program to add capacity through operational improvements as well as building the Dedicated Freight Corridor of some 2,762 km. That is equivalent to building a new railway from Boston to Albuquerque in the United States or further than that from Paris to Moscow.

Recognizing the need to eliminate the remnants of the colonial bureaucracy, projects are being conceived, planned and implemented in short periods of time. The Off-Shore Container Terminal at Mumbai Port and the new Indian Customs and Excise Gateway are prime examples of this effort to quickly move India into the 21st century. In each instance, the democratic process is being protected. Stakeholders are aggressively sought out for their input and participation. The results are projects that move forward quickly based on a comprehensive understanding of the interests, concerns and expectations of those who will either directly or indirectly be involved in the project.

Singapore

Although the beginnings of Singapore as an independent nation were rocky, this island nation has accomplished much in four-and-one-half decades. The public declaration of Singapore's severance from Malaysia in 1965 by then Malaysian Prime Minister Tunku Abdul Rahman on national television prompted a distraught and emotional reaction from Prime Minister Lee Kuan Yew.

"For me, it is a moment of anguish. All my life, my whole adult life, I believed in merger and unity of the two territories..." said Singapore former Prime Minister Lee Kuan Yew, during the televised declaration of Singapore's separation from Malaysia.[20]

Mr. Lee, Singapore's first Prime Minister, knew of the battles that lay ahead for Singapore, a small city-state without a hinterland and without the security of the British army. He had three main concerns—national security, the economy, and social issues. He had to find the quickest way possible to build up the armed forces, attract foreign investors, clean up the city, and manage international relations, among others. The following quote clearly indicates the focus and commitment of Singapore to become the best: "If there was one formula for our success, it was that we were constantly studying how to make things work, or how to make them work better." Soon after independence, Lee took the strategic route of implementing strict regulations that enabled Singapore to aggressively invest in infrastructure, subsidize its system of education, maintain an open and corruption-free economy, and establish sovereign wealth funds that made a wide variety of investments.

That focus and commitment has not changed in the intervening decades. In 2001, Dr. Kaizad Heerjee, Assistant Chief Executive of On-line Development, IDA Singapore, gave a speech in which he stated, "To ensure that we remain competitive, Singapore cannot compete simply on labor costs. We must ride on our strengths as a trusted business, financial

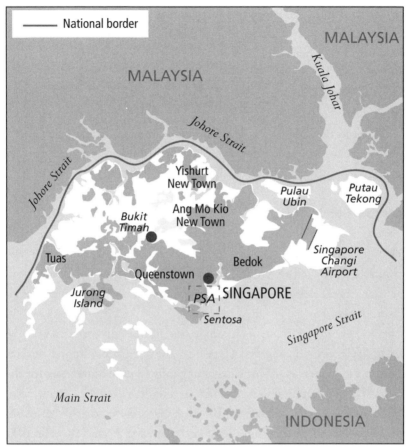

Singapore

and logistics hub to leapfrog the competition, and transform Singapore into Asia's key Collaborative Manufacturing Services Hub. Singapore can also be an attractive option for those industries that requires a high level of system efficiency and network connectivity."[21] That multi-disciplinary approach is emblematic of Singapore, a country committed to creating an integrated foundation on which a wide variety of economic activities are coordinated and focused on creating economic and social benefits for its population.

Off the southern tip of the Malaya Peninsula sits one of the world's top logistics hubs. A brief look at the historical development of Singapore highlights the developments of transport and logistics facilities and services. It is on this foundation that Singapore now claims to be one of the world's highest per capita gross national incomes and is recognized as the world's best location for doing business.[22] The recession of 2008 left Singapore relatively unscathed. In September 2008, Singapore's economy slipped into a recession due in part to slumps in manufacturing and exports.[23] But in less than a year, Singapore's economy recovered. Gross domestic product grew an annualized, seasonally adjusted 14.2 percent in the 3rd quarter, following a jump of 21.7 percent the previous quarter, according to the Trade and Industry Ministry.[24]

Transport and Logistics

On average, a vessel calls at Singapore's port every four minutes, every day of the year.[25] At its airport, an aircraft lands or takes off every two minutes.[26] Many of the 5 million people who live and work in Singapore carry on a centuries-old tradition of supporting transportation and logistics services.

From the first settlements in Singapore in the 2nd century AD, the Malay Archipelago has served as an entrepôt, supply point, and rendezvous for the sea traders. Three flows of goods laid the foundation for the creation of ports on the island and the surrounding area. Fish, fruit, rice, pepper and spices from Java and the Molcuccas were borne by fleets of swift inter-island craft. From the west, Indian and Arab traders brought cotton textiles, Venetian glass, incense and metal products, while Chinese junks carried silks, damasks, porcelain, pottery, and iron to seaports that flourished on the Malay Peninsula and the islands of Sumatra and Java. The merchants and sailors from these distant lands brought not only their trade goods but also their cultures, languages, religions, and technologies for exchange in the bazaars of this great crossroads.[27] The island was an outpost of the Sumatran Srivijaya empire and originally had the Javanese name Temasek ("sea town").

Visionary leaders from Thomas S. Raffles to Lee Kuan Yew have recognized the location's value and pushed forward plans and projects that have established and created Singapore as a hub of transport and logistics whose links touch all regions of the world. Between January 29, 1819, when Raffles landed on the island, and 1869, Singapore evolved from an isolated settlement of tents to a British Colony of 100,000 inhabitants. Ninety years later, Singapore was a self-governing state, a member of the British Commonwealth. Singapore officially gained sovereignty on August 9, 1965, and Lee Kuan Yew became the first prime minister of the Republic of Singapore.

An indication of Singapore's constant reach for the future is reflected in its physical growth. In the 1960s the land area was 581.5 km^2 (224.5 sq mi). Early in the 21st century, it is 704 km^2 (271.8 sq mi). There are plans to add another 100 km^2 (38.6 sq mi) by 2030.[28] But that determined push for growth and development does not end with expanding the size of the island; it pervades all sectors of the economy and society.

Singapore is the world's fourth leading financial center. Its economy is often ranked among the world's top 10 most open, competitive, and innovative. Even before independence in 1965, Singapore was one of the richest states in East Asia due to its strategic location as a port. Singapore's per capita GDP in 1965 was $511, the third highest in East Asia after Japan and Hong Kong. After independence, foreign direct investment into Singapore and a state-led drive for industrialization based on plans by Dr. Goh Keng Swee created a modern economy focused on industry, education, and urban planning.

Seaport

The commitment by leaders to create the best possible environment for seaborne trade is reflected in the following brief history of the development of port facilities at Singapore.

The East India Company trading station established by Raffles in 1819 thrived because of the massive volume of cargo that passed through its port. By 1822, more than 130 square-rigged vessels had entered the port of Singapore. The arrival of steamships, which were bigger in capacity and size compared to the square-rigged vessels, posed a serious threat of increasing congestion and destabilizing trade. To avert this scenario, a survey for a new harbor was begun in 1849. In 1852, New Harbor was built, which later became known as Keppel Harbor.

Meanwhile, Malaysian company Guthrie Group Limited (which introduced rubber and palm oil in Malaysia) decided to piggyback on

Singapore's remarkable success and partnered with Singapore-born Chinese merchant Tan Kim Ching to form Tanjong Pagar Dock Company in 1864. By 1868, Tanjong Pagar's dock operations were in full swing and the company inaugurated its first dry dock, the Victoria Dock. By 1870, tonnage of steamships surpassed that of sailing ships. Around the same time, another dock operations company, Paten Slip & Dock Co., opened its first dry dock. Four years later, the amount of cargo handled at Tanjong Pagar wharves had grown to 800 tons per a day.

By 1880, Singapore tonnage reached 1.5 million net registered tonnage (NRT), with steamships accounting for about 80 percent. By the beginning of the 20th century, Singapore's port tonnage had risen to 5.7 million NRT annually. In 1912, the port operations were taken over by the Singapore Harbor Board. The Board replaced old wooden wharves with concrete ones and enhanced system processes to improve port operations. The restructuring clearly paid off because by 1916, Singapore emerged as the seventh largest port in the world.

After the defeat of the Japanese in 1945, the people of Singapore set about rebuilding Keppel Harbor, where almost 70 percent of warehouses had been destroyed. The harbor also was cluttered with sunken vessels. In spite of a string of plagues and hardships—severe food shortages; outbreaks of disease, crime and violence; malnutrition; destruction of rubber plantations and tin mines; and stoppages in public transport, public services and the harbor—Singapore's port pulled through. In 1947, the port handled 20.4 million NRT. Even as the political landscape of Singapore underwent changes, its port continued to flourish and reached 82.9 million NRT in 1963. In 1964, Lee Kuan Yew formed the Port of Singapore Authority (PSA) to manage the port operations.

The following picture illustrates the size of the port and the volume of traffic that passes across its docks.

Port of Singapore   Source: en.wikipedia.org

The Maritime and Port Authority of Singapore (MPA) was established on February 2, 1996. Its mission is to develop Singapore as a premier global hub port and international maritime center. It also is charged with advancing and safeguarding Singapore's strategic maritime interests. MPA partners with the industry and other agencies to enhance safety, security and environmental protection in port waters, facilitate port operations and growth, expand the cluster of maritime ancillary services, and promote maritime research and development and manpower development.[29]

The MPA is pursuing a strategy composed of five elements known as the "5 P's." Those elements are:

1. Nurturing Competent and Committed People
2. Building Strong Partnerships
3. Developing a Pro-Business Environment
4. Improving Operational Processes
5. Achieving International Prominences

The port of Singapore comprises a number of facilities and terminals that handle a wide range of cargo transported in different forms, including containers as well as conventional and bulk cargo. The terminal operators include PSA Corporation and Jurong Port Pte Ltd.

As the following table illustrates, total tonnage grew by 54 percent between 2002 and 2008 at the Port of Singapore. Containerized cargo accounted for about 57 percent of the total traffic, while oil volume ave-

Singapore Port Traffic (millions of tonnes)				
	General Cargo		Bulk	
Year	Total	Containerized	Conventional	Oil	Non-Oil
2002	335.16	183.95	14.57	120.67	15.97
2003	347.69	191.69	14.76	123.37	17.87
2004	393.42	223.50	17.38	129.33	23.21
2005	423.27	241.97	20.29	137.83	23.18
2006	448.50	258.55	22.84	153.03	14.08
2007	483.62	289.09	25.82	157.38	11.32
2008	515.42	308.49	27.93	167.32	11.67
2009	472.30	262.90	17.45	177.32	14.63

Source: The Maritime and Port Authority website, 2010

raged about one-third of the traffic. Singapore is the largest ship refueling station in the world.

Another example of Singapore's commitment to the future is represented by the 3rd Maritime Research and Development Advisory Panel, which was established in April 2007 for a two-year term. The panel's Terms of Reference included:

1. Develop a vision for maritime technology and research and development (R&D) in the next 15 years based on global trends of the maritime industry;

2. Develop strategies for making Singapore a center of excellence for maritime R&D, and identify factors to intensify R&D partnerships and investment in Singapore;

3. Identify trends in the Port, Shipping and Offshore Marine and Engineering sectors and use the R&D program(s) to address these trends, new operating environment and new commercial requirements and conditions; and

4. Identify emerging technologies (e.g., nanotechnology, photonic, biotechnology, fuel cell) for maritime R&D and their specific potential applications by the maritime industry.

The panel recommended that Singapore develop its maritime industry beyond its current core maritime businesses by promoting the growth of more knowledge-based activities to add diversity and gain competitive advantage. Specifically, the 3rd MRDAP recommended the establishment of a Singapore Maritime Cluster (SMC) Vision 2025 of "A Global Maritime Knowledge Hub Shall Propel the Singapore Maritime Cluster" to sustain competitiveness in the maritime sector and attract maritime companies to Singapore on a global level.[30]

The following diagram illustrates the scale and complexity of the Singapore Maritime Cluster and interaction of various elements. The needs and operations of the four primary groups—port, shipping, offshore and maritime services—must be coordinated and accommodated if the cluster is to operate successfully. As in many other aspects of its economic and social fabric, the Singapore government is creating and implementing a comprehensive plan for the optimal benefit of all of the members of the cluster.

Singapore's Maritime Cluster

PORT

Petro-chemicals

Importers

Other Transport Freight Forwarding

Storage & Warehousing

Cargo/Passenger Terminals
Ship Chandlers
Ship Bunkering
Inland Water Transport

SHIPPING

OFFSHORE & MARINE

Cruises

Ship Management Services

Offshore

Ship Broking & Chartering Services

Insurance, Reinsurance & P&I
Maritime Legal Services
Maritime Related Finance
Government Agencies
Education and Training
Maritime Related R&D/IT
Maritime Logistics & Supporting Services

Wholesale/Retail of Marine Equipment/Accessories

Shipping Lines/ Ship Owners

Shipbuilding & Repair

Defense

Shippers

Exploration

Other Logistics Services

Ship Agency Services

Class Societies & Marine Surveying Services

Labour Suppliers

Material Suppliers

MARITIME SERVICES

Source: Maritime & Port Authority of Singapore, www.mpa.gov.sg/sites/research_and_
development/introduction_to_maritime_r_d/maritime_r_d_framework.page

The MPA has established a US$100-million MINT Fund to support development programs for the maritime technology cluster. This includes the Maritime Industry Attachment Program, the Joint Tertiary & Research Institution and MPA R&D Program, the Maritime Technology Professorship, and the Platform for Test-bedding, Research, Innovation and Development for New-maritime Technologies (TRIDENT).

Airport

Just as Singapore has a history of creating and implementing facilities to support and encourage sea borne trade, its actions toward aviation have followed a similar track. Since 1928, Singapore has always been conscious of the future needs of commercial air service and has proactively developed facilities.

With the advent of commercial aviation, Singapore's role as a major point on the emerging transport's network quickly evolved. A vision similar to that for ocean traffic has emerged, with a string of ever-larger facilities built to handle commercial airliners and the increasing flow of passengers, mail and cargo. The first airport, at Seletar on the northeast coast of the island, was established in 1928 as a Royal Air Force base for sea and land planes and opened to commercial services two years later. The first commercial service at Seletar was a KLM flight on February 11, 1930, from Amsterdam to Batavia (now known as Jakarta). Three years later, Imperial Airways (now known as British Airways) began services from London and India, and on December 17, 1934, the Imperial Airways service, in conjunction with Qantas Empire Airways, was extended to Brisbane. By 1934, it took eight days via 22 intermediate stops over 13,612 kilometers (8,458 miles) to complete the journey from London to Singapore at a cost of £180 (US$900).[31]

Because of growth and the consequent conflict between military and commercial aviation operations, a new airport, to be located at Kallang, was announced in 1931. It opened in 1937 and remained as Singapore's primary airport until 1955, when it was replaced by an even larger facility at Paya Lebar. Between 1955 and 1975, annual passenger numbers rose dramatically, from 300,000 to 4 million. In 1981, Changi International Airport, located on the site of the infamous Japanese prison camp, was opened as the newest international airport to serve Singapore. It sat on 5,200 hectares (12,850 acres) of landfill and sea-fill after six years of construction. As of mid-2010, Changi handles more than 5,000 arrivals and departures each week. It is the home base for a number of airlines, including Singapore Airlines, SilkAir and Tiger Airways. It is also the major secondary hub of Qantas Airways, which uses Singapore Airport as a hub on the "Kangaroo Route" between Australia and Europe.

Growth in Traffic and Connectivity at Singapore Changi Airport			
Indicator	1981	1990	2008/2010(*)
Passengers (millions)	8.1	15.6	37.7
Air Cargo ('000 tonnes)	193.0	623.8	1,883.9
Country Links	43	53	60 (*)
City Links	67	111	>180 (*)
Airlines	34	52	82 (*)
Weekly Scheduled Flights	1,200	2,000	>5,000 (*)

Sources: Airports Council International, www.aci.aero;
Changi International Airport, www.changiairportgroup.com

The first Singapore Airlines A380, 9V-SKA, parked at Terminal 2
Source: en.wikipedia.org

In 2009, the airport handled more than 37 million passengers, making it the world's 21st busiest airport and the fifth largest in Asia. In the same year, 1.66 million tons of cargo passed through Changi. As the following table shows, traffic at Changi International has experienced significant growth since its first year of operation.

With a commitment to provide up-to-date facilities and support for air operations, and recognition of the economic value (13,000 jobs and an estimated $4.5 billion to Singapore's GDP) of the airport, a new S$300 million (US$216 million) fund was created in 2007 to strengthen Changi as a hub. The airport has a development policy of building years ahead of demand to help avoid congestion problems common to major airports and to maintain high service standards.

While the original master plan included two passenger terminals, it also provided for long-term expansion initiatives, including the allocation of space for a third terminal with a physical configuration mirroring that of Terminal 2. Terminal 3 was opened in January 2008 and an improvement plan for Terminal 1 was announced. A fourth terminal, dedicated to low-cost carriers, was opened in 2006, as well as a third runway. The plan is to double the size of Changi in anticipation of rising traffic flows.

Road and Rail

Johor-Singapore Causeway
Source: en.wikipedia.org

The earliest roads in Singapore were laid out in 1822 in a grid system. The original design was for carriage roads that were 15 m (48 feet) wide; for horses, 4 m (12 feet) wide; and for pedestrian paths, 1 m (6 feet) wide. Macadam (asphalt) surfacing was used on High Street while the remainder was unsurfaced. In 1924, the Johor-Singapore Causeway was built as part of the 340 km (212 miles) of roads built to that date. In contrast, more than 2,000 km (1,250 miles) of roads were built between 1965 and 2005. The 1,056-meter Johor-Singapore Causeway links the town of Woodlands in Singapore to Johor Bahru in Malaysia. The causeway serves as a road, rail, and pedestrian link, as well as piping water into Singapore. An estimated 60,000 vehicles use the causeway daily. The current road system includes a network of expressways.

A bus service and a heavy rail passenger Mass Rapid Transit metro system provide public transport. A Light Rail Transit system increases access to housing estates around the island nation. Another example of innovation occurred in 1975 when Singapore introduced congestion pricing to control road usage during rush hours and in the city center.

Between 1900 and 1902, the Singapore-Kranji Railway, also known as the Singapore Government Railway and the Singapore-Johore Railway at various times, was constructed with services in full operation along the 16 miles of line by April 1903. A ferry at Kranji linked Singapore to the Malayan mainland. By 1907, the railway was nearly 20 miles long. With construction of the Johor-Singapore Causeway, train service for goods began on September 17, 1923, and passenger trains began running on October 1, 1923. The main railway station for Singapore at Tanjong Pagar was completed in 1932. Tanjong Pagar railway station (also called Keppel Road railway station or Singapore railway station) is owned by Keretapi Tanah Melayu (KTM), the main railway operator in Malaysia. The land on which the station and the KTM railway tracks in Singapore are situated has been held by KTM on a 999-year lease. Following an agreement between Malaysia and Singapore that was reached on May 24, 2010, railway operations into the station will cease by July 1, 2011. KTM's southern terminus will then be relocated to the Woodlands Train Checkpoint.

Multimodal Transport

As the preceding sections illustrate, the individual transport modes in Singapore provide a multimodal framework for trade. As one of the original members of the Association of South East Asian Nations (ASEAN), Singapore has leveraged its own transport framework with other members to provide an excellent base for transport and logistics companies to serve the growing economies north to Mongolia.

In November 2005, the ASEAN ministers of transport signed a comprehensive multimodal transport agreement. That agreement incorporated three objectives, including:[32]

- Provide the minimum requirements for registration of ASEAN multimodal transport operators;
- Define the liability and limit of liability of multimodal transport operators and consignors; and
- Unify the legal principles to institutionalize multimodal transport operations in ASEAN.

The need for this agreement was driven by the Asian Highway project, which began in 1958 under the auspices of the United Nations Economic and Social Commission for Asia and the Pacific. In 1992, the Asian Highway project was integrated into the Asian Land Transport Infrastructure Development (ALTID). The ALTID includes the highway project, the Trans-Asian Railway and facilitation of land transport projects. As of 2005, the Asian Highway comprised a total of 140,000 kilometers (86,992 miles) in 32 countries, stretching from Indonesia in the southeast to Europe. The Trans-Asian Railway (TAR), begun in the 1960s, is aimed at providing a continuous rail link that stretches from Singapore to Istanbul. The TAR project is focused on providing access to landlocked countries and handling larger volumes of traffic than is reasonable by truck. An agreement between 18 Asian governments was signed in November 2006 to coordinate the development of the Trans-Asian Railway.

The expectation of the ASEAN Multimodal Transport Agreement is to increase efficiency and reduce costs of multimodal transport operators. With respect to Singapore, the Agreement is expected to create a competitive alternative for the movement of goods between Singapore, Malaysia and Thailand—by road instead of by sea or air.

An example of the Agreement's benefits is the road service in Southeast Asia created by TNT. Prior to the January 1, 2010, activation of new trade deals between ASEAN and China and India, TNT had been building up its road services across Southeast Asia, China and India to boost the volumes moving through its global network, partly in anticipation of the more competitive environment, said regional TNT Regional MD Onno Boots. "My focus over the last few years has been to anticipate the further evolution of these trade agreements," he said. "We expanded the road network—we now cover most of the ASEAN countries—and we link them to China by road and air, and with Europe via air."[33]

The service, marketed as the Asia Road Network (ARN) was in operation by mid-2008 between Singapore and southern China. The service linked 125 cities in seven countries along a 5,000-km route, handling 90 percent of the TNT parcel volume in the region versus 70 percent in TNT's European road system.[34]

Impact on the Economy

The strength of Singapore's transport and logistics system is reflected in the manufacturing operations that exist and thrive there. A unique approach by Singapore is to leverage its location in Southeast Asia and build on its history as an entrepôt and center of trade. Specifically, multinational companies can use Singapore as a base and harness the strengths of neighboring countries. The multi-cultural social structure of Singapore allows companies based there to easily integrate inputs, including labor-intensive manufacturing in China and elsewhere in Asia, the software expertise of Indian companies, and the product design capabilities found in Japan.

"Today, competition is no longer between companies but between supply networks," Dr. Heerjee says. "Supply chain management must be transformed from a one-entity effort into a cooperative effect, where all partners in the chain join forces to create and share the value created."[35] With that recognition and focus, Singapore's economy is vibrant, proactive and flexible.

Singapore's Petrochemical Hub on Jurong Island is another example of the state's innovative spirit. Singapore has grown to one of Asia's—and one of the world's—leading and most cost-effective locations for producing petrochemicals. What started as a group of small islands has, through land reclamation, become Jurong Island. More than 95 companies from the U.S., Europe and Asia invested more than US$30 billion and by the end of 2009, employed some 8,000 people in the complex.

Creating the island from scratch allowed Singapore to cater to investors' requirements, such as basic infrastructure, services and access to feedstocks, as well as a highly educated workforce. Singapore offers investors what it calls "plug and play," emphasizing the ease with which major projects can be developed and become operational. The next phase in the development of the petrochemical hub is to improve integration for greater operating efficiencies and to attract new entrants.[36]

Prior to the recession of 2008, Singapore's Industrial Development Agency initiated the formation of an e-Supply Chain Task Force, with a mandate to examine three areas of interest. The three areas included the creation of e-Business standards for development of an industry-shared service platform for supply chain management and product design collaboration, development of a framework to benchmark the e-Business and e-Supply Chain readiness of Singapore companies, and third, to determine how IDA could assist Singapore companies in developing and implementing e-Business programs, such as manpower training. By implementing such a program, Singapore companies were ready with new dynamic approaches and systems to deal with the recession of 2008 and to quickly respond and recover from its impact.

As a result of this long-term initiative, as well as more focused programs including the Jobs Credit program that supported companies so they could minimize layoffs, Singapore was able to shrug off the recession of 2008 in less than one year. As of mid-2010, economists forecast that Singapore's economy will expand by 7-9 percent. The sector leading Singapore's economy out of the short recession is manufacturing exports, led by electronic and pharmaceutical production, with a growth rate of 16.7 percent.[37]

Conclusion

From its beginnings, Singapore has been a center for transport and logistics. Its location on the southern end of the Malay Peninsula on the Malacca Straits that link the Indian Ocean with the South China Sea has been leveraged for thousands of years. Arab and Indian traders from the west met and traded with Chinese merchants from the north and east, while those from Malaysia and Indonesia brought spices, pepper and fish to the mix.

Since the early 18th century, Singapore has been established as a major transport center, first for sea borne trade and then for air services. With ships arriving every four minutes and planes arriving and departing every two minutes, the seas and air around this island nation are full of commerce. Facilitating this flow of commerce has been a constant progression of investment fulfilling the vision of and commitment by colonial and independent leaders. Whether it is the road system, the seaport or the airport, Singapore is known around the world for its state-of-the-art infrastructure that is constantly being upgraded and expanded.

Since the mid-1960s, Singapore also has been recognized for its corrupt-free, transparent and highly effective government and civil service. Private businesses are supported, encouraged and left alone to compete as hard as they can, so long as they obey the rules.

While Singapore experienced the global recession of 2008, it quickly enacted programs, such as the Jobs Credit Scheme, to assist companies in keeping their employees. Taking advantage of its location in Southeast Asia and a stable and highly effective workforce, Singapore's brush with the recession was short-lived.

The role of Singapore as a model for developing nations is well regarded. The East African nation of Rwanda has solicited counsel and advice from Singapore. Rwanda's focus on eliminating corruption and establishing a private-public partnership environment reflects the success of Singapore.

In a speech entitled "Asia and Africa: Past Lessons, Future Ambitions" that was delivered at the National University of Singapore on February 26, 2010, the former Secretary-General of the United Nations, Kofi Annan, noted that "Singapore is a shining example of Asia's growing economic and political success and an impressive testimony to the vision, courage and commitment that is found here in such abundance."[38] He went on to say that while many Asian governments base their legitimacy and reasons for retaining power on their economic growth, poverty reduction and expanding opportunity, too many governments in Africa after coming to power believe that only they can be trusted to rule their countries and thus their focus is on the ruling elite rather than society as a whole.

The vision of Singapore's leaders and implementation of their plans has led to the economic miracle at the end of the Malay Peninsula. The vision and the resulting infrastructure reinforces Singapore's role as one of the world's major transport and logistics hubs.

United Arab Emirates

A vast desert stretches as far as the eye can see. In the blinding sun and scorching heat it is punctuated by some isolated settlements and a few roads. Along the 1,318-km coast where the desert meets the sea are most of this country's 41 airports, all of its 19 seaports and terminals, 30

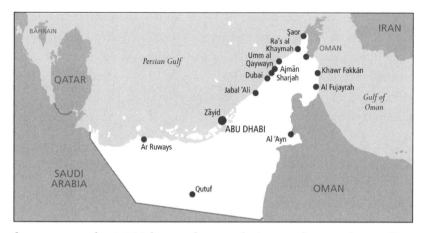

free zones, and a 4,080-km road network. Many of its nearly 5 million people who live and work here are focused on international trade. If your mind cannot fathom these contrasts, chances are you haven't been to the United Arab Emirates (UAE).

The UAE is composed of seven states called "emirates." They are Abu Dhabi (the capital), Dubai, Sharjah, Ajman, Umm Al Quwain, Ras Al Khaima, and Fujairah. Even though the UAE has limited manufacturing capabilities or naturally produced articles of trade, the combination of its geographic location and the vision and investment commitment of its rulers has been rewarded by ever growing levels of traffic.

While dhows, whose basic design can be traced back centuries, ride at anchor in Dubai and represent the history of transportation in the

Dhow in Indian Ocean

Source: en.wikipedia.org

country, modern airlines carrying hundreds of passengers or tons of cargo fill the skies. The largest ships that ply ocean routes and the largest aircraft that fly around the world serve the ports and airports in the UAE, attracting an influx of people who are seeking the hundreds of thousands of jobs that are tied to the huge volumes of cargo and passengers passing through the country.

As the world bears witness to the rise of the UAE as a world-class business hub, those within and outside of the transport logistics industry wonder: What does the future possibly hold for a nation that has made global headlines with the magnitude of its success in such short period of time?

This chapter examines how transport logistics elements played a huge part in the UAE's current economic standing, and the probable missing link that could make the country the preferred center for global trade.

World-Renowned Seaports

Seaports have been a major development priority in the UAE, since all emirates and major cities and towns are located on the coastline. The sea borne trading roots of the UAE can be traced to fishing and pearl diving. Scholars agree that its maritime history started in the small stream of Dubai Creek. This protected waterway on the southern shore of the Arabian Gulf was a focal point for fishermen and traders alike. Because their land was too barren to support agriculture, they turned to the sea for their livelihoods.

As demand for pearls grew during the 18th and early 19th centuries, Dubai Creek became the country's center of trade. Merchant ships from China and the Indian Subcontinent docked with their silk and spices. Those were sold to traders from Europe and the Middle East. Reclamation and further construction provided purpose-built Abra (small passenger boats) Boarding Stations, plus cargo handling and storage areas on the side of the creek. These added facilities enabled the growth of trade.

Although the pearl industry declined with the onset of the Great Depression in 1929 and the Japanese invention of cultured pearls in the early 1930s, regional trade continued. The 1962 discovery of oil prompted resurgence of the UAE's maritime fortunes. In 1970, the United Arab

Emirates was formed. That led to a major spurt in infrastructure investment, including schools, housing, hospitals and roads—and, as expected, the development and expansion of its sea ports.

In the 1950s, encroaching sand dunes began to fill in Dubai Creek, and affected trade. In response, the late Ruler of Dubai, Rashid bin Saeed Al-Maktoum, ordered the creek to be dredged. At that time, nobody but the late Sheikh believed that this same place would be the origin of the UAE's remarkable journey to becoming one of the world's busiest ports. Expanded port facilities first occurred at Port Rashid in Dubai and Mina Zayed Port in Abu Dhabi in the early 1970s, shortly after the founding of the UAE as a unified country. With both ports located near their respective city centers, and oil reserves as the main product of trade, the country's stature as a trading hub was re-established.

While much attention and investment focus in the UAE has been on larger ports, all facets of sea borne activity have been supported. An example is Al Hamriya Port—a small port located at the northeastern coast of Dubai. In 1975, the Government of Dubai provided 20 million dirhams (US$5.4 million) to develop the small port to handle small fishing ships, as well as to accommodate some of the commercial ships destined for the emirate.

Jebel Ali Port
www.theworldonline.ae/?p=1113

Even while the port business was thriving, it was recognized that growth was limited. By this time, it was again the vision of the late Sheikh that gave way to an even more ambitious project: construction of the world's largest man-made harbor at Jebel Ali. When completed in 1979, Jebel Ali Port ranked alongside the Great Wall of China and the Hoover Dam as one of only three man-made objects that could be seen from space.

And so began the history of one of the largest port conglomerates in the world—Dubai Ports World (DP World). DP World is a leading global port operator based in Dubai, UAE. It currently manages port terminals of Dubai, Abu Dhabi and Fujairah, as well as ports in the

Middle East, Asia, Europe, Australia and Latin America. The following table provides a brief summary of the accomplishments of DP World that have shaped the country's port industry.[39] Indeed, DP World made it possible for the UAE, led by Dubai, to become well known for world-class port facilities and services. In 2009, Dubai ranked seventh among the Top Ten Container Ports in the World based on its Twenty-Foot Equivalent Units (TEUs) throughput.[40]

Year	Accomplishments
2009	Achieved ISO 10002:2004, Customer Service Complaint Management Certification
2007	10 million TEU handled
	Ranked as 7th largest container port in the world
2006	8.92 million TEU handled
	Ranked as 8th largest container port in the world
	ISO 28000:2005 Supply Chain Certification
	DP World acquires P&O Ports
2005	7.62 million TEU handled
	Ranked as 9th largest container port in the world
	DPI Terminals and DPA merge to form DP World
2004	6+ million TEU handled
	DPI Terminals acquired CSX World Terminals
2002	TEU volume up 20% over 2001
1997	DPA ranked as 10th largest port in world
1996	2+ million TEU handled
1991	Jebel Ali and Port Rashid merged to form Dubai Ports Authority (DPA)
1985	Jebel Ali Free Zone opens
1979	Jebel Ali Port opens
1972	Port Rashid first stage opens

As much as DP World dominates the local and regional port playing field, another big player in the industry ensures the northern part of the UAE is also covered—Gulftainer Company Limited. Gulftainer's primary role is to manage and operate the container terminals in Port Khalid and Khorfakkan on behalf of Sharjah Port Authority, as well as Ruwais in Abu Dhabi. Gulftainer, like DP World, is also recognized as a global player in the field of port and terminal operations. Just recently, transport and shipping analysts Dynaliners (Dynamar BV in the Netherlands) revealed that Gulftainer's Sharjah Container Terminals (in particular the flagship Khorfakkan) moved dramatically up the list of major terminal operators in 2009. Sharjah/Khorfakkan ranked number 39 in the "league table" of major worldwide terminals.[41]

With two world-class port operators managing the coastline of the country, coupled with port expansions, particularly in Port Khalifa in Abu Dhabi and Port Khor Fakkan in Sharjah, the UAE continues to hold a slot at the top of the global seaport industry, as well as in the region.

Free Zones

The large number of free zones in the region, particularly in the UAE, has opened doors and created opportunities for a wide range of businesses that were once inconceivable. An integral component of the success of Dubai's port operations is the Jebel Ali Free Zone (JAFZA). Operations began in 1985, providing offices and warehouse space to companies seeking to handle freight moving through the adjacent port. Between 1985 and 2009, the number of companies at JAFZA grew from 19 to more than 6,402.[42] A stimulus for growth was inclusion of light industrial operations.

In the early 21st century, JAFZA became one of the world's largest and fastest growing free zones. Like other free zones (also known as duty free zones in some countries), JAFZA provides an open business environment for companies that locate there. Some of the features afforded to companies in JAFZA include exemption from corporate tax for 15 years, no personal income tax, no import or export duties, no restriction on currency, and easy labor recruitment.

Businesses in free zones in the UAE have many advantages, including:
- 100 percent tax free
- 100 percent foreign ownership
- No corporate tax
- No custom duty
- Full currency convertibility
- No restrictions on capital, trade barriers or quotas
- Hassle-free company registration

- Hassle-free company laws and legal framework
- Flexible labor laws for recruiting during part-time projects
- 24-hour visa service and fast-track immigration process

The following table lists the 30 free zones in the UAE.

Existing UAE Free Zones

City	Free Zone
Abu Dhabi	Abu Dhabi Airport Free Zone
	Higher Corporation for Specialized Economic Zones
	Industrial City of Abu Dhabi
	Khalifa Port and Industrial Zone
	Twofour54 Media and Production Free Zone
Dubai	Dubai Airport Free Zone
	Dubai Car and Automotive City Free Zone
	Dubai Flower Center Free Zone
	Dubai Gold and Diamond Park
	Dubai Health Care City
	Dubai Industrial City
	Dubai International Financial Centre
	Dubai Internet City
	Dubai Knowledge Village
	Dubai Media City
	Dubai Multi Commodities Centre
	Dubai Gold and Commodities Exchange
	Dubai Silicon Oasis
	Dubai Technology and Media Free Zone
	Economic Zones World
	Jebel Ali Free Zone
Ajman	Ajman Free Zone
Fujairah	Fujairah Free Zone
	Fujairah Creative City
Ras Al Khaimah	RAK Free Trade Zone
	RAK Investment Authority Free Zone
	Ras Al Khaimah Media Free Zone
Sharjah	Hamriyah Free Zone
	Sharjah Airport International Free ZoneUmm Al
Quwain	Ahmed Bin Rashid Free Zone

Data as on March 19, 2010,   Source: www.dubaifaqs.com/free-zones-uae.ph

In addition to the existing free zones, 18 more are in various stages of planning.

List of future free zones in the UAE

City	Free Zone
Dubai	Dubai Aid City
	Dubai Auto Parts City
	Dubai Biotechnology & Research Park Dubiotech or Dubai Biotech
	Dubai Carpet Free Zone
	Dubai International Arbitration Center
	Dubai Maritime City
	Dubai Outsource Zone
	Dubai Studio City—Dubailand
	Dubai Techno Park
	Dubai Textile Village
	eHosting Data Fort
	Heavy Equipment & Trucks Free Zone
	International Media Production Zone
	Mohammad Bin Rashid Technology Park—Jebel Ali Area
	Free Zone
Ras Al Khaimah	RAK Center for Business Excellence or RAK Training Center for Business Excellence
	RAK Education Zone
	RAK Financial Center
	RAK Industrial and Technology Park

Source: www.dubaifaqs.com/free-zones-uae.php, March 19, 2010

First-Rate Airports

In addition to the country's port terminals and facilities, international trade and commerce is handled at a collection of airports in the UAE. Dominated by Dubai, they are recognized around the world for their state-of-the-art facilities and extensive services that link them to points around the world.

Aviation has a long history in the UAE. One of the first landing fields was built in 1932 at Sharjah by Imperial Airways (now known as British Airways). The field was constructed as a technical stop on the fledgling air service between England, India, Singapore and Australia.

Dubai Cargo Village, Dubai International Airport

Source: www.dubaiairport.com/dia/DubaiAirports/
English/MediaGallery/Flower%20Centre/Dubai%20
Cargo%20Village.jpg

The largest airport is Dubai International Airport. It was established in 1959 and 10 years later was connected to 20 destinations by nine airlines. By 2004, Dubai International was linked to more than 160 destinations by 107 airlines. In anticipation of the travel demands of the 21st century, the Dubai Department of Civil Aviation launched an expansion program in 1997. The program included upgrading existing terminals and creating a new third terminal, as well as two new concourses and a new cargo terminal. On October 14, 2008, the new US$4.5-billion Terminal 3, built exclusively for the Dubai-based Emirates Airlines, opened. Concourse 3, which is part of Terminal 3, is on track to be completed by 2011, exclusively for the Emirates Airbus A380.

Since 2002, Dubai International Airport has been ranked as one of the world's busiest airports. According to surveys and data collected by Airports Council International and BAA (British Airports Authority), the airport placed among the top 30 in terms of passenger traffic from 2007-2010 and also among the world's top 30 busiest airports by cargo traffic from 2002-2009. As the following tables illustrate, Dubai International has risen through the rankings year after year.

The second largest international airport in the UAE is Abu Dhabi International Airport, the home base for the UAE's second largest airline—Etihad Airways. Initially built in 1982 to handle a maximum of 5 million passengers a year, the airport went under a major expansion program in the mid-1990s. Ever growing traffic levels have made Abu Dhabi International one of the world's fastest growing airports. In January

Dubai International Airport, one of Top 30 World's Busiest Airports By Passenger Traffic		
Year	Rank	Total Passengers
2010 (YTD)	11	7,501,848
2009	15	40,901,752
2008	21	37,441,440
2007	27	34,348,110

Dubai International Airport, one of Top 30 World's Busiest Airports By Cargo Traffic		
Year	Rank	Total Cargo (Metric Tons)
2009	7	1,927,510
2008	11	1,824,992
2007	13	1,668,505
2006	17	1,503,697
2005	18	1,314,906
2003	18	956,795
2002	21	784,997

2009, the airport's newest terminal, Terminal 3, started operations, increasing the airport's passenger capacity to approximately 12 million. By 2012, when the Midfield Terminal is expected to be in service, the airport's passenger capacity should exceed 20 million per year.

Sharjah International Airport was formally established in 1977, during the heydays of the oil boom in the UAE, with an annual capacity of 2 million passengers. Since its opening in 1979, capacity improvements have included the UAE's first cargo terminal and larger passenger facilities. By the onset of the new millennium, the construction of cargo Terminal 4 was completed and in 2005, the Institute of Transport Management (ITM) in London named Sharjah International Airport as the "Best Global Airport of the Year." A new expansion program, focused on passenger facilities, was launched in 2007. The airport's master development plan incorporates additions to the facility's capacity, including expanded aircraft parking bays, taxiways, aprons and passenger facilities by 2017.

The next largest airports among the 38 other UAE facilities are Al Ain, Fujairah International and Ras Al Khaimah. There are two all-cargo airlines based at Al Ain, while limited regional/international services are handled at Fujairah.

Headline-Grabbing Airlines

With the significant economic growth in the oil and non-oil sectors, UAE aviation has prospered. Local businesspersons and freight logistics providers no longer have to fight for cargo space. A combination of business expansion and its geographic position has supported the emergence of the UAE as one of the fastest-growing global airline hubs. Some of the biggest air cargo and passenger carriers are based in the UAE. It is also served by most of the world's airlines. In mid-2010, Dubai-based Emirates Airlines operates more than 2,200 passenger flights per week to 108 destinations in 60 countries across six continents.

Emirates Airlines, founded in 1985, captured international attention in 2007 with an announcement of ordering/signing aircraft contracts worth an estimated US$34.9 billion for 120 Airbus A350s, 11 A380s and 12 Boeing 777-300ERs. In June 2010, the airline announced its intent to buy an additional 32 A380 jets from Airbus SAS, valued at US$11.5 billion. Emirates Airlines was named the seventh largest airline in the world in 2009 in terms of international passengers carried and the fourth largest in terms of scheduled international passenger-kilometers flown.[43]

Abu Dhabi-based Eithad Airways was established in 2003. As of mid-2010, it had a fleet of 53 aircraft that operated 147 daily flights serving an international network of 63 destinations in 42 countries.

The emirate of Sharjah paved the way for the first and now largest regional low-cost airline—Air Arabia. Air Arabia commenced operations in October 2008 and has expanded to three operational hubs: Sharjah (serving 46 destinations in 22 countries in the Middle East, North Africa, the Indian subcontinent, Central Asia and Europe), Casablanca (11 destinations in 10 countries), and Alexandria (two destinations in two countries). Dubai also launched its own LCC in 2008, and named it FlyDubai. The airline's intent was to make travel within a four-and-one-half-hour flight radius of Dubai easier, more accessible and more affordable. As of mid-2010, FlyDubai had a network of 21 destinations with a goal of expanding to more than 25 destinations by year's end. In all, it is clear that the UAE aviation industry players mean serious business.

While many foreign-based airlines have come and gone in response to demand, local airlines are committed to developing and expanding aviation in the Gulf region. In addition to these four airlines, there are more than 25 other UAE-based airlines.

UAE—A Sea-Air Hub

At the 2008 World Air Cargo Event in Bahrain, the "sea-air" concept was discussed at length. To most countries in the world, the sea-air combined transport was a novel idea. Not in the UAE.

The sea-air transport concept is not new. One of the earliest operations was in Canada in the early 1970s. Known as "Manchester Flying Fish," it linked Asia with Europe by a combination of ocean services to the Port of Vancouver and then air service. The economic fundamentals of a sea-air system comprised an efficient seaport in close proximity to a major airport, excess airlift priced aggressively, and facilities and manpower where ocean containers would be unpacked and the shipments prepared for air shipment.

At a time when the Far East, particularly China, surged as a global manufacturing haven, the main traffic lane for sea-air cargo moving through the UAE is the Far East to Europe. With many air freighters returning with light loads from the Gulf region to Europe, along with highly efficient seaports and airports, the sea-air system was formed in the UAE. Africa has emerged as a growth market and because of its size, several landlocked countries have benefited from sea-air services based in the UAE. Apart from this, the government is enthusiastic about lending support to sea and airfreight businesses. About 20 airlines ply the UAE-Africa route, covering most of the African continent. More importantly, as discussed earlier, the country has an open sky policy and efficient customs facilitation—all adding up to the mechanism of making the sea-air combined transport concept work.

UAE of the Future

All governments have an agenda. But not all government leaders would put their visions for their countries into a book and bravely publish it for the world to read and critique. This is exactly what HH Sheikh Mohammed bin Rashid Al Maktoum, UAE Vice President and Prime Minister and Ruler of Dubai, did when he published in February 2007 the controversial *Dubai Strategic Plan of 2015*. The booklet discussed future projects to be undertaken by the government of Dubai to complement the UAE's objectives in five specific sectors, including Economic Development; Social Development; Infrastructure, Land and Environment; Security, Justice and Safety; and Government Excellence.

One such project in Dubai is construction of the ambitious Dubai World Central-Al Maktoum International (DWC-AMI). The multiphase development of six clustered zones also includes Dubai Logistics City (DLC), Commercial City, Residential City, Aviation City and Golf City. The 140-sq-km development, in addition to housing what will one day be the world's largest airport, also will be the region's first integrated, multimodal transportation platform. On completion, the entire development will be 10 times larger than Dubai International Airport and Dubai Cargo Village combined. The first phase of the airport is a single runway capable of A380 operation, a terminal with a capacity of 5 million passengers per year, and a cargo terminal with a capacity of 250,000 tons per year (expandable to 600,000). Eventually, Al Maktoum International Airport will accommodate 160 million passengers and a cargo capacity of 12 million tons annually. This is considerably more than the world's current busiest passenger and cargo airports.

A message posted on the personal web site of HH Sheikh Mohammed bin Rashid Al Maktoum reflects the flexibility of Dubai to review and possibly revise its long-term plans at the onset of the global economic downturn. "In 2005, we were successful in achieving the objectives of the 2010 plan. Therefore, we had to revise our plan, coming up with the 2006-2015 plan. Following a similar logic, the implications of the global financial crisis required that we revise our 2015 plan. The plan is currently under a careful review, wherein we are monitoring all the developments in the financial markets and the global economy. Should we feel that the timelines set for our initiatives need to be adjusted, we will adjust them in order to maintain a reasonable and actionable plan, and ensure the achievement of its objectives."[44]

In an example of his visionary drive, HH Sheikh Mohammed, the

Ruler of Dubai and Prime Minister of the UAE, stated that "I don't call it a recession, I call it a challenge," and said that everyone around the world had to deal with the situation to the best of their abilities. He went on to say that it was important to grab hold of opportunities and not wait, but to execute the plan. Recognizing the impact of the "challenge," he noted that companies such as Dubai World had "to stop and restructure."[45] As others, including the Chairman of HSBC noted, the UAE, especially Abu Dhabi and Dubai, has created the needed infrastructure and is poised to take advantage of the next phase of economic growth. As an example of taking advantage, it was noted that the region's largest airline, Emirates, had placed some US$26 billion worth of airplane orders since "9-11" (the attack on the World Trade Towers in New York City) and was expected to sign an additional order during the 2010 Farnborough Air Show in England.

The Missing Element: Rail Transport

On September 9, 2009, the first driverless, fully automated urban train network on the Arabian Peninsula was launched in Dubai—the Dubai Metro. The Dubai Metro was established to accommodate the anticipated 15 million annual visitors as of 2020. The combination of a rapidly-growing population and severe traffic congestion necessitated the building of an urban rail system to provide additional public transportation capacity, relieve motor traffic, and provide infrastructure for future development. When completed, Dubai Metro will have 70 kilometers (43 mi) of lines, and 47 stations (including nine underground). It will be the world's longest automated metro network, 3 km longer than the Vancouver Skytrain system. There are ongoing discussions of a proposed line from the Dubai International Airport to Al Maktoum International Airport.

The Gulf Cooperation Council (GCC), which includes the UAE, Saudi Arabia, Kuwait, Bahrain, Qatar, and the Sultanate of Oman, has initiated feasibility studies for a regional rail network linking all member countries. Discussions about such a project will unfold for some years now. It would link all major cities and logistics hubs in the GCC, and would complete the multimodal transport and logistics system of the UAE.

Conclusion

When oil was discovered in the Gulf in the late 1960s, entrepreneurs flocked to the region. While the oil boom continued, these business persons guaranteed that they would stay to grow with the local economy. It was hoped that increased business would help to address one of the greatest freight transit imbalances. Local freight logistics providers had to put up with soaring airfreight rates and constant changes in service patterns of air and ocean services.

Since the 1990s, non-oil sectors have emerged in these petroleum-rich economies. Once again, the whole world has turned its eyes to the Gulf countries, awed by the exceptional economic boom the region has experienced with its infrastructure, tourism, real estate and, most importantly, transport hub operations. The region's industry players took the reins to ensure that the imbalance that existed in the 1970s—freight transit of 90 percent in and 10 percent out—would not happen again. A balanced freight movement has been developed in the Gulf.

What sets the UAE apart from other nations is its fearless execution of plans. The country's focus on the cultivation of its transport logistics industry has been supported by the implementation of several infrastructure projects. These have prompted a ripple effect that allowed other economic sectors to flourish—travel and tourism, banking and finance, retail, construction, real estate, and even the proliferation of Internet use. Led by Dubai and Abu Dhabi, the UAE is constantly reinforcing its position as one of the world's leading transport logistics hubs. With grand projects such as DWC-AMI and other developments listed in the Dubai Strategic Plan 2015, the country will continue to position its residents and traders for future growth.

[1] Peter Jess, President, Jessco Logistics Ltd., March 2010

[2] www.bhpbilliton.com/bb/ourBusinesses/diamondsSpecialtyProducts/ekatiDiamondMine/aboutEkati.jsp

[3] www.diavik.ca/ENG/whoweare/index_whoweare.asp

[4] Nuna Logistics, Inc., www.nunalogistics.com/services/ice_roads_runways.html).

[5] Iglauer, Edith, Denison's Ice Road, 2007, Map pgs 10-11

[6] Richard Molyneux, *Catching A Dream,* (De Beers Canada, Inc., 2008), 99

[7] J.R.K. Main, *Voyageurs Of The Air,* (Ottawa: Queen's Printer, 1967), 65-66

[8] Ibid. 67

[9] "For want of a drink—A special report on water," *The Economist,* May 22, 2010, 4

[10] "Sin aqua non," *The Economist,* April 11, 2009, 59

[11] "For want of a drink—A special report on water," *The Economist,* May 22, 2010, 9

[12] Ibid. 8

[13] Indian Railways, Yearbook 2007, New Delhi, 2008

[14] Mumbai Port Trust, Docks Department, "Container Operation After Taking Over of BPS Berth by OCT Operator," Press Release No. TMP/P/19-28/9982, January 11, 2008

[15] "Historical Background of Railway Electrification," Central Organization for Railway Electrification, Ministry of Railways, Government of India, www.core.railnet.gov.in/general/Brief

[16] Indian Railways, Official Web Site of Ministry of Railways, www.indianrailways.gov.in

[17] Indian Railways, Official Web Site of Ministry of Railways, www.indianrailways.gov.in

[18] Dedicated Freight Corridor Corporation of India Ltd., http://dfccil.org

[19] Central Board of Excise and Customs, "Citizen's Charter," December 1, 2008

[20] Lee Kuan Yew, *From Third World to First, The Singapore Story: 1965-2000,* Singapore, 687

[21] Dr. Kaizad Heerjee, "Singapore as Collaborative Manufacturing Services Hub," IDA Singapore, October 26, 2001

[22] World Bank Group, *Doing Business 2010: Reforming through Difficult Times,* (World Bank, 2009), 150

[23] Shamim Adam, "Singapore's Economy Probably Slipped Into Recession," Bloomberg, www.Bloomberg.com (September 26, 2008)

[24] "Singapore moves out of recession," *Telegraph.co.uk, www.telegraph.co.uk*/news/worldnews/asia/singapore/6603425/Singapore-moves-out-of-recession.html (November 19, 2009)

[25] The Maritime and Port Authority of Singapore, www.mpa.gov.sg/sites/port_and_shipping/port_and_shipping.page

[26] Changi Airport Group, 2010

[27] Barbara Leitch Lepoer, ed. *Singapore: A Country Study,* (Washington: GPO for the Library of Congress, 1989)

[28] Ministry of the Environment and Water Resources, "Towards Environmental Sustainability, State of the Environment 2005 Report (PDF)," Singapore, http://app.nea.gov.sg/counter/nea_soecover.asp

[29] The Maritime and Port Authority of Singapore, www.mpa.gov.sg

[30] The Maritime and Port Authority of Singapore, www.mpa.gov.sg/sites/pdf/annex_1.pdf

[31] Anthony Sampson, *Empires of the Sky: The Politics, Contests and Cartels of World Airlines,* (London: Hodder and Stoughton, 1984)

[32] Cheong Yun Wan, in consultation with Stanley Lim and Thomas Sim, *The Practitioner's Definitive Guide: Multimodal Transport,* (Singapore Logistics Association, 2008) 196

[33] Mike King, "Slowly but surely the key to Asia expansion," ifw-net.com, (March 2, 2010)

[34] Donald Urquhart, "TNT Express Taps New Markets," *Payload Asia,* Singapore, August 2008

[35] Dr. Kaizad Heerjee, "Singapore as Collaborative Manufacturing Services Hub," October 26, 2001

[36] Muriel Axford, "Jurong Island: Singapore's Petrochemical Hub," chemicals-technology.com (March 16, 2010)

[37] Alex Kennedy, "Singapore analysts expect economy to surge 9 percent in 2010 as manufacturing soars," Associated Press, June 9, 2010

[38] Kofi Annan, "How Asia and Africa Can Help Each Other," Forbes.Com Daily Newsletter, February 26, 2010

[39] DP World, www.dpworld.ae

[40] Central Intelligence Agency, *The World Factbook*

[41] Gulftainer Company Limited, www.gulftainer.com

[42] Jebel Ali Free Zone (JAFZA), www.jafza.ae

[43] World Air Transport Statistics (WATS) 54th Edition, International Air Transport Association, www.iata.org

[44] "Prime Minister's First e-Sessions with the Public," www.uaepm.ae

[45] "Dubai's Sheikh Mohammed: It's not a recession, it's a challenge," CNN Marketplace Middle East, June 25, 2010

Transport
Logistics
– the Wheel of Commerce

SECTION V
CONCLUSION

The close interplay between transport and logistics services and commercial and industrial activity is pervasive around the world. Globalization of enterprises has been supported by the development of a multimodal transport system that links points around the globe. The huge volume of merchandise trade reflects the flow of components from one factory to another, as well as finished goods to consumers everywhere.

The expansion of trade during the last few decades of the 20th century has created new opportunities for people in developing economies. The shift of manufacturing to countries with lower labor costs has been aided by an extensive network of transport and logistics services that operate on the basis of high reliability.

The first recession of 2008 created a plethora of opportunities and challenges for the world's transport and logistics industry. While the trough of the recession has not yet been identified, successful companies are already planning for the recovery. Because of this recession's magnitude, it is highly unlikely that recovery will be fast and dramatic. Many economic and fiscal structural issues remain to be addressed. Consumption funded by debt has run its course, but until the capital and credit markets return to health, questions remain as to how demand for goods and services can be stimulated and sustained without adding to mountains of sovereign debt.

Globalization pervades all sectors of the world. While most people think of the highly complex networks of production and distribution operations as well as the supporting transport and logistics systems, financial markets have similarly evolved with the advent of computers and reliable communications services.

2008 Recession

In March 2007, the first disturbing indications of highly interdependent financial markets were observed when two previously considered independent indices moved in tandem after the so-called "Shanghai surprise." Analysts noted that the US Dollar-Japanese Yen exchange rate and the Standard & Poor's 500® market index mirrored each other. After careful analysis, they determined that movement in the S&P 500 index contributed to 40 percent of the movement in the USD-JYP exchange rate index.

This and other close associations among the world's financial markets meant that when the U.S. financial markets finally succumbed to the dramatic devaluation of the U.S. housing market, that in turn pulled down the value of securitized mortgages. Then the banks and insurance companies that had issued them or written policies in capital markets around the world also fell. The recession, first identified in Denmark in the 2nd quarter of 2008, was by the 4th quarter in full force in most other countries around the world. Even those countries that continued to record economic growth experienced slowdowns.

As a result, what could have been an isolated correction in one sector of one market morphed into a worldwide recession on a scale not seen since the 1930s. The consequent decline in asset values and credit for consumption led to a general reduction of demand for goods. Manufacturing plants closed or curtailed their operations. The demand for transport and logistics services experienced severe drops.

Transport indices like the Baltic Dry Index and the HARPEX heralded the declines as ocean freight fell when production companies reacted quickly by scaling back their operations. Hundreds of ocean freighters of all types and sizes were taken off line and put in anchorages with only maintenance crews to keep them ready to return to service at some later date. Hundreds of commercial airplanes, some of them brand new, joined older aircraft in storage as the airlines likewise cut back services in response to lower demand.

After two years in the recessionary period, the outlook for a recovery is patchy and confused. Some regions, especially in East and South Asia, have weathered the economic storm, while the high-income economies are dealing with higher-than-normal unemployment levels, rising government debt resulting from aggressive fiscal stimulus programs, and post-stimulus declines. What was accepted as normal in the last half of the 20th century—continued economic growth, emerging globalization, reduction of world population in poverty, rising asset values—is no longer valid. The once dominant economies of the United States, Japan and Europe are being challenged by those of Brazil, China and India.

These changes will alter the world's transport and logistics industry. More flexible multimodal systems will emerge to respond quickly and efficiently to shifting levels and areas of demand. Ocean services will carry an increasing percentage of consumer products that previously were carried by airfreight. All of these changes will occur within a macroeconomic environment.

The challenge then becomes how to plan for and predict the future. Forecasting tools for transport and logistics managers in the 21st century include the OECD Composite Leading Economic Indicators, merchandise trade statistics, crude oil prices, and a number of key exchange rates.

Finally, all managers must be willing to be highly flexible and focus on short- and medium-term plans. A state of an ever-rising growth road has been replaced by a bumpy, ever changing path. Forecasting the future based on past performance and experience is no longer valid. In an environment of variability, only those who are aware of changes and willing to adapt to changes will survive.

Country Studies

Each of the country studies illustrates a unique aspect of the interplay between transport and logistics systems and economic and social activities that represent the fundamental elements of commerce. The review of the development of the wheel described the contribution of this universal transport component to the emergence of the industrial revolution and the expansion of trade that now involves all regions of the world. In the 21st century, transportation and logistics are essential aspects of everyone's lives. Whether it is fresh flowers or produce delivered from the southern to northern hemisphere, cocoa beans that find their way from a farm in Africa to a luxury chocolatier in Brussels, fresh lobster caught off the Kenya coast that grace a restaurant table in Hong Kong, or water collected at the face of a glacier in Chile that slakes thirsty workers in the UAE, the transport and logistics industry is key to managing the flow of goods from one part of the world to another.

Among the many study projects are those in various stages of development. They represent the future.

- **Burundi**: logistics cluster in Bujumbura on Lake Tanganyika and Central Rail Corridor
- **Chile**: transport of fresh glacier melt water in bulk around the world
- **Ethiopia**: agricultural projects, Addis Ababa-Djibouti railway
- **Ghana**: improved farming and inland water and railway transport
- **India**: dedicated freight corridor, computer-based customs system
- **Singapore**: expansion of Changi International Airport
- **Tanzania**: Mtwara Development Corridor, developing Mnazi Bay gas field
- **United Arab Emirates:** Dubai International Airport, Abu Dhabi International Airport, Sharjah International Airport, GCC rail project, Al Maktoum International Airport

The potential for a logistics and distribution cluster in Bujumbura to serve the countries that ring Lake Tanganyika reflects both a belief in the potential of economic development in the region and the challenges of relying on transport and logistics services that are based in adjoining countries. To access extra-African markets, Burundian importers and exporters employ a variety of transport alternatives including trucks, the existing rail service from Dar es Salaam and Kigoma, and lake services.

This situation requires close coordination between governments and transport operators to ensure that the flow of goods moves unimpeded.

In order to develop and operate the cluster, an open and transparent business environment must be created and maintained. Establishing a public-private enterprise that manages and operates the Port of Bujumbura symbolizes the potential for creating the required environment. The local and Burundian national authorities must reinforce and protect this environment if the cluster is to develop and grow to its full potential.

With a seamlessly integrated transport and logistics system, access to raw materials in the DRC and Zambia would be improved. This would make it easier to increase the flow of those materials. If the transport and logistics system was sufficiently efficient and reasonably priced, more refining and manufacturing locations could be added, increasing the number of jobs for citizens, income for the companies, and the GDP of the countries. The increased production also would lead to increases in imported goods to meet the needs of the higher production levels and those of the workers.

The benefits also would accrue to Burundi and Tanzania. The higher flows of goods would increase the demand for more transport and logistics services. At the same time, the improved logistics systems should translate into lower costs for goods imported to the interior locations. The demand for the goods would increase, thus creating increased income and employment in Burundi.

Another landlocked country, Ethiopia, has leveraged its natural bounty to become a dominant supplier of a wide variety of flowers and foodstuffs, including coffee, beans and vegetables. With limited surface transport alternatives, Ethiopia has turned to its airline to move precious exports. Ethiopian Airlines is one of the continent's leading air carriers, operating the largest all-cargo fleet and providing direct links to Ethiopia from North America, Europe, the Middle East and Asia as well as throughout Africa. While the air system is providing a critical link for Ethiopia, the rest of the logistics and transport system in Ethiopia must not be ignored. The higher capacity, lower cost modes of rail and road need to be developed. The critical road and rail link to the port of Djibouti requires significant investment. Making improvements to road links to surrounding countries as well as to the domestic transport network will increase access and facilitate economic and social expansion within Ethiopia. Another critical part of the logistics system that needs to be addressed is the lack of international banks; this limits the nation's financial and trade development.

There is no disputing the importance of cocoa to Ghana as a source of employment and input to the nation's GDP. In order to realize even more economic and social benefits, investment in transport and logistics as well as production is essential. Ghana once operated a large and efficient railway network. Now it barely exists and Ghana is poorer for it. The proposed improvements are essential for the long-term growth of the nation. The benefits, both social and economic, that would arise from an efficient and effective railway operation will be wide ranging. Larger quantities of goods can be transported at lower costs. If the Ghanaian system is linked to those of adjacent countries, the ports of Tema and Takoradi can become major gateways to other West African nations, generating jobs and income for Ghana.

Inland water transport is another transportation mode that needs to be developed. The primary route exists but the waterway needs to be prepared and maintained to handle commercial traffic that would likely be faster and cost less than the rail system. The result would be to open up the interior of Ghana. The social and economic benefits of such developments would include higher incomes and improved lifestyles as goods (primarily agricultural products) can be more easily moved to Tema for export while imported goods can more cheaply be taken inland.

The combination of an efficient rail system and inland waterway would provide a means to move more cocoa products less expensively from the collection points to the processing facilities and port.

The majority of the growers of cocoa in Ghana are small and thus inefficient. There is an innovative Ghanaian-based concept to create large farm-holdings and derive economies of scale for both revenues and costs. Larger farms not only generate more crops but also become traffic generators that attract transport and support logistics enterprises. As the volumes become concentrated, the efficiency of the transport and logistics system rises. As these efficiencies rise, rates can be cut and profits, which ensure continued operation, can also increase. Additionally, as profits rise, tax revenues also can increase, and if properly managed, can bring benefits to the entire nation.

In East Africa, the entrepreneurial spirit is evidenced by a Kenyan businessman who exports the bounty of the Indian Ocean. The company relies on independent fishermen to catch the seafood, and a transport and logistics network of boats, trucks, and processing facilities to prepare shipments that are exported by air to the Middle East, China and Singapore.

As Mr. B. builds his business, Kenya has created and is implementing a comprehensive program that will raise the nation's growth rate to one of the highest in the world. Vision 2030 is addressing a broad array of issues, many of which affect or enhance transport and logistics infrastructure and services in Kenya, including the creation of a common portal for handling and managing the flow of import and export shipments. Historically, Kenya has been a primary entry point into Africa. As illustrated by the statistics, the Port of Mombasa is a transit point for East Africa. As Kenya improves its transport and logistics network and works to create a "single portal" to manage the flow of goods through its ports and seaports, the benefits will expand beyond its borders. Not only will this bolster the economies of surrounding countries, their economic expansion will generate higher trade flows that will create business, revenues and tax income for Kenyans.

Building an infrastructure requires a long-term perspective. While small business owners learn how to optimize their available resources, many are unable to create comprehensive networks, and so they have to rely on those that are created by the government or other service providers. An essential role of every government is ensuring that its political environment supports the development of this essential component of modern-day economies. Kenya has embarked on its journey to establish and protect such an environment. Small businessmen like Mr. B. and his customers around the world are among the many beneficiaries.

Rwanda's national focus on addressing corruption head-on is an overt recognition that the short-term benefits of these added payments are not in the population's and nation's long-term interests. While Rwanda cannot directly change the situation outside its borders, as represented by the extra costs incurred by truckers moving shipments from the nearest seaports, it can influence changes throughout the East African Community. The benefits of reducing corruption are well known and documented by the World Bank, Transparency International and others. And although conceptually it might sound easy to eliminate this corrosive state of affairs, the simple fact is that the situation is ingrained, and eliminating these extra payments will require decisive leadership and constant monitoring.

In spite of being a landlocked country, Rwanda has set out on a course that involves innovative public and private partnerships to aggressively develop its economy and the social well being of its citizens. Using the model of Singapore, a small city-state in Southeast Asia, Rwanda is on track to become a shining light in East Africa. The focus on improving the transport and logistics infrastructure will facilitate economic development. By providing and maintaining a transparent environment, businesses will be attracted to Rwanda. Those investments will contribute to rising incomes with myriad benefits that will spread throughout the country.

In Tanzania, a comprehensive program known as the Mtwara Development Corridor encompasses industrial, agricultural, extractive and transport investments. The full potential of this concept is based on adopting a series of public-private partnerships. Specifically of interest is how to maximize the economic value of the Mnazi Bay gas field and to ensure that the Mtwara Port is expanded to meet the growing needs of the Mtwara administrative region, southern Tanzania and the surrounding countries.

Solutions exist that do not involve exclusively seeking financial support from donors around the world. Establishing an open, transparent and welcoming political and legal environment that supports public-private partnerships is the optimal approach. The long-term focus of governments is best employed in building and maintaining long-lasting infrastructure components where rates of return are measured not exclusively in terms of short-term financial gain, but in terms of increased employment, rising per capita income and rising tax revenues. This approach can be meshed with the faster, more flexible, more aggressive focus of private investors whose horizons are much shorter, but who have the ability and skills to bring new projects on line and create businesses that employ the newest technology, create jobs, and generate incomes. The plan for the Mtwara Development Corridor recognizes this mix in terms of the traffic-producing ventures, like the mines, plantations and farms. But it is within the transport and logistics arena where the public-private partnership also can be applied for the benefit of many.

The simple dirt road to Mnazi Bay, built with private funds, is but a small link in the entire network. It is important because it demonstrates the potential of public-private partnerships. The road was built with private funds, when there would have been no justification based on a traditional public cost-benefits analysis. Also, now that it is built, there is the potential for the local government to take over the maintenance and upgrade efforts, especially when tax revenues grow from the increasing gas output from the Mnazi Bay gas field. In the end, the local inhabitants should see the greatest benefits of this development.

Addressing the multiple challenges of vast distances, difficult topography, a harsh climate and the concerns of Native Canadians, the development of mines and oil and gas fields continues in the Canadian Arctic. The lessons learned by the logistics experts in meeting and overcoming the natural challenges of this world region are applicable around the world. Ice roads are used for 1-2 months each year, while water transport operates in another 1-2 months. Throughout the year, air services provide the vital lifelines to remote mines and oil and gas fields. In spite of some of the worst weather in the world, Canadian logistics firms, airlines, trucking companies and vessel operators provide safe and reliable services to a growing array of companies that are attracted to Canada's Arctic and the natural wealth that lays beneath the surface of some of the oldest parts of the earth's crust.

As more detailed geological surveys are conducted in the Canadian Arctic, additional rich mineral deposits of all kinds will be uncovered. While the process of exploration, permitting and construction can take years, and, in some cases, decades, the need for specialized logistics experts and firms in the Canadian Arctic is not likely to decline. Each

new location brings with it a new operational challenge. Adapting existing equipment and services is what the Canadian Arctic logistics experts
thrive on. Moving hundreds of thousands of tons of equipment and supplies, along with thousands of prospectors, engineers, managers and
operating employees is an ongoing, never ending activity in one of the
coldest parts of the world.

Water is essential to life on Earth. Access to water is limited or even
non-existent in many regions of the world. If life is to continue, fresh
water must be available where it is needed. Moving vast quantities of
fresh water from a source to an area of demand is a transportation and
logistics challenge, especially when the quantities exceed the typical
volumes associated with bottled water. Only 1.2 percent of the world's
water is freely available for the needs of humans and animals. With a
world population that exceeds 6.5 billion and is predicted to rise by
almost 50 percent in the next 40 years, the demand for water continues
to grow. But the supply of readily available, safe, fresh potable water is
not expanding. Faced with this dilemma, a Chilean company has secured
rights to capture melt water from one ice field. The quantity of water is
sufficient to satisfy the thirst of hundreds of thousands, if not millions,
in the world where access to potable water is limited.

Waters of Patagonia is developing a program to ship high quality fresh
water from a melting glacier around the world. Capturing the water is
relatively simple. Bottling the water is likewise a straightforward process.
Moving very large bulk shipments of fresh water over long distances is a
challenge that has been accomplished only for petroleum products. The
company is much more than a supplier of water; it is a logistics company.
It has designed a family of transport and logistics solutions to move
different quantities and categories of its fresh water. They range from
0.5-liter bottles, small bulk shipments in specially equipped 20-foot
ocean containers, adaptation of crude oil tankers, and even a massive
towed bag that can accommodate 30,000 cubic meters of fresh water.

In India, the world's largest democracy and so long associated with
suffocating bureaucracy, is quietly, but effectively, implementing a series
of programs that are facilitating the economic growth and social development that have positioned the country as one of the world's economic

engines. India faces many challenges in order to achieve everything it must do to create a state-of-the-art transport and logistics system. Its airports and ports are being overwhelmed by growth rates and volumes not considered possible as recently as two decades ago.

Developments at ports, on the railway and within Excise and Customs reflect not just the extensive array of projects, but also the speed at which these projects are being planned and completed. Building the Off-Shore Container Terminal at Mumbai Port in less than five years; conceiving, building and expanding a completely new port (Jawaharlal Nehru Port) to rank within the world's top 25 in two decades; creating a completely new freight-only railway across the sub-continent in a 11 years (planned); and introducing a state-of-the-art computerized shipment clearing system in five years are all examples of the commitment within India to build the necessary transport and logistics infrastructure to support the commercial activity of the nation.

These and other programs are designed to handle traffic volumes that India could never have imagined in the early 1990s. Through the implementation of policies that loosened the shackles on the natural inventiveness and entrepreneurial spirit of Indians, the nation is benefiting. Domestic companies once thought to need protection behind high tariffs and trade restrictions have embraced the new market openness and are now trawling the world, acquiring companies on every other continent. While restrictions continue, such as those concerning establishing stores, international trade and investment in India is exploding.

In recognition of the need to eliminate the remnants of the colonial bureaucracy, projects are being conceived, planned and implemented in short periods of time. The Off-Shore Container Terminal at Mumbai Port and the new Indian Customs and Excise Gateway are prime examples of this effort to quickly move India into the 21st century. In each instance, the democratic process is being protected. Stakeholders are aggressively sought out for their input and participation. The result are projects that move forward quickly, based on a comprehensive understanding of the interests, concerns and expectations of those who will be directly or indirectly involved in the project.

Based on its location at the southern end of the Malaysian Peninsula on the Malacca Straits, Singapore has since the 2nd century AD been a major transport hub. Arabs from the Gulf Region and Indian traders from the west met and traded with Chinese merchants from the north and east, while those from Malaysia and Indonesia brought spices, pepper and fish to the mix. With ships arriving every four minutes and planes arriving and departing every two minutes, the seas and air around this island nation are full of commerce. Facilitating this flow of commerce has been a constant progression of investment fulfilling the vision and commitment by colonial and independent leaders. Whether by its road system, the seaport or the airport, Singapore is known around the world for its state-of-the-art infrastructure that is constantly being improved and expanded.

Since the mid-1960s, Singapore also has been recognized for its corrupt-free, transparent and highly effective government and civil service. Private businesses are supported, encouraged and left alone to compete as hard as they can, so long as they obey the rules.

While Singapore experienced the global recession of 2008, it quickly enacted programs such as the Jobs Credit Scheme to help companies keep their employees. Taking advantage of its location in Southeast Asia and a stable and highly effective workforce, Singapore's brush with the recession was short-lived.

The role of Singapore as a model for developing nations is well regarded. The East African nation of Rwanda has solicited counsel and advice from Singapore. Rwanda's focus on eliminating corruption and establishing a private-public partnership environment reflects the success of Singapore.

In a speech entitled "Asia and Africa: Past Lessons, Future Ambitions" that was delivered at the National University of Singapore on February 26, 2010, the former Secretary-General of the United Nations, Kofi Annan, noted that "Singapore is a shining example of Asia's growing economic and political success and an impressive testimony to the vision, courage and commitment that is found here in such abundance."[1] He went on to say that while many Asian governments base their legitimacy and reasons for retaining power on their economic growth, poverty reduction and expanding opportunity, too many governments in Africa after coming to power believe that only they can be trusted to rule their countries, so their focus is on the ruling elite rather than society as a whole.

The vision of Singapore's leaders and implementation of their plans has led to the economic miracle at the end of the Malay Peninsula. The vision and the resulting infrastructure reinforces Singapore's role as one of the world's major transport and logistics hubs.

In the United Arab Emirates (UAE), a vast desert stretches as far as the eye can see, punctuated by some isolated settlements and a few roads. Along the 1,318-km coast where the desert meets the sea are most of this country's 41 airports, all of its 19 seaports and terminals, 30 free zones, and a 4,080-km road network. Many of its nearly 5 million people who live and work here are focused on international trade. If your mind cannot fathom the contrasting representations of this prominent business hub, chances are you haven't been to the UAE.

What sets the UAE apart from other nations is fearless execution of its plans. The country's focus on the cultivation of its transport logistics industry has been supported through the implementation of several infrastructure projects. These have prompted a ripple effect for other economic sectors to flourish—travel and tourism, banking and finance, retail, construction, real estate, and even the proliferation of Internet use. Led by Dubai and Abu Dhabi, the UAE is continually reinforcing its position as one of the world's leading transport and logistics hubs. With grand projects such as Dubai World City-Al Maktoum International Airport and other developments listed in the Dubai Strategic Plan 2015, the country will continue to position its residents and traders for future growth.

In spite of a combined 70-plus years of experience in the transport and logistics industry around the world, our experience in researching and writing this book has opened our eyes to new opportunities and challenges. The work reinforces our belief that transport and logistics services are the glue of economic development around the world.

As the book illustrates through the country studies, many barriers and hurdles must be addressed on a daily basis. Some of those barriers require a commitment by political and business leaders to address the issues for everyone's benefit. Many of the barriers cannot be eliminated in a short period of time, but require thoughtful and prolonged attention and action. But without that commitment, attention and action, progress cannot and will not be recognized. Small steps taken—not just studied—are the key. Tapping the fundamental belief of everyone that tomorrow will be better than today is essential to achieving success.

The book has focused most of its attention on Africa. Its nations are blessed with a bounty of natural resources and young and vibrant populations. Just as the UAE and Singapore have prospered because of visionary leadership and relentless pursuit of their plans, we are confident that individual nations, by adopting similar measures, will finally begin to realize their potential and emerge from the Dark Continent.

A key element to success is a robust and state-of-the-art transport and logistics infrastructure supporting innovative services. Transport and logistics services are what make the Wheel of Commerce turn, and generate benefits for individuals and nations alike.

---

[1] Kofi Annan, "How Asia and Africa Can Help Each Other," Forbes.Com Daily Newsletter, February 26, 2010

ABBREVIATIONS

3PL	third party logistics provider
4PL	fourth party logistics provider
AGCC	Arabian Gulf Cooperation Council
B2B	Business to Business
CSI	Container Security Initiative
FDI	foreign direct investment
FLP	freight logistics provider
FMCG	fast-moving consumer goods
GDP	gross domestic product
JIT	just-in-time
NGO	non-governmental organization
NVOCC	non-vessel operating common carrier
SCM	supply chain management
TEU	twenty-foot equivalent unit
ULD	unit load device
VMI	vendor-managed inventory

Organizations

ASEAN	Association of Southeast Asian Nations
COMESA	Common Market for Eastern and Southern Africa
ECOWAS	Economic Community of West African States
FIATA	International Federation of Freight Forwarders Associations
GCC	Arabian Gulf Co-operation Council
ISO	International Organization for Standardization
NAFTA	North American Free Trade Agreement
SACU	Southern African Customs Union
SADC	Southern African Development Community
TIACA	The International Air Cargo Association
WCO	World Customs Organization
WTO	World Trade Organization

GLOSSARY

B2B (Business to Business) A strategy whereby a company sells products or services directly to another company, rather than to consumers, often through Internet commerce.

break-bulk cargo Loose cargo (i.e., cartons), which is stowed directly in a vessel's hold as opposed to containerized or bulk cargo.

bulk cargo An unpacked commodity (i.e., grain, oil, ore).

clustering The practice of locating a business in or near a specific geographic area with advanced physical infrastructure and a concentration of innovative, similar companies, specialized suppliers, service providers, and skilled knowledge workers.

electronic data interchange (EDI) Systems that allow computers to conduct business transactions over telecommunications networks. EDI is an electronic commerce technique for re-engineering trade processes, and it is especially useful in streamlining customs procedures.

fast-moving consumer goods (FMCG) Packaged commercial products that are consumed through use (i.e., pre-packaged food and drinks, alcohol, health and beauty items, tobacco products, paper products, household cleansers and chemical, animal care items). Unlike consumer durables (i.e., clothing, electronics, DVDs, and small appliances), FMCG are inexpensive products that consumers constantly re-buy.

fourth party logistics provider (4PL) Company that provides the supply chain leadership and analytical skills necessary to integrate all of the companies involved in the supply chain. 4PLs plan, steer, and control all logistics procedures but do not usually own assets in the supply chain. Also known as lead logistics providers.

freight forwarder Traditional transport intermediary who arranges transport for his customers' cargo, finding the fastest and most cost-effective route by utilizing his buying power with carriers. Also provides customs clearance services.

freight logistics provider (FLP) Freight forwarder who has evolved to offer value-added logistics services to customers (i.e., warehousing, distribution, pick/pack, labeling, etc.) in addition to traditional clearing and forwarding tasks.

freight pipeline System by which encapsulated freight travels in underground tunnels with the aid of either **pneumatic propulsion**, electrical power, a hydraulic system, or linear induction motors.

Incoterms Standard trade definitions devised by the International Chamber of Commerce and commonly used in international sales contracts. Among the best known: EXW (Ex works), FOB (Free on Board), CIF (Cost, Insurance and Freight), DDU (Delivered Duty Unpaid), and CPT (Carriage Paid To).

just-in-time (JIT) System in which inventory is kept at a minimum in small lots, and products are supplied on demand rather than stocked in large quantities. JIT allows capital reduction, plant throughput, quality assurance, and market responsiveness.

International Organization for Standardization (ISO) A network of the national standards institutes of 153 counties. ISO members have reached consensus agreements on specifications and criteria which are applies consistently in materials classification; the manufacture, supply, testing and analysis of products; terminology and service provision.

logistics Process of planning, implementing, and controlling the efficient flow and storage of goods and their related information.

multimodalism Transfer of freight from one transport mode to another.

non-vessel operating common carrier (NVOCC) Companies that book space on ships in large quantities at lower rates and then sell space to shippers. NVOCCs consolidate small shipments into full container loads (FCL) that are transported under one bill of lading. The shipper in turn gets the benefit of cheaper rates.

open skies Policy that allows the aircraft of one nation to fly into or over another nation's territory.

postponement logistics System that provides manufacturers with a cost-effective method of mass customizing a product. The idea is to maintain the product in a neutral or non-committed state for as long as possible, delaying its differentiation to the last possible moment.

procurement The purchase of merchandise or services at the best possible total costs, in the correct quantity and quality.

roll on/roll off (ro-ro) Combined transport whereby vehicles drive onto a ferry, train, or plane at the beginning of the journey, and then drive off at the destination.

rolling motorway (ro-mo) Accompanied combined transport whereby a truck and its driver are transported by rail from Terminal A to Terminal B, at which point the truck is unloaded and the driver continues its road journey.

route-kilometer A unit of distance that measure the distance by rail between two points on a railway network.

supply chain Network of retailers, distributors, transporters, storage facilities, manufacturers, and suppliers that participate in the production, sale, and delivery of a particular product to its consumer.

supply chain enterprise portal (SCEP) Integrated database that is capable of supporting each function in the supply chain.

supply chain management (SCM) software applications Applications that automate and improve supply chain activities in order to achieve inventory efficiency; faster information flow; more accurate determinations of when and how much material/capacity must be purchased, produced, or moved; and supply chain events monitoring.

supply hub Set up by a 3PL on or near a manufacturer's site in order to warehouse and manage the inventory needed for production and distribution. The 3PL has a ready stock of parts for the manufacturer, so that neither the 3PL nor the manufacturer has to rely on extensive transport networks for delivery. The 3PL may provide the other value added services, such as procurement, purchase order management, invoicing of supplier goods, and transport to and from the supply hub.

TEU Twenty-foot equivalent unit, used to describe a 20-foot dry cargo container.

third-party logistics provider (3PL) Company that manages and executes particular logistics tasks (using its own assets and resources) on behalf of another company.

tonne-kilometer One metric tonne transported one kilometer.

trade bloc A regional economic partnership formed to promote trade between member states.

unit load device (ULD) Container of loading unit used for air cargo.

vendor-managed inventory (VMI) System that gives the supplier (vendor) the responsibility and authority to manage the entire replenishment process. He monitors the buyer's inventory levels, makes re-supply decision, and initiates transactions that would previously have been completed by the buyer.

A NOTE ON WEIGHTS AND MEASURES

Short ton (net ton)	United States	2,000 lbs	907.185 kg
Long ton (British ton, Imperial ton)	United Kingdom	2,240 lbs	1,016.05 kg
Metric tonne (T)	2,204.62 lbs	1,000 kg	

BIBLIOGRAPHY

"A bad climate for development—Developing countries and global warning," *The Economist*, September 19, 2009, 69-70

"A catastrophe is looming—East Africa's drought," *The Economist*, September 26, 2009, 59-60

"A glimmer of hope?" *The Economist*, April 25, 2009, 13-14

"A good example—Democracy in Africa," *The Economist*, October 24, 2009, 20

"A plan to unlock prosperity—The Panama Canal," *The Economist*, 5 December 2009, 45-47

"A stimulating question—Can emerging economies now afford counter-cyclical policies?" *The Economist*, December 13, 2008, 90

"A world apart—India and capital flows," *The Economist*, October 31, 2009, 83-84

About.com: Inventors, http://inventors.about.com/od/cstartinventions/a/Car_History.htm

Adam, Shamim, "Singapore's Economy Probably Slipped Into Recession," *Bloomberg*, www.Bloomberg.com (September 26, 2008)

Aerotropolis Business Concepts, LLC™

Africa Competitiveness Report, World Economic Forum, June 10, 2009

Africa Development Indicators 2008/09, The World Bank, 2009

Africa @ Risk, *World Economic Forum*, 2008

"After the storm—The new economic landscape will be grim unless policymakers act to foster growth," *The Economist*, October 3, 2009, 11

"Air to ocean shift—the facts behind the hype," *Air Cargo News*, April 5, 2010, 15

"Air freight and the economy," *Cargo Facts*, September 1, 2009, 19

"Air India Cargo goes solo from struggling parent," *Air Cargo News*, February 26, 2010, 8

"An astounding rebound—Asia's emerging economies are leading the way...," *The Economist*, August 15, 2009, 9

Anklesaria, Jimmy, "Identifying Critical Costs in the Supply Chain," *Supply Chain Quarterly*, Qrtr. 2, 2009, 64-74

Annan, Kofi, "How Asia and Africa Can Help Each Other," Forbes.Com Daily Newsletter, February 26, 2010

"Asian economies—Troubled tigers," *The Economist*, January 31, 2009, 75-77

Authers, John, "Market Forces," *Financial Times*, May 22, 2010, Life & Arts 1-2

Autoevolution, www.autoevolution.com/news/history-of-the-wheel-7334.html

Axford, Muriel, "Jurong Island: Singapore's Petrochemical Hub," chemicals-technology.com (March 16, 2010)

Bailey, Medina, "Wildest Dreams," *Water Innovation*, March–April 2010, 20-25

Bew, Robin, "Not So Fast," *The Economist*, January 2010

Bekele, Kaleyesus, "Ethiopian: Africa's Rising Airline," *Airline Fleet Management*, Qrtr. 4/2009, 46-50

BHP Billiton, www.bhpbilliton.com/bb/ourBusinesses/diamondsSpecialtyProducts/
ekatiDiamondMine/aboutEkati.jsp

"Briefing: The Panama Canal, A Plan to Unlock Prosperity," *The Economist,* December
5, 2009, 45-47

"Business and water—Running Dry," *The Economist,* August 23, 2009, 53-54

Cai, Solomon, "Expecting an economic turnaround," WCA News, April 5, 2010

"Canada's Arctic policy—Harper of the melting North," *The Economist,* August 29,
2009, 34

Cates, Andrew, "Tectonic economics—productivity," *UBS,* October 14, 2009

Caves, Richard E., Ronald W. Jones, *World Trade and Payments: An Introduction,* (Boston:
Little, Brown, 1977), 160

Central Board of Excise and Customs, "Citizen's Charter," December 1, 2008

Central Intelligence Agency, *The World Factbook*

Changi Airport Group, 2010

"Chile's new government—Running to rebuild a shaken country," *The Economist,*
March 20, 2010, 43

"Chile's wine industry—If one green bottle," *The Economist,* April 10, 2010, 39-40

"China-Africa-India—The "Silk Road" revisited," *WCA News,* April 5, 2010, 8

Cipolla, Carlo M., ed., Before the Industrial Revolution, (Fontana Press 1973), 196,
198-199, 208, 211

"Climate change—When glaciers start moving," *The Economist,* April 11, 2009, 61

Coffee Board of Burundi, 2007

Collier, Mike, "Recession arrives in Estonia," The Baltic Times, ww.baltictimes.com/
news/articles/21072/(August 13, 2008)

"Congo's oil—We got it too," The Economist, April 10, 2010, 52

Conway, Peter, "Tewolde Gebremariam—Ethiopian Airlines," Air Cargo News,
November 13, 2009, 6-7

"Crash landing for Latvia's housing market, Global Property Guide, www.
globalpropertyguide.com/Europe/Latvia (January 26, 2009)

"Crouching tigers, stirring dragons—Asian economies," The Economist, May 16,
2009, 79-81

"Damage assessment—How much will the financial crises hurt America's economic
potential?," *The Economist,* August 16, 2009, 84

"Dangerous froth—The world economy," *The Economist,* November 14, 2009, 83-84

"Dangerously hopeful—Ghana and oil," *The Economist,* 2 January 2010, 36

Dave, Damini, "Neither Dark Art nor Infallible Science," *Air Cargo World,* January 1,
2010, 21-27

"Dealing with America's fiscal hole," *The Economist,* November 21, 2009, 13

Deck, Mark, "Taming Turbulence," *World Trade,* September 1, 2009, 30-33

Dedicated Freight Corridor Corporation of India Ltd., http://dfccil.org

"Denmark in recession after first quarter contraction," *EU business,* www.eubusiness.

com (July 1, 2008)

Deutsche Bahn Consulting, "Etude de Faisabilité du Projet Ferroviaire Isaka-Kigali/ Keza-Gitega-Musongati," 2009, Table 14-24, 158

"Developing countries and global warming—A bad climate for development," The Economist. March 27, 2010, 69-70

Dictionary.com, http://dictionary1.classic.reference.com/help/faq/language/e37. html

"Dishdashed—The repercussions of Dubai," The Economist, December 5, 2009, 79-81

"Doing Business 2010—Reforming through Difficult Times," The World Bank," 2009

DP World, www.dpworld.ae

DP World, Port of Djibouti—Port History, www.dpworld-djiboutiport.com

DP World, Port of Djibouti—Statistics, www.dpworld-djiboutiport.com

"Dubai's debts—Finding the ripcord," The Economist, March 27, 2010, 82-83

"Dubai's Sheikh Mohammed: It's not a recession, it's a challenge," CNN Marketplace Middle East, June 25, 2010

Dupin, Chris, "Transatlantic belt-tightening," American Shipper, January 2010, 28-29

Dupin, Chris, "Speed-to-market: Crowley offers frequent service for 'perishable' products," American Shipper, April 2010, 52-55

East African Community, Common External Tariff, 2007 Version

East African Community Customs Union, www.eac.int/customs/

East African Community, EAC Trade Guide, www.customs.eac.int/index. php?option=com_content&view=article&id=101&Itemid=103 East African Community Secretariat, Protocol On The Establishment of the East African Customs Union, March 2, 2004, 1-2

Edinformatics, www.edinformatics.com/inventions_inventors/

Edward J., Richard L. Morrill and Peter R. Gould, Transport Expansion in Underdeveloped Countries: A Comparative Analysis, (American Geographical Society, 1963)

eHow, www.ehow.com/about_4658773_invention-wheel.html

El-Husseini, Ibrahim & Maidalani, Fadi & Borgogna, Alessandro, "Filling the Gulf States' Infrastructure Gap," Strategy + Business, September 22, 2009

Ellis, Simon, "The Case for Profitable Proximity," Supply Chain Quarterly, Qrtr. 2, 2009, 56-63

Embassy of Ethiopia, Washington, DC, www.ethiopianembassy.org/pdf/Flower%20 Combo.pdf

"Eurozone officially in recession," BBC News, http://news.bbc.co.uk/2/ hi/business/7729018.stm (November 14, 2008) and Jan Strupczewski, "Euro zone recession confirmed," Reuters, www.reuters.com/article/ idUKTRE4B32JK20081204 (December 4, 2008)

"Faced with a gun, what can you do?—War and militarisation of mining in eastern Congo," Global Witness, July 2009

"Fare well, free trade," The Economist, December 20, 2008, 15

"Fatalism v fetishism—How will developing countries grow after the financial crisis," *The Economist*, June 13, 2009, 82

"For want of a drink—A special report on water," *The Economist*, May 22, 2010, 4

Foster, V., Butterfield, Wm., Chen, C., & Pushak, N, Building Bridges—China's Growing Role as Infrastructure for Sub-Saharan Africa, *The World Bank*, 2009

"Food aid in Africa—When feeding the hungry," *The Economist*, March 20, 2010, 52

"From slump to jump—Asia's economies," *The Economist*, August 1, 2009, 36

"GDP Forecasts," *The Economist*, September 5, 2009, 101

"GDP Forecasts," *The Economist*, October 17, 2009, 117

"GDP growth forecasts 2010," *The Economist*, January 2, 2010, 69

"Germany and France's recoveries won't help the US much in the near term," *The Kiplinger Letter*, August 14, 2009, 2

"German economy officially in recession," *FRANCE 24*, www.france24.com/en/20081113-german-economy-officially-recession-financial-crisis-europe (November 13, 2008)

Ghana Cocoa Board

"Ghana Railway," www.Ghana-Net.com

"Ghana to Upgrade Railways," *Railways Africa*, www.railwaysafrica.com (September 8, 2009)

"Global Growth @ Risk 2008," *World Economic Forum*, June 30, 2008

"Global Logistics and Trade Management—Making Globalization Profitable and Reducing Supply Chain Risk," *The Supply Chain Digest* Letter, May 2008, 1-4

Global Risks 2009, *World Economic Forum*, 2009

"Globalisation and trade—The nuts and bolts come apart," *The Economist*, March 28, 2009, 79-81

"Globalisation stalled," *Economist Intelligence Unit*, May 2009

Great Idea Finder (The), www.ideafinder.com/history/inventions/wheel.htm

"Guide to Economic Indicators-Making Sense of Economics," *The Economist*, 2007, 55

Gulftainer Company Limited, www.gulftainer.com

Haggett, Peter, *Locational Analysis in Human Geography*, (London: Edward Arnold, 1969), 3, 5, 79

Haggett, Peter, Richard J. Chorley, *Network Analysis in Geography*, (London: Edward Arnold, 1969), 109, 111, Appendix One

Heerjee, Dr. Kaizad, "Singapore as Collaborative Manufacturing Services Hub," IDA Singapore, October 26, 2001

Heim, Kristi, "Bill introduced to curb mineral trade that fuels war and rape," *Seattle Times*, November 18, 2009

Hill, John, "Armageddon or Schumpeter redux?—Trade Forecast 2009," *American Shipper*, 2009

HIS Global Insight, "International Containerized Ocean Freight Volumes Trade Forecast 2009," *American Shipper*, September 2009

Historical Background of Railway Electrification," Central Organization for Railway Electrification, Ministry of Railways, Government of India, www.core.railnet.gov. in/general/Brief

Holcomb, Mary C. & Foggin, James A., "A Framework For Network Optimization," *Supply Chain Quarterly,* Qtr. 2, 2009, 72-77

"Hope at last—The world's biggest economy has begun a much-need transition,"The Economist, April 3, 2010, 13

"Hong Kong slides into recession," *BBC News,* http://news.bbc.co.uk/2/hi/ business/7729652.stm (November 14, 2008)

Hoyle, B.S., *Transport and Economic Growth in Developing Countries:The Case of East Africa,* (London: MacMillan, 1973)

HubPages, http://hubpages.com/hub/Invention-of-the-Wheel

Iglauer, Edith, *Denison's Ice Road,* Harbour Publishing, 2009

"India's evolving conglomerates—Avantha's advance," *The Economist,* April 10, 2010, 68-69

"Indian Infrastructure Ripe for Renovation," *Air Cargo World,* September 2009, 8-9

"India's Industrial Output Surges," *World Trade,* November 2009, 12-13

"India @ Risk 2008," *World Economic Forum,* 2008

Indian Railways, Official Web Site of Ministry of Railways, www.indianrailways.gov.in

Indian Railways,Yearbook 2007, New Delhi, 2008

International Cocoa Organization, 2006

International Monetary Fund, 2007

"It's cargo for openers at "airport of the future," *Air Cargo World,* April 2010, 9

"Is It Smooth Sailing and Clear Skies for Ocean and Air Cargo?," *SupplyChain Brain,* March 2010, 62-65

Jacoby, David, "Guide to Supply Chain Management," *The Economist,* September 2009

Jansen, Gert-Jan, "Air to ocean shift-the facts behind the hype," *Air Cargo News,* April 5, 2010, 15

Jebel Ali Free Zone (JAFZA), www.jafza.ae

Jenoside, Kigali Memorial Centre, Kigali, 2004, pg. 22

Jess, Peter, President, Jessco Logistics Ltd., March 2010

Johnson, Eric, "Oceania/North America stability reigns," *American Shipper,* December 2009, 32-33

Johnson, Eric, "Slow Burn," *American Shipper,* January 2010, 34-45

Johnson, Eric, "Unlucky year or bad business? (CSAV—Chile)," *American Shipper,* April 2010, 34

Johnson, Eric, "Slow steaming changes game," *American Shipper,* April 2010, 42-44

Kennedy, Alex, "Singapore analysts expect economy to surge 9 percent in 2010 as manufacturing soars," *Associated Press,* June 9, 2010

King, Mike, "Slowly but surely the key to Asia expansion," ifw-net.com, (March 2, 2010)

Kollewe, Julia, "Ireland falls into recession," guardian.co.uk, www.guardian.co.uk/business/2008/sep/25/recession.ireland (September 25, 2008)

Kolisch, Erik, "Recession rebound—sourcing shifts," *American Shipper*, November 2009, 8-15

Kolisch, Erik, "Infrastructure in political divide," *American Shipper*, April 2010, 6-13

Kolisch, Erik, "Bubble ready to burst?" *American Shipper*, April 2010, 25

Kuan Yew, Lee, *From Third World to First, The Singapore Story: 1965-2000*, Singapore, 687

"Land of eastern promise-India," *The Economist*, 21 November 2009, 47

Leitch Lepoer, Barbara, ed. *Singapore: A Country Study*, (Washington: GPO for the Library of Congress, 1989)

"Look south—Who's doing well in Africa?," *The Economist*, 3 October 2009, 62

MacDonald, Andrea, "NAFTA: A Delicate Balance," *American Shipper*, October 2009, 30-33

MacDonald, Andrea, "Southeast Asia—A new look at an "old" market," *World Trade*, December 2009, 46-47

Main, J.R.K., *Voyageurs Of The Air*, (Ottawa: Queen's Printer, 1967), 65, 66, 67

"Manufacturing activity," *The Economist*, August 8, 2009, 82

Maritime and Port Authority of Singapore, www.mpa.gov.sgm, www.mpa.gov.sg/sites/port_and_shipping/port_and_shipping.page, www.mpa.gov.sg/sites/pdf/annex_1.pdf

Martichenko, Robert A. & von Grabe, Kevin, "Mapping A Lean Strategy," *Supply Chain Quarterly*, Qrtr. 2, 2007, 52-59

McCone, Dan, "The New American Hub," *World Trade*, November 2009, 14-22

McKinsey Quarterly, "Six steps to energy-efficient supply chains," *Supply Chain Quarterly*, Qrtr. 3, 2009, 12

"Measuring what matters—Man does not live by GDP alone," *The Economist*, September 19, 2009, 88

"Merchant ships," *The Economist*, December 12, 2009, 105

MergeGlobal Value Creation Initiative, "In search of growth," *American Shipper*, June 2008, 6-27

MergeGlobal Value Creation Initiative, "Beyond the recession," *American Shipper*, March 2009, 18-25

"Mining in Ghana—Carats and sticks," *The Economist*, April 3, 2010, 68

Ministry of the Environment and Water Resources, "Towards Environmental Sustainability, State of the Environment 2005 Report (PDF)," Singapore, http://app.nea.gov.sg/counter/nea_soecover.asp

Moberg, Christopher & Pienaar, Abre & Stank, Theodore & Vitasek, Kate, "Time for a New Supply Chain Model," *Supply Chain Quarterly*, Qrtr. 3, 2008, 36-49

Molyneux, Richard, *Catching A Dream*, (De Beers Canada, Inc., 2008), 99

Mongabay.com, www.Global.Mongabay.com

"Much ado about multipliers—Who do economists disagree so much on whether fiscal stimulus works?" *The Economist,* September 26, 2009, 90

Mumbai Port Trust, Docks Department, "Container Operation After Taking Over of BPS Berth by OCT Operator," Press Release No. TMP/P/19-28/9982, January 11, 2008

Murphy, Jean, "Logistics Companies Emerge from Recession Leaner, Wiser and Ready for Better Times," SupplyChain Brain, March 2010, 46-49

Narayanan, Arun, "India poised for Air Cargo Revolution," *Air Cargo World,* September 2009, 20-23

Natarajan, Chandrashekar & Hales, Lee, "Six Steps to Effective Network Planning," *Supply Chain Quarterly,* Qrtr.1, 2008, 58-71

National Bureau of Economic Research

National Development Corporation of Tanzania, "Draft Strategic Perspective of the Mtwara Development Corridor

Ncube, Bekezela, "Ethiopia," http://fic.wharton.upenn.edu/fic/africa/Ethiopia%20Final.pdf (2007)

"New Dubai airport set to open in June," *Air Cargo News,* April 5, 2010, 3

"New rules for a new era," *Air Cargo News,* November 13, 2009, 1

"New Silk Roads: Roads, railways and pipelines are redefining what we mean by Asia," *The Economist,* April 10, 2010, 48

"New-year irresolution ," *The Economist,* January 2, 2010, 55

"Not just straw men—BRICSs, emerging markets and the world economy," *The Economist,* June 20, 2009, 63-65

"Not quite as bloody as before—Strife in eastern Congo," *The Economist,* 28 November 2009, 54

Nuna Logistics, Inc., www.nunalogistics.com/services/ice_roads_runways.html

"On the up—Gulf carriers survive slump," *Air Cargo World,* April 1, 2010, 30-34

"Opening the floodgates—Imports can be as useful to developing countries as exports are," *The Economist,* May 9, 2009, 82

Organization for Economic Cooperation and Development, "Economics: Growth Rising Faster Than Expected but Risks Increasing, Too," OECD Economic Outlook, May 25, 2010

Parekh, Deep, "5 trends for 2010 and beyond," *American Shipper,* December 2009, 16-17

Port of Bujumbura

Prahalad, C.K. & Bhattacharyya, H., "Twenty Hubs and No H.Q.," *Strategy + Business,* Spring 2008, 24-29

Prasso, Sheridan, "Ambassador for the Asian Century," *Strategy + Business,* Spring 2008, 84-89

Preuninger, Jim, "Next Generation of Global Trade Management Software Navigates

Complex Trade Rules to Streamline the Import Supply Chain," *The Supply Chain Digest Letter,* May 2008, 3-10

Private Sector Federation—Rwanda, "Assessment of Non Tariff Barriers (NTB's) Along the Northern & Central Corridors-EAC," 2008, 5, 21, 22, 28

Process in Tanzania," August 14, 2006, 11

"Productivity growth—slash and earn," *The Economist,* March 20, 2010, 75-76

Profitt, Michael, "MNCs are global trade drivers, not countries," Payload Asia, October 2009, 33-35

"Raw deal—Higher commodity prices may not be good news," *The Economist,* June 6, 2009, 72

Rau, Hertwig, "Risk Management in the Air Cargo Industry {Revenue Management, Capacity Options and Financial Intermediaries," *WHU,* July 2009

"Record Trade Deficit for Canada," *World Trade,* November 2009, 12

"Redefining recession," *The Economist,* September 13, 2008, 82

"Reforming through tough times—The World Bank's Doing Business report," *The Economist,* September 12, 2009, 71

Republic of Rwanda, Rwanda Vision 2020, 15, 16, 18

Railway Gazette, "Grand designs from Ethiopian Railway Corp.," www.railwaygazette.com (September 11, 2009)

Rio Tinto, www.diavik.ca/ENG/whoweare/index_whoweare.asp

Rosenzweig, Paul, "Why the U.S. doesn't trust Canada," *MacLean's,* 12 October 2009, 33-35

Rutas De Chile, COPEC, 2010

Saddi, Joe & Sabbagh, Karim & Shediac, Richard, "Oasis Economies," *Strategy + Business,* Spring 2008, 44-57

Sadlovska, Viktoriya, "Global Supply Chain Management: Demand-Supply Networks: Success Factors in 2010," *Global Supply Chain Management,* March 18, 2010

Salvucci, Dawn, "Leveraging Supply Chain Optimization and Transportation & Logistics Management Solutions t Manage a Complex Global Environment," *The Supply Chain Digest Letter,* May 2008, 11

Sampson, Anthony, Empires of the Sky: The Politics, Contests and Cartels of World Airlines, (London: Hodder and Stoughton, 1984)

Samson Fatokun, Oldadele, African air transport in the 21st century: A case study of the contrasting experience of Nigeria and Kenya—M.Sc. Thesis, *Cranfield University—School of Engineering,* September 2005

Savage, Luiza Ch., "Canada's biggest problem? America," *MacLean's,* October 12, 2009, 28-31

"Sea of troubles—Shipping in the downturn," *The Economist,* August 1, 2009, 55-56

Seabury Group, "International Air Freight Forecast," *American Shipper,* August 2009

Shah, Prof. Janat & Suresh, Dr. D.N., "Global Perspectives-India," *Council of Supply Chain Management Professionals,* 2009

Sheng, Andrew, "Financial Crisis and Global Governance: A Network Analysis,"
    Globalization and Growth, (Washington, DC, World Bank, 2010), 72-75
"Shifting flower power," Freighters World,"September 2009, 15-23
"Sin aqua non," The Economist, April 11, 2009, 59
"Single market bargaining," The Economist, November 14, 2009, 65
Singapore moves out of recession,"Telegraph.co.uk, www.telegraph.co.uk/news/
    worldnews/asia/singapore/6603425/Singapore-moves-out-of-recession.html
    (November 19, 2009)
Singh, Manfred, "The "Pride of Africa" is set to shine—Kenya Airways," Payload Asia,
    November 2009, 28-31
Smithsonian Magazine, www.smithsonianmag.com/science-nature/A-Salute-to-the-
    Wheel.html
"Smoothing out the spikes," WCA News, April 5, 2010
Société Concessionnaire de l'Exploitation du Port de Bujumbura (EPB), www.pmaesa.
    org/media/docs/burundi.pdf
Sowinski, Lara L., "Big Red Sets Up Shop in Michigan,"World Trade, March 2009, 22
"Spectre of nationalism," The Economist, January 24, 2009, 82
Spence, Michael, Globalization and Growth—Implications for a Post-Crisis World,
    The World Bank, April 15, 2010
SpeedNews, www.speednews.com, January 2010
Steyn, Mark, "Is Canada's Economy a Model for America?," Imprimis, January 2008
"Stakes and mistakes—India," The Economist, 14 November 2009, 74-75
"Stemming the tide—America's fiscal deficit," The Economist, November 21, 2009,
    25-28
"Stumble of fall?—Emerging markets," The Economist, January 10, 2009, 63-64
"Suddenly vulnerable," The Economist, December 13, 2008, 15
"Surviving the slump," The Economist, May 30, 2009
"Sweden stumbles into recession,"The Local, www.thelocal.se/15998/20081128/
    (November 28, 2008)

Tanzania—Country Brief, The World Bank, 2009
"Tap that water—Dams in Africa," The Economist, May 8, 2010, pg. 49
Teravaninthorn, Supee & Raballand, Gael, "Le prix et le coût du transport en Afrique,"
    The World Bank, 2009
Terreri, April, "Delivery Supply Chain Excellence," World Trade, March 2010, 24-29
"The BRICs—The trillion dollar club," The Economist, April 17, 2010, 64-66
"The clean water challenge—An integrative approach can solve a three-pronged
    problem that affects billions," Global Outlook, February 2010
"The collapse of manufacturing," The Economist, February 21, 2009, 9
"The dollar will bounce around a while longer then move to the upside," The Kiplinger
    Letter, August 21, 2009, 2
"The game has changed—Consumer goods in recession," The Economist, August 22,
    2009, 55-56

The Global Enabling Trade Report, *World Economic Forum,* 2009

"The global slumpometer," *The Economist,* November 8, 2008, 92

"The Great Stabilisation," *The Economist,* December 19, 2009, 15

"The humbling of Detroit North—Canada's stalled economy," *The Economist,* August 1, 2009, 31-32

The Little Data Book on Africa, *The World Bank,* 2009, Pg. 36

"The recession—When did it end?" *The Economist,* April 17, 2010, 30-32

"The resilient dollar," *The Economist,* October 4, 2008, 84

"The return of economic nationalism," *The Economist,* February 7, 2009, 9-10

"The US is headed for the sharpest drop in the trade deficit in 18 years," *The Kiplinger Letter,* August 14, 2009, 2

"Thriving on Adversity-Some Companies are Finding Opportunities in the Recession," *The Economist,* October 3, 2009, 82

Thuermer, Karen E., "Say it with Flowers, Say it with Logistics," *World Trade,* September 2009, 20-25

Tibbit to Contwoyto Winter Road Joint Venture, Facts, http://jvtcwinterroad.ca/

"Time to Rebalance-A Special Report on America's Economy," *The Economist,* April 3, 2010, 3

Tompkins, Jim, "The riddle of Supply Chain Cost Reduction," *Tompkins Associates,* February 4, 2009

"Towards a Sustainable Cocoa Chain," Oxfam International Research Report, January 2008

Transport Intelligence, "Slow Growth Forecast for Forwarders," *Air Cargo World,* December 2009, 48-50

"Turning their backs on the world-globalization," *The Economist,* February 21, 2009, 59-61

"U, V or W for recovery," *The Economist,* August 22, 2009, 10-11

"Uganda's Oil—A bonanza beckons," *The Economist,* April 3, 2010, 49-50

"Unpredictable tides," *The Economist,* July 25, 2009, 67-68

"Unrepentant bears—The end is nigh (again)," *The Economist,* October 3, 2009, 83-84

UN Development Programme, "Human Development Index," *The Economist,* October 10, 2009, 102

"UK economy 'Weakest in 30 Years,'" *BBC News,* http://news.bbc.co.uk/1/hi/business/8015704.stm (April 24, 2009)

Urquhart, Donald, "TNT Express Taps New Markets," *Payload Asia,* Singapore, August 2008

U.S. Department of Commerce press release, May 18, 2010

USAID, "Comparative Transportation Cost Analysis in East Africa, Final Report," Technical Paper No. 22, April 1997

Veloso, Paulina, Tortel—wood culture of the austral fiords, *Andros Impresores,* December 2007

Wallop, Harry, "Japan joins growing list of countries to fall into recession,"Telegraph. co.uk, www.telegraph.co.uk/news/worldnews/asia/japan/3472608/Japan-joins-growing-list-of-countries-to-fall-into-recession.html, (November 17, 2008)

Wan, CheongYun, in consultation with Stanley Lim andThomas Sim, *The Practitioner's Definitive Guide: Multimodal Transport*, (Singapore Logistics Association, 2008) 196, 197

"Wanted: new customers—Manufacturing's future," *The Economist*, October 3, 2009, 36-37

Water—a shared responsibility, The United Nations World Water Development Report 2. United Nations Educational, Scientific and Cultural Organization (UNESCO), 2006

"Water—sin aqua non," *The Economist*, April 11, 2009, 59-61

"Water rights—Awash in rights," *The Economist*, April 11, 2009, 13-14

"Water Tech," *Kiplinger Letter*, April 16, 2010, 4

Waters of Patagonia, World's Fresh Waters—Briefing Guide, March 2010

"When a flow becomes a flood—Global economic imbalances," *The Economist*, January 24, 2009, 74-75

"When fortune frowned," *The Economist*, October 11, 2008

"When the rains fail—India's water crisis," *The Economist*, September 12, 2009, 27-30

Wikipedia, http://en.wikipedia.org/wiki/Chariot

Wikipedia, http://en.wikipedia.org/wiki/Wheel

Wikipedia, http://en.wikipedia.org/wiki/Industrial_Revolution

Wikipedia, http://en.wikipedia.org/wiki/Timeline_of_the_late_2000s_recession

Wilson, Rosalyn, "20th State of Logistics Report—Riding OutThe Recession," *CSCMP*, June 17, 2009

World Air Transport Statistics (WATS) 54th Edition, International Air Transport Association, www.iata.org

World Bank Group, *Africa's Infrastructure: A Time for Transformation,* (World Bank, December 2009), 1, 2, 3, 5, 7, 13, 211, 212, 222, 229, 232, 235, 236, 249, 259, 262, 268; Figure 10.4, 218

World Bank Group, *Doing Business 2010: Reforming through Difficult Times,* (World Bank, 2009), 4, 150

World Bank, "Global Economic Prospects—Crisis, Finance and Growth 2010," Washington, DC, Table O.1, 3

World Bank, *World Development Indicators 2009,* (World Bank, April 2009), 218

World GDP, *The Economist*, December 19, 2009, 173

World Trade Organization, "International Trade Statistics 2009," 1

www.washingtonpost.com/wp-dyn/content/article/2008/12/01/ AR2008120101365.html (December 1, 2008)

Yarusso, Lowell, "3 steps to strategic sourcing," *Supply Chain Quarterly,* Qrtr.3, 2009, 54-61

Zenebe, Wudineh, "Dry Ports to Receive 220 Million Br Expansion," http://allAfrica. com (April 6, 2010)

Zeng, Douglas Zhihua, "Africa—Knowledge, Technology and Cluster-based Growth," *The World Bank,* 2008

Zhihua Zeng, Douglas, ed., *Knowledge, Technology, and Cluster-Based Growth in Africa,* (World Bank, February 2008), 1, 3

INDEX